30 EVENTS
THAT SHAPED THE
CHURCH

30 EVENTS

THAT SHAPED THE

CHURCH

LEARNING *from* SCANDAL,
INTRIGUE, WAR, AND REVIVAL

ALTON GANSKY

BakerBooks

a division of Baker Publishing Group
Grand Rapids, Michigan

© 2015 by Alton Gansky

Published by Baker Books
a division of Baker Publishing Group
P.O. Box 6287, Grand Rapids, MI 49516-6287
www.bakerbooks.com

Printed in the United States of America

Library of Congress Cataloging-in-Publication Data

Gansky, Alton.
    30 events that shaped the church : learning from scandal, intrigue, war, and revival / Alton Gansky.
        pages cm
    ISBN 978-0-8010-1608-0
    1. Church history—Miscellanea. I. Title. II. Title: Thirty events that shaped the church.
BR153.G36 2014
270—dc23   2014028822

Scripture quotations are from the New American Standard Bible®, copyright © 1960, 1962, 1963, 1968, 1971, 1972, 1973, 1975, 1977, 1995 by The Lockman Foundation. Used by permission.

Scripture quotations labeled KJV are taken from the King James Version of the Bible.

Published in association with MacGregor Literary Agency.

15   16   17   18   19   20   21   7   6   5   4   3   2   1

Contents

Contents

the church to meet freely and expand throughout the Roman Empire.

Contents

Contents

Introduction

Imagine standing on a barren shoreline staring across the smooth waters of a massive lake. Poking out of the depths are small islands that seem to float independently of all the others, but a closer look reveals causeways connecting one island not just to its nearest neighbor but also to scores of others. There is something important on each of those islands, something worth investigating. History is like that vast lake, and this book is about that lake.

We are all products of history. The cities or towns where we live exist because people in our past chose to settle there. The medicines we take were created on knowledge learned by scientists and doctors decades and even centuries ago. The places we work, the way we travel, and the entertainment we enjoy all have history.

Appreciating history is a nice sentiment, but the twenty-first century is a demanding place filled with distractions, challenges, and sometimes mentally and physically taxing effort just to get by. Still, we are the product of the past. Every new day, year, decade, and century is rooted in its past, and—at the risk of sounding like a history professor on the first day of class—that past is important.

The late Michael Crichton (1942–2008) is known for his works of fiction: not for his medical degree, not for being a Harvard graduate, but for his ability to spin captivating tales. He said, "If you don't know history, then you don't know anything. You are a leaf that doesn't know it is part of a tree." This book is about that tree.

Church history is a broad topic spanning two thousand years. Unlike the timelines we all learned in junior high school, history is more of a web than a straight line, more mountains and hills than open plains. It has twists and sudden turns and unexpected happenings that resonate for centuries.

Of the seven billion people in the world, over two billion are connected to a church. Christianity is the largest religious system in existence. Christian history is *everyone's* history, not just those in the pews but those who have never crossed the threshold of a sanctuary. Even the most anti-church individual must admit that Christianity has changed and continues to change the world.

It may seem odd to quote a Hindu in a book about Christian events, but Mahatma Gandhi's (1869–1948) words could certainly apply to the events that shaped the church: "A small body of determined spirits fired by an unquenchable faith in their mission can alter the course of history." This book is about those "determined spirits."

30 Events That Shaped the Church is the companion book to *60 People Who Shaped the Church*. In the first book I focused on the people who helped or hurt the Christian cause. In this book, I focus on events that continue to shape our Christian behavior and thinking.

"Events" can be misleading. The word conjures up an occurrence that happened at some moment in time, but events can slowly rise from the depths, break the surface, and last for years. I use the term liberally here. At times I discuss events that happened over a period of hours, and at others events that are still ongoing.

"Those who don't know history are doomed to repeat it," or so said Edmund Burke. This sentence is often uttered as a warning, a way of saying, "Wake up, pay attention, or you will make the same mistakes as those who came before you." True as that is, some history deserves to be repeated. The examples of the brave, the determined, and the dedicated are worth emulating.

Selecting which events to include in this book was difficult. I started with a much longer list, then began paring it down. With every event

I removed from the list, I felt I was leaving something important on the cutting room floor. For every bit of joy I felt over what remained, I felt guilt for those left behind. Even after the list was set it began to change. During the writing of this book I dropped some events to make room for others.

In the end, I believe this is a good sample of key events in church history, drawn from both the distant past and modern times. It is my hope that this book will help the reader get a sense of the people, times, and events that make the church what it is today.

Alton Gansky

1

Pentecost

(AD 30)

Fifty days after the crucifixion, the inner circle of disciples watched the resurrected Jesus ascend to heaven. Before leaving, the Messiah told them they would be witnesses to the world. Since that moment they had waited, as they had been told to do, in Jerusalem, uncertain what would happen next.

Outside their doors the people who had chanted for Christ's crucifixion carried on their daily lives as if nothing had happened two months before. The Jewish leaders who orchestrated his arrest and the Roman leader who allowed it all to happen—all were still in place. The danger remained.

The leaders of the fledgling church, people we think of today as brave, bold, unrelenting in their duties, and ready to die for the cause of Christ, started off as timid, uncertain, confused, and frightened.

But what happened at Pentecost would change them—and the world—forever. The church did not come on the scene quietly. Its birth was loud. Chaotic.

Jesus practiced an itinerant ministry, walking from town to town preaching and performing miracles. This created a variety of interested parties. Some came out to hear and behold the spectacle that often followed Christ. Others believed his message but continued their daily lives as before. There is no evidence that they gathered for fellowship or worship.

Then there was the larger group of disciples, those who were closer to Jesus, who supported and aided him in his work. When we hear the word *disciple* we often think of the twelve men who were part of Jesus' ministry. The Bible sometimes refers to them as "the Twelve." (Mark 4:10 mentions the Twelve and "His followers.") The New Testament reveals Jesus' followers numbered 120 people, which included the Twelve and a group of women. Still, there is no indication that, other than the Twelve, they considered themselves as part of an organization or community. The idea of a "church" was foreign to them. Jesus said the word *church* only twice in the Gospels (Matt. 16:18; 18:17). He visited synagogues and, when in Jerusalem, the temple. This was no oversight; it was part of the plan. Jesus came to teach, to die, to be raised from the dead, and then to ascend to heaven to take his seat at the right hand of God. The establishment of the church wouldn't come until after those accomplishments. The rest was in the hands of his followers.

At Pentecost the church and its leaders received a spiritual power that allowed them to do what they never could have done before. Prior to that, Jesus' followers had been a *congregation* but not a *church*.

Timeline

A timeline helps us link separate occurrences into a unified series of events. Jesus begins a public ministry that lasts three years. During Passover, he is arrested in Jerusalem, endures three trials, and is crucified and buried in a borrowed tomb. His followers are scattered and directionless. Three days later, Jesus rises from the dead, and over the next forty days he appears to his followers—and only his followers—as many as five hundred at one time (1 Cor. 15:6).

At the end of the forty-day period following the resurrection, he calls the Twelve (technically the Eleven after Judas' suicide) and gives them their final marching orders. Then Jesus, in full view of his disciples, ascends into heaven. It is interesting that their first question reveals their lack of understanding of Jesus' overall goal. They ask about an earthly kingdom, with Jesus on the throne. This misunderstanding would continue until Pentecost.

It is in Jesus' last words that we get a hint at what was changing. There are two accounts of this event recorded in the Bible:

> Now He said to them, "These are My words which I spoke to you while I was still with you, that all things which are written about Me in the Law of Moses and the Prophets and the Psalms must be fulfilled." Then He opened their minds to understand the Scriptures, and He said to them, "Thus it is written, that the Christ would suffer and rise again from the dead the third day, and that repentance for forgiveness of sins would be proclaimed in His name to all the nations, beginning from Jerusalem. You are witnesses of these things. And behold, I am sending forth the promise of My Father upon you; but you are to stay in the city until you are clothed with power from on high."
>
> And He led them out as far as Bethany, and He lifted up His hands and blessed them. While He was blessing them, He parted from them and was carried up into heaven. And they, after worshiping Him, returned to Jerusalem with great joy, and were continually in the temple praising God. (Luke 24:44–53)

> The first account I composed, Theophilus, about all that Jesus began to do and teach, until the day when He was taken up to heaven, after He had by the Holy Spirit given orders to the apostles whom He had chosen. To these He also presented Himself alive after His suffering, by many convincing proofs, appearing to them over a period of forty days and speaking of the things concerning the kingdom of God. Gathering them together, He commanded them not to leave Jerusalem, but to wait for what the Father had promised, "Which," He said, "you heard of from Me; for John baptized with water, but you will be baptized with the Holy Spirit not many days from now."

So when they had come together, they were asking Him, saying, "Lord, is it at this time You are restoring the kingdom to Israel?" He said to them, "It is not for you to know times or epochs which the Father has fixed by His own authority; but you will receive power when the Holy Spirit has come upon you; and you shall be My witnesses both in Jerusalem, and in all Judea and Samaria, and even to the remotest part of the earth."

And after He had said these things, He was lifted up while they were looking on, and a cloud received Him out of their sight. And as they were gazing intently into the sky while He was going, behold, two men in white clothing stood beside them. They also said, "Men of Galilee, why do you stand looking into the sky? This Jesus, who has been taken up from you into heaven, will come in just the same way as you have watched Him go into heaven." (Acts 1:1–11)

Waiting

The disciples were to stay in place for ten days. It is doubtful they fully understood what would happen, but they were obedient nonetheless. Waiting can be hard work, but it often has a reason. Why wait for the coming of the Holy Spirit? Why would Jesus order his disciples to bide their time in a hostile city—the same city where he was tortured and crucified? The answer is timing.

They were to wait for the arrival of the Holy Spirit, who would grant them supernatural power. This part was not new to them. Most scholars link the start of Jesus' public ministry with his baptism at the hands of John the Baptist. John fit the mold of the Old Testament prophet. He lived an ascetic life, like a desert monk, but preached to the masses the need for repentance and baptism. He said, "As for me, I baptize you with water for repentance, but He who is coming after me is mightier than I, and I am not fit to remove His sandals; He will baptize you with the Holy Spirit and fire" (Matt. 3:11). There it is, the mention of fire and the Holy Spirit. John was speaking of an event that wouldn't happen for three years. But the disciples would recognize it when it came.

This commission must have sounded overwhelming to them. They were, Jesus said, to become witnesses in four geographical arenas: Jerusalem, Judea, Samaria, and the ends of the world. The last one must have made them pause. It was one thing to follow Jesus around the Holy Land for three years, but the "ends of the world" would have been too much to imagine. After all, Jesus never left his home country.

Of course, there was a reason for this. His mission centered on presenting God's plan to the Jews first (Matt. 15:24). The global mission would spread out from there. At the right time, they were to evangelize in Jerusalem, the city they were in, then move to regional but still local areas, then to the outliers in Samaria—a place religious Jews of the day avoided—then out to the world. The New Testament book of Acts is outlined on this structure.

While Jesus had many friends, the real core of his followers numbered 120, the size of a small church, and the real outreach would be done by the remaining members of the Twelve, with the later addition of the apostle Paul.

This mission would be done with first-century technology: walking, riding, traveling by ship, and small-group communicating. No armies would march ahead of them to subdue the people in advance. That was Rome's way. Jesus' way was much simpler but had a much longer life, and it continues today.

The 120 waited in the upper room, probably the same upper room where Jesus instituted the Lord's Supper. They stayed busy with prayer and filled Judas' spot with Matthias (Acts 1:23–26). In some ways they were acting like a small church and, against the custom of the day, included the female followers of Jesus. In that number were his mother Mary and most likely Mary Magdalene. Jesus' ministry crossed gender lines. The first people to see the resurrected Jesus were women (Luke 24:1–12).

Pentecost

Pentecost is a Greek term for one of the Jewish feast periods. The ancient Jews referred to it as the Feast of Weeks and later as Shavuot.

The first name refers to a "week of weeks," that is, forty-nine days. Adding Passover to that raises the number to fifty, hence, "Pentecost." The word *pentecost* comes from the ancient Greek meaning "fiftieth" day.

For the Jews it was a time to celebrate the first harvest and offer the "firstfruits" to God as a sacrifice. Later the feast became associated with the giving of the Law on Mount Sinai.

The church was born on this particular Pentecost, and it came about in a remarkable way. The disciples were all in one place. There is some debate as to where that place was. It is generally assumed they were in the upper room because the phrase "whole house" is used. Some scholars think the phrase refers to the temple as the house of God, but there is no mention in the text of the disciples leaving the upper room to go to the temple after supernatural events began. Acts 2 relates the whole story.

Whether in the upper room or somewhere on the temple grounds, the disciples were together, probably a huddle of 120 or more people. There came an audible event: the sound of rushing wind filled the whole house. Then a visual event followed: tongues of fire appeared and rested on them. Both fire and wind are emblems of the Holy Spirit, that is, symbols of the third person of the Trinity. As promised by Jesus, the Holy Spirit descended upon them, at a time and in a place where thousands of people would see.

There were more attention-getting happenings. The disciples began to speak in other languages. And not just speaking, but preaching as the Spirit gave them utterance. The hook here is that the disciples, all from Galilee, were speaking the home languages of all the pilgrims at the temple. Centuries of invasions had scattered Jews around the known world, many of whom would return to Jerusalem during the holy feast days, especially Passover and Pentecost. The population of Jerusalem would swell by tens of thousands. Many pilgrims camped outside the city walls. Jerusalem and its environs were packed with travelers who lived most of the year in distant lands. As observant Jews they would have learned Hebrew, but their daily language would be that of the land they lived in.

It was not uncommon for people in the first century to speak multiple languages. In the case of the disciples, they would have been familiar with Hebrew, the language of religious worship and rites; Latin, the language of the Roman oppressors; and Aramaic, the common language for Jews of the day. Some were also familiar with Greek, which would become the language of the New Testament. There were a great many other languages in the world that were beyond their experience.

Hearing people from Galilee speaking languages common to what is now Turkey, Iran, Iraq, Egypt, and other parts of North Africa must have been surprising. It wasn't that the languages were strange, it was who was speaking them. Add to that, they were speaking a Christian message. This was so startling that some people assumed the cacophony was fueled by early morning drinking (Acts 2:13). These were not ecstatic utterances but the voicing of known languages. Luke, the author of Acts, records the languages by listing the countries they were associated with. Most of these countries border the Mediterranean Sea.

First Sermon

The disciples were changed by the arrival of the Holy Spirit. That morning they had awakened as cautious, fearful people who harbored grave concerns about their safety and future. They knew that the religious leaders who conspired against Christ, the Romans who crucified him, and the crowd who had chanted, "Crucify Him!" were still walking the streets of Jerusalem. Even at several hundred strong, they were a tiny minority compared to those around them.

But things changed dramatically with the arrival of the Holy Spirit. Those same disciples who had abandoned Christ after his arrest became very different people: boldness replaced fear. The greatest change came in Peter, who had, a few weeks before, publicly denied knowing Jesus.

Peter had been the center of the disciples, at times showing great courage and insight and at other times making blunders. He was

19

always deeply committed. As if unwinding his weakest and darkest moment, publicly denying Christ, Peter steps up and delivers the first sermon of the church age. What makes it a "church age" sermon?

First, it is Bible-based. Peter quotes from the Old Testament book of Joel and several psalms (Joel 2:28–32; Ps. 16:8–11; 110:1; and others).

Second, the message is Christ-centered, not Law-centered. The Mosaic Law was the heart of Jewish life. Its codes and commandments were clearly established (although embellished through the centuries): "This is what God expects; this is what you must do." Peter's message focused on Jesus, hitting on all the key issues: Christ came for a purpose, worked miracles, was delivered up by the plan of God to death, was raised from the dead, ascended to heaven, and sits at the right hand of God.

He closed with, "Therefore let all the house of Israel know for certain that God has made Him both Lord and Christ—this Jesus whom you crucified" (Acts 2:36). "Lord and Christ"; Master and Messiah.

Peter pulled no punches. He laid blame for the crucifixion on the people and called for public repentance. It is interesting that the church was planted and grew in the place most hostile to it.

The sermon was direct, harsh, accusatory, and struck at the heart of the hearer. It was longer than what is recorded in Acts (2:40), but the material we have shows a change in preaching that has lasted for two thousand years. In seminaries around the world, professors of preaching teach this account to their students.

The people responded to it—at least three thousand of them committed to repentance and baptism. The church would continue to grow daily (v. 47). We have no way of knowing how many of those same people were in the crowd shouting for Jesus' crucifixion two months earlier.

A Church Pattern Is Established

What was it like to be a part of the first church? There were no church manuals. No seminaries to train pastors. No denominations.

Everything was new. Acts 2:46–47 lists the key habits of the first church, customs that remain to this day:

"One mind." They cultivated and maintained unity, something that would be tested in the years ahead.

"In the temple." In the early days of the church, believers in Jerusalem would gather at the temple. Over time, Christians would meet in homes and later in rented buildings.

"Breaking bread from house to house." They celebrated the Lord's Supper in private homes. Church buildings were a thing of the future. The Lord's Supper (the Eucharist) is distinctly Christian and portrays the broken body and shed blood of Christ, not something that would fit with temple rituals.

"Taking their meals together with gladness and sincerity of heart." Fellowship was a priority, and sharing meals was an important social ritual. It built friendship and kinship.

"Praising God." Praise has always been a part of worship. Public singing is common today (although there were periods of history where singing was prohibited). In the first church, praise was a daily habit, not something reserved for a special day of the week.

"Having favor with all the people." Their behavior was Christlike, portraying Jesus in their words and in the way they treated others.

The contemporary church has changed in many ways, and some of the ways it expresses itself in worship have changed. A few things, like breaking bread from house to house, may have disappeared, but the principles behind them have remained.

The church did not slowly rise in history, it exploded on the scene, accompanied by a miracle. What had been a ragtag band of Jesus' followers became an organized force in the world that has continued to alter human history for two millennia. The meek became the brave, the uncertain became the confident, and the world became a mission field.

That hasn't changed.

2

The Conversion
of Paul

(AD 35)

F ew things are as dangerous as a zealous man with the wrong
idea. Paul, formerly Saul, was one such man, and many paid a
dear price because of it. Yet this man who admitted to persecuting
the church to the death and imprisoning men and women (Acts 22:4)
became the most important person in the development of the church.
It is no exaggeration to say that he, more than any other person apart
from Jesus himself, did more to advance the cause of Christ, solidify
the doctrine of the church and open its doors to people around the
world, and clarify what it means to be a follower of Christ.

True as all that is, no one saw it coming. His brilliance was recognized early by his Jewish teachers and his zeal was observed throughout Jerusalem, yet he would not have been singled out to become
a man who would influence billions of people for two millennia.
Today, he remains the most-read man in history. Bruce Shelley said it
best: "No one did more for the faith, but no one seemed less likely."[1]

The Pre-Converted Paul

"Some," wrote Shakespeare, "are born great, some achieve greatness, and some have greatness thrust upon 'em."[2] Paul was not born great, but he did manage the other two items in Shakespeare's list.

All that we know of Paul comes from his own testimony. The most complete version is recorded in the New Testament's history book, Acts. It is a testimony given in a moment of great danger. Paul and others were in Jerusalem with a mob of angry men ready to kill them. Paul had gone to the temple to participate in purification rites when a group of Jews from Asia recognized him and stirred the crowd to a murderous pitch. We can almost hear them screeching: "Men of Israel, come to our aid! This is the man who preaches to all men everywhere against our people and the Law and this place [the temple]; and besides he has even brought Greeks into the temple and has defiled this holy place" (Acts 21:28).

The crowd rushed him, and they dragged him from the temple with murder on their minds. It is ironic that, prior to his conversion, Paul might have been one of those egging the mob on. Instead, he was the object of persecution. Only the intervention of Roman soldiers could keep the victim from the enraged mob. Protected by armed men, Paul asked the commander for permission to speak to the people. Approval was granted. Paul faced the angry mob and spoke to them in Hebrew. That caused the crowd to settle a little. He then told the story of his background and conversion. From Acts 22 and other passages we learn several things.

First, Paul stated he was a Jew born in Cilicia, a coastal region in the south of Asia Minor. His city of birth was Tarsus, an ancient city of what is now Turkey. It was a city with roots that reached back four thousand years before Paul's day. It was also known as an educational town. More important to his attackers, however, was the revelation that Paul had been educated under Rabbi Gamaliel, one of the greatest Jewish religious thinkers in history.

Paul added a few words about his zeal for God and Jewish law. Paul would later write to the church at Philippi reminding them of

23

his deep Jewish grounding. In that letter he wrote: "If anyone else has a mind to put confidence in the flesh, I far more: circumcised the eighth day, of the nation of Israel, of the tribe of Benjamin, a Hebrew of Hebrews; as to the Law, a Pharisee; as to zeal, a persecutor of the church; as to the righteousness which is in the Law, found blameless" (Phil. 3:4–6). He was a Pharisee, a conservative group of Jewish believers and the ones who most tormented Christ. They orchestrated the arrest that led to the crucifixion of Jesus.

Paul had all the elements necessary for greatness in the Jewish world: sound family lineage, the best in education, a lifetime adherence to the Mosaic laws and Jewish practices, and a determination to serve God—no matter who it hurt. He admitted to persecuting the church in Jerusalem and jailing men and women. He told of how he had letters of authority from religious leaders to expand his persecution to Damascus, a city about 140 miles from Jerusalem. He would get to Damascus, but not in the way he thought.

Paul, ever the evangelist, had quieted the mob with his brief biography. Then he told them the rest of the story. He related his conversion to Christ and then called on the mob to repent and be baptized. That went badly. Again, the soldiers were the only thing between him and a brutal death. The Romans carted him off for his own protection.

The Damascus Road Turnaround

The first line of Acts 9 pulls no punches: "Now Saul [was] still breathing threats and murder against the disciples of the Lord." Threats and murder. There might be a tendency to want to soft-pedal Saul's persecution of the church, but he never did, nor did Luke, the author of Acts. Luke was one of the apostle Paul's traveling companions. We can assume they had become friends as well as coworkers in the gospel. Still, Luke is blunt about his activity. Persecuting Christians in Jerusalem was not enough; Saul was ambitious and wanted to cast a wider net. To do this he needed letters from the high priest to extend the persecution. These letters would give him access to synagogues and legal right to take Christians prisoner and drag them back to Jerusalem.

Saul believed he was doing God a favor, extracting the impurities from the faith. Those impurities were people who belonged to the Way, the term the first Christians used to describe themselves (Acts 22:4). Saul did not see himself as a tormentor but as the man who would save traditional Judaism from being diluted with heresy. In his mind, he was the good guy; the Christians were the ones in the wrong.

Not long before his expedition to Damascus, he participated in the stoning death of the deacon Stephen. Stephen's crime was preaching the gospel. In one of church history's great ironies, Paul would, about sixteen years later in Lystra, be stoned, dragged outside the city perimeter, and left for dead. His crime? Preaching the gospel.

Someplace on the road from Jerusalem to Damascus, Saul and his band of enforcers were stopped in their tracks. Acts 9 and Paul's testimony in Acts 26 tell the story from Saul's point of view. Light flashed around him with such intensity that Saul was knocked to the ground and blinded. Paul described the light as "brighter than the sun" (26:13). The light encompassed him and his travel companions. And then he alone heard a voice.

"Saul, Saul, why are you persecuting Me? It is hard for you to kick against the goads" (v. 14).

This was more than a question—it was an accusation. The way the question is framed is condemning. Jesus didn't ask why Saul was persecuting the church; he asked why Saul was persecuting *him*. Then came a statement that puzzles the modern mind: "It is hard for you to kick against the goads." A goad is a long, sharp stick used to move an ox forward. The beast's owner would poke the ox to make it move or to change its direction. The statement implies that something had been goading Saul. His conscience? An expert in the Tanakh, the Hebrew Bible, was he seeing a connection between the prophecies of the coming Messiah and Jesus? Had Jesus tried a gentler form of persuasion that Saul ignored? We're not told. Animals like oxen often kicked against the goad, which brought even more goading.

Saul had been doing the same, and now the time came when goading was done and direct confrontation was needed.

Saul asked, "Who are You, Lord?"

The answer must have melted his heart: "I am Jesus whom you are persecuting" (v. 15). It isn't difficult to imagine what Saul's next few thoughts were. In an instant, Saul was humbled and stripped of everything he valued: his pride, the sense of duty he used to justify throwing men and women in jail and stoning an innocent man to death, and his understanding of God and his service to him. Saul learned in a moment that he had been wrong about everything, and shame, regret, and guilt came with that realization.

It's possible that Saul believed he would die on that road. But that was not to be. Paul gives a more detailed account of Jesus' response:

> Get up and stand on your feet; for this purpose I have appeared to you, to appoint you a minister and a witness not only to the things which you have seen, but also to the things in which I will appear to you; rescuing you from the Jewish people and from the Gentiles, to whom I am sending you, to open their eyes so that they may turn from darkness to light and from the dominion of Satan to God, that they may receive forgiveness of sins and an inheritance among those who have been sanctified by faith in Me. (26:16–18)

The encounter left Saul blind, and he had to be led into Damascus. He had planned to arrive in strength, but now he could not move forward without help. Saul was led into the city and situated in a house owned by a man named Judas (not the traitor; see Acts 9:11). For three days he neither ate nor slept. He did nothing but wait and live with his thoughts and his past. Guilt weighed on him; regret ate at him.

A Christian in Damascus named Ananias received a vision in which Christ appeared and told him to go to Saul and lay hands on him so that he would regain his sight. Ananias was not keen on the idea. Who would be? Saul's reputation preceded him. Jesus insisted: "Go, for he is a chosen instrument of Mine, to bear My name before the

Gentiles and kings and the sons of Israel; for I will show him how much he must suffer for My name's sake" (9:15–16).

Another piece of irony appears here. Saul had come to Damascus to find Christians and drag them back to Jerusalem. Most likely, one of the names on his list was Ananias. A man Saul would gladly have plucked from his home and imprisoned would be the conduit for his healing. This was not missed by Saul. Ananias prayed for Saul, and the former tormentor of the church was healed. Saul spent several days in the company of the Damascus disciples.

During those days, Saul reconsidered his enormous theological knowledge, but this time with Christ as the Messiah. He began preaching in the synagogues, proclaiming Jesus as the Son of God. Those were the same synagogues the high priest had given him authority to search.

Saul was now Paul the apostle.

A Different Kind of Apostle

Paul was a man of great pride. Even after his conversion he could come across as self-important. In his case, he was more important than even the people of his day knew—perhaps more than he himself knew. Prior to his encounter with Christ on the road to Damascus, he must have been quite arrogant. That arrogance morphed into a commitment to serve Christ and his church. He traveled without delay and preached without hesitation. Still, a reading of his letters shows a man who, although forgiven by Jesus, could not forgive himself. "For I am the least of the apostles, and not fit to be called an apostle, because I persecuted the church of God" (1 Cor. 15:9). Like Peter, who it seems could never forgive himself for denying Christ, he carried the baggage of regret with him. Perhaps that regret was some of the fuel that saw him through horrible times of rejection, beatings, and near-death events. Still, he never felt subservient to the other apostles (2 Cor. 11:5).

Paul had not traveled with Christ, had not sat at his feet during his three years of earthly ministry, and may have never seen Jesus in the flesh. Although born in Tarsus, he spent many of his educational years in Jerusalem studying under Gamaliel. Still, he seems to be absent from the Holy City during Christ's ministry. Perhaps he had returned to his family home in Tarsus, or perhaps, as an evangelizing Pharisee, he was away on missionary trips—not for the Christian church, but for Judaism. Jesus mentions traveling Pharisees in one of his condemnations of their behavior: "Woe to you, scribes and Pharisees, hypocrites, because you travel around on sea and land to make one proselyte; and when he becomes one, you make him twice as much a son of hell as yourselves" (Matt. 23:15).

Although Paul was not present during the twelve resurrection appearances of Christ (Jesus only appeared to supporters and family), he nonetheless saw the risen Christ: first on the road to Damascus and also while in a trance (Acts 22:17–21). Paul claimed to have seen Jesus in 1 Corinthians 9:1 and 15:8–9. In the 1 Corinthians 15 passage, he refers to himself as "one untimely born," that is, one who didn't fit the usual definition used to describe an apostle. In selecting a replacement for the traitor Judas, the remaining disciples created a set of criteria: the replacement (1) must have been present with Jesus during his entire earthly ministry; and (2) must have been a witness to Jesus' ascension into heaven. Paul met neither of these criteria.

This doesn't mean he had no qualifications. Certainly Jesus thought him to be the right man for the job. Paul would, more than any other apostle, shape the church.

Paul was a true apostle. The word means "he that is sent"—very much like an ambassador from one country to another. Paul described himself as an ambassador of the gospel (Eph. 6:20). He made three missionary trips around the Mediterranean and may have traveled as far as Spain.

The man who started off as the great persecutor would become greatly persecuted for the very cause he had attempted to stamp out. In a letter to one of the early churches, he listed the abuses he had been forced to face during his work:

> In far more labors, in far more imprisonments, beaten times without number, often in danger of death. Five times I received from the Jews

thirty-nine lashes. Three times I was beaten with rods, once I was stoned, three times I was shipwrecked, a night and a day I have spent in the deep. I have been on frequent journeys, in dangers from rivers, dangers from robbers, dangers from my countrymen, dangers from the Gentiles, dangers in the city, dangers in the wilderness, dangers on the sea, dangers among false brethren; I have been in labor and hardship, through many sleepless nights, in hunger and thirst, often without food, in cold and exposure. Apart from such external things, there is the daily pressure on me of concern for all the churches. (2 Cor. 11:23–28)

Ultimately, Paul would be arrested, and since he was a Roman citizen, he was allowed to appeal his case to Rome. It would be his last journey. After a period of "house arrest" in Rome, where he continued his ministry, he was beheaded. Had he not had Roman citizenship, he would have been crucified as so many Jewish Christians were.

Just What the Church Needed

Paul's life is the stuff of movies, filled with advances and setbacks, achievements and rejection. This Jew of Jews was just what the church needed, not only in the first century but in every century that followed. His résumé was remarkable.

As a missionary he became the primary evangelist to the Gentiles but always preached to the Jews first. As a scholar he established the basic doctrine that the two-thousand-year-old church holds today. As a church planter he established churches, trained leaders, left them in capable hands, and, like a mother hen, brooded over them, always concerned about their spiritual state. He served as the poster boy for redemption. If the former persecutor of the church could have a spiritual turnabout, anyone could. Although he never considered himself so, Paul was a gifted speaker. Perhaps his gifts were not in the Greek tradition of oratory that was so valued in his day, but he delivered sermons and lessons that people could understand and respond to. As a writer, he penned a body of work that formed the belief system of the church. He was the defender of the outcast, championing the cause of the Gentiles and defending them against the Judaizers who desired them to become Jews first. He leveled the playing field for everyone. As a martyr, like other martyrs, he showed that the message of Christ was worth dying for. And if it was worth dying for, it was also worth living for.

Paul Shaped the Church with His Theology

Theology is the study of God. Doctrine is the set of Christian beliefs. Paul, using his deep understanding of the Jewish Scriptures, showed that Christianity was forever rooted in Judaism. He opened the Old Testament passages to show Christ being revealed there. He was a scholar of the first order. The new church had the teachings of Jesus thanks to four people—Matthew, Mark, Luke, and John—who recorded much of what Jesus did and said. This would provide the basis for Christian belief, but Paul solidified early doctrine. Much of his writing, although often intended for other purposes, forms the core of contemporary Christian thinking. Every Sunday, preachers stand behind pulpits proclaiming truth based on what Paul wrote.

Paul Continues to Shape the Church through His Writing

Paul did so much good that most people are reluctant to single out his greatest work. His most enduring effort, however, gets almost no debate. Paul was a scholar, church planter, preacher, missionary, church starter, and teacher, but most of all he was a writer. There are twenty-seven books in the New Testament, and thirteen were written by Paul. Scholars debate the author of Hebrews, but many, if not most, believe Paul penned that book also. If so, then that brings the number of New Testament books written by Paul to fourteen—over half. That half comprises about 40 percent of the New Testament's content. The book of Acts was written by

Luke, a travel companion of Paul. Approximately sixteen chapters of that book deal with Paul's missionary journeys and other material regarding his conversion.

Paul's books are a collection of epistles (letters) written to churches. In most cases, the letters are corrective, warning Christians away from the cult of the Gnostics and the legalism of the Judaizers. He also defended himself against rumor and called for moral and doctrinal purity, all delivered with large measures of encouragement. He did not set out to write a theology text, although the New Testament books of Hebrews and Romans come pretty close. Still, by challenging false doctrine, he presented correct teaching. For example, the clearest teaching about the nature of Christ is found in his letter to the Colossians, a book designed to disarm Gnostics and other groups upsetting the understanding of the Christians.

These letters were widely copied and circulated among the first-century church and were later collected in what became the New Testament. Peter refers to Paul's style of writing:

> Therefore, beloved, since you look for these things, be diligent to be found by Him in peace, spotless and blameless, and regard the patience of our Lord as salvation; just as also our beloved brother Paul, according to the wisdom given him, wrote to you, as also in all his letters, speaking in them of these things, in which are some things hard to understand, which the untaught and unstable distort, as they do also the rest of the Scriptures, to their own destruction. (2 Pet. 3:14–16)

Paul's writings were not always easy to fathom. He thought at a much higher level than the average person. Even Peter admits that some of Paul's prose was difficult to understand. Nonetheless, Peter, in this passage, equates the missionary's writing with Scripture.

Our understanding of Christ, the importance of the resurrection, salvation by faith and not works, and scores of other foundational concepts would be much thinner had Paul not put his thoughts down in writing. His written words have outlived the churches he founded, but the church as a whole has spread across the planet.

On a stretch of road leading from Jerusalem to Damascus, a flash of light and a pressing question changed the church and the world forever. Paul wrote like no other, spoke like no other, and worked like no other—and billions of lives have been changed over the centuries because of his work for the gospel.

Gentiles and Judaism
Showdown in Jerusalem

(AD 50)

The church as we know it almost ended before it started. Had it not been for the actions of one man, the church might have been little more than a sect of Judaism.

The world was a tumultuous and uncertain place for most first-century people, the most secure being Roman citizens in and around Rome. Much of the rest of the world, while under Roman rule, clung to some of their own traditions. This was especially true for Jews who were famous for their intractability regarding their religious beliefs. Not even the fear of imprisonment or death could budge them. Rome learned to tolerate the Jews. They also learned to hate them as a people.

For centuries, Jews had been taught to observe a set of strict laws that dictated their daily lives. Unlike other groups, they had rigid rules about diet and about how one served God. While non-Jews were polytheistic, with a constellation of pagan gods to worship, Jews were strictly monotheistic. Daily they would repeat the Shema:

"Hear, O Israel! The LORD is our God, the LORD is one!" (Deut. 6:4). Morning and night they would repeat these words, as many still do today. It is a confession of faith. Those words are followed by a list of commands:

> You shall love the LORD your God with all your heart and with all your soul and with all your might. These words, which I [God] am commanding you today, shall be on your heart. You shall teach them diligently to your sons and shall talk of them when you sit in your house and when you walk by the way and when you lie down and when you rise up. You shall bind them as a sign on your hand and they shall be as frontals on your forehead. You shall write them on the doorposts of your house and on your gates. (vv. 5–9)

Those commands were given 1,400 years before Christ, and the Jewish commitment to the practice outlined in those words had not waned. As with any group, there are those who were more devout than others, but the percentage of practicing Jews was very high.

The Jews were a separated people, chosen by God from all other nations to be unique and holy in God's eyes. To them, there were only two types of people: Jews and Gentiles. Their lifestyle, diet, worship, and circumcision set them apart from all other groups and made them appear to others as aloof, clannish, and arrogant. This was fine with them. They were being obedient to God's commands, and what others thought mattered little.

This bifurcated view threatened to hamstring the fledgling church. After Christ's death and resurrection and the Pentecost experience, thousands joined the church, causing it to grow from a few hundred adherents to a megachurch overnight. Many of these new believers came from the priestly caste and other segments of the religious society. This included people from one of the most conservative branches of Judaism: Pharisees. During Jesus' ministry, his most vocal opponents came from the Pharisees. Pharisees can be considered the conservative party, holding to a strict practice of Jewish law.

While the church remained Jewish, all was fine, but Jesus never intended for the church to be confined within Judaism. While it is true that the gospel was to be delivered to the Jews first, then to the Gentiles, it had always been part of the divine plan to reach into all nations (Rom. 1:16; 2:9, 10). Therein lay the problem. Jesus was Jewish, all his disciples were Jewish, Pentecost occurred in Jerusalem, and the first church was born in the heart of the most Jewish city in the world.

Yet it was clear that God had a wider view in mind. In a vision, Peter was led to understand that the message of Christ was meant for Gentiles too (Acts 10:1–48). Peter said, "I most certainly understand now that God is not one to show partiality, but in every nation the man who fears Him and does what is right is welcome to Him" (vv. 34–35).

While Peter was the first to understand the all-inclusive nature of the gospel, it would fall upon the apostle Paul—a very Jewish man—to become the leader in that movement.

Jewish Openness to the Gospel

The Jewish people were a natural place to start with the gospel. First, they were already the covenant people of God. The Messiah would come from their ranks and be a descendant of King David (Isa. 9:7). They understood the Old Testament prophecies and teaching. Much of the New Testament is rooted in the Old Testament. The book of Hebrews is a good example. It cites numerous Old Testament passages. First-century Jews had spent their lives exposed to these teachings, so they needed very little training in understanding the Old Testament. They were intellectually primed to understand.

They were also spiritually primed, having been taught that God would send his "anointed One," the Messiah. Many Jews expected and longed for a conquering Messiah to free them from the bondage and oppression of the Romans, and many could understand the numerous passages foretelling a suffering Messiah (e.g., Ps. 22; Isa. 53).

Also, Jews were everywhere in the empire. Jews could be found in every major city; perhaps as much as 7 percent of the population in each of those cities was Jewish. Paul used this fact to his advantage, often establishing churches in crossroad cities, first by preaching in the synagogues and then taking the message to the wider audience of Gentiles.

Gentile Openness to the Gospel

Gentiles proved to be open to the message of Christ. Gentiles were religious people but in a very different way from the ancient Jews. Jews had the writings of Moses and the Prophets, and therefore had a solid basis for their belief. They could cite passages to back up their beliefs. Polytheistic Gentiles had scores of gods to worship, most from Greek mythology, which the Romans had adopted and changed. The idea of a Jewish God would not be surprising. In his sermon on Mars Hill, Paul pointed to a statue for an unknown god (Acts 17:22–34). Apparently there was a fear of offending some god unknown to them. The tricky part was persuading polytheists that there was only one God.

The message of Christ was tolerated by some Gentiles and dismissed as meaningless talk by others, but many responded to the call and churches sprang up around the empire.

Fear of the Different

After generations of seeing themselves as separate from other nations and uniquely called, it was hard for some Jews to accept Gentile believers. Gentiles were pagans and great sinners. Paul wouldn't argue that fact. In his letter to the church at Corinth, he wrote, "Or do you not know that the unrighteous will not inherit the kingdom of God? Do not be deceived; neither fornicators, nor idolaters, nor adulterers, nor effeminate, nor homosexuals, nor thieves, nor the covetous, nor drunkards, nor revilers, nor swindlers, will inherit the kingdom of God. *Such were some of you*; but you were washed, but you were sanctified, but you were justified in the name of the Lord

36

Jesus Christ and in the Spirit of our God" (1 Cor. 6:9–11, emphasis added). The common habits and the sexual behavior that many Gentiles practiced were what Jews had been avoiding all their lives. Gentiles had a lot of learning to do, and many Jewish Christians were not convinced they could do it.

Those brought up in Jewish homes learned that faith was worked out through prayer, righteous living, and animal sacrifices. Some Gentile cults had similar practices, but not to the extent or depth of meaning of the Jews. How could a Gentile properly earn salvation without being Jewish? This thinking led to the rise of the Judaizers, and with them the first doctrinal clash in the church.

Some of the Jewish Christians were willing to accept Gentile believers if they would first become Jews. It was not unusual for Gentiles to convert to Judaism. The purity of the faith was attractive to many, but since a full conversion meant undergoing circumcision, a painful commitment for adult males (and a repulsive concept to many Gentiles), many chose to adopt the belief and practices without undergoing circumcision. These men were called "God-fearers" (Acts 17:4).

There is more to this thinking. What the early Judaizers were teaching was a works-based salvation based on a works-centered Judaism. Keeping the law of Moses required effort and commitment. To hear that salvation came through faith and not works was difficult, if not impossible, to accept. Could God have changed his plan that much? Did this mean that all the years of disciplined living and sacrifice meant nothing? Letting go of something held so tightly for so long was difficult. To some, Christianity was an extension of Judaism. The new covenant of Christ was a structure built on the foundation of the old covenant. This is mostly correct. Jesus made no comments about abolishing the Mosaic law, but he did speak of fulfilling it (Matt. 5:17).

Trouble came in the Syrian city of Antioch, three hundred miles north of Jerusalem. As the first wave of persecution swept through Jerusalem and surrounding regions, many Christians fled, taking the message of Christ with them. Some ended up in Antioch where they preached the gospel, but only to Jews. Others arrived and shared the same message with Gentiles, many of whom readily took the message to heart. Word of all this reached church leaders, who sent Barnabas to investigate. He found an impressive group of Gentile believers in the city. Barnabas went in search of Paul and brought him back to the city to help in the evangelistic and discipling work. The pair ministered in the city for a year. The term "Christian" was coined in Antioch (see Acts 11:26).

Then the Judaizers arrived, teaching that unless you are circumcised according to the custom of Moses, you cannot be saved. This didn't go over well with Paul and Barnabas and became the first major doctrinal dispute of the church.

Head-to-Head in Jerusalem

Acts 15 gives the account. Paul, Barnabas, and a few others made the three-hundred-mile journey to Jerusalem to meet with church leaders. Paul presented the problem to the church as a whole but gave an "executive session" account to church leaders like Peter and James. The issue was debated until Peter reminded the group that he had been the first to present the gospel to the Gentiles and that they gave every evidence of having received the same Holy Spirit as Peter and the others had on Pentecost. Then he made an interesting remark: "Now therefore why do you put God to the test by placing upon the neck of the disciples a yoke which neither our fathers nor we have been able to bear? But we believe that we are saved through the grace of the Lord Jesus, in the same way as they also are" (vv. 10–11). That comment and the account Paul and Barnabas gave about God's work in Antioch sealed the deal. The first and most important church council had met and made its decision.

James, the half-brother of Jesus and now a leader of the church, then composed a letter to be delivered to the church in Antioch. It contained a few requests:

Since we have heard that some of our number to whom we gave no instruction have disturbed you with their words, unsettling your souls, it seemed good to us, having become of one mind, to select men to send to you with our beloved Barnabas and Paul, men who have risked their lives for the name of our Lord Jesus Christ. Therefore we have sent Judas and Silas, who themselves will also report the same things by word of mouth. For it seemed good to the Holy Spirit and to us to lay upon you no greater burden than these essentials: that you abstain from things sacrificed to idols and from blood and from things strangled and from fornication; if you keep yourselves free from such things, you will do well. Farewell. (vv. 24–29)

The letter put an end to the conflict at Antioch, but the work of Judaizers would continue and play a significant role in church history. It is interesting to note that those who had traveled to Antioch with their faulty message had not been sent from Jerusalem. They were working on their own. The letter also praises Barnabas and Paul for their work and willingness to risk their lives for the gospel. While the pressure to first become Jews was removed, several requests were made. The council asked that their Gentile brothers abstain from food that had been offered to idols, from consuming blood as food, from eating things that had been strangled to death, and from sexual sins. Three out of four requests had to do with Mosaic dietary laws. All four items were abhorrent to Jews and forbidden in Leviticus 17 and elsewhere.

The purpose of the request was not to force Gentiles to observe the dietary laws of the Jews, or to make them think that to do so was a requirement for salvation. The intent was to help Gentiles understand that these were matters of concern to their Jewish brothers, and by avoiding such things they could create a strong fellowship and establish a church where Jew and Gentile could worship together.

The council had an effect on the apostle Paul, who was an independent personality, driven in his work, and who held an unswerving desire to reach Gentiles. This alone is interesting since Paul was, prior to his dramatic conversion on the road to Damascus, a Jew's Jew. No one could claim to be a better Jew, and for the first part of his life he took great pride in his Jewish standing and his unceasing devotion to keeping every aspect of the Law. He was one of the earliest persecutors of the church, but once he became the very kind of person he had been persecuting, he put those energies into mission work. It's ironic that a man with deep Jewish roots and a—albeit misplaced—zeal for all things Jewish would become the protector of Gentile Christians.

Paul and later church leaders would face many attacks against the basic doctrine of the church, the two most prevalent being Gnostics and Judaizers. Later centuries would see other issues resolved by councils, such as the Trinity and the nature of Christ. Some issues were never solved in council but fragmented the church: Calvinism versus Arminianism, the inerrancy of the Bible, the proper mode of biblical baptism, slavery, the nature of missions, and many more. The Roman Catholic Church called twenty-one councils over a 1,700-year period. After the Reformation, individual denominations would hold similar meetings, although with much less formality. There is no major denomination that does not have some level of disagreement in its ranks.

Still the church continues forward, and it does so with a global mind-set. Over two billion people are associated with a Christian church of some sort, comprising about a third of the world's population—the majority of which are Gentiles. It is startling to see how Christianity has spread over the last century. In 1910, 27 percent of the population in the Americas was associated with the Christian church; in 2010, that number had grown to nearly 39 percent. Sub-Saharan Africa has grown from 1.4 percent to over 23 percent. Asia-Pacific numbers have nearly tripled from 4.5 percent to over 13 percent. Europe, on the other hand, declined from 66 percent to 26 percent. The Middle East has remained the same.[1]

Gentiles make up the bulk of Christian churches. The realization that the gospel was meant for the world was known from the beginning. Before Jesus' ascension, he told his disciples, "Go therefore and make disciples of all the nations, baptizing them in the name of the Father and the Son and the Holy Spirit, teaching them to observe all that I commanded you; and lo, I am with you always, even to the end of the age" (Matt. 28:19–20). The word Jesus used for "nations" is *ethnos*, the same word used for "Gentiles." Tradition has the disciples traveling the known world, reaching as far as Spain in the West and India in the East.

The first church was Jewish, but under Christ's command it spread to Gentile countries around the world. That was God's plan all along.

4

When Rome Burned

(AD 64)

It could have been a scene from Dante's *Inferno*: a man standing on a rooftop as the sky above roiled with thick smoke. Black ash and orange embers rained from the sky. In one hand he held his pride and joy, a lyre; with the other he plucked at its seven strings. From his elevated position, he sang to the city. His song mixed with the fearful wails rising from the streets below. He sang an ode to Troy, another devastated city.

The man performing is Lucius Domitius Ahenobarbus.

Later he took the name Nero Claudius Caesar Augustus Germanicus. Today we just call him Nero. The year was AD 64.

Nero watched Rome burn. Citizens, soldiers, and firefighters waged war with the unstoppable flames and Nero could do nothing but lament the loss—a loss he may have brought about.

Nero was a mere twenty-seven when one of the worst urban fires in history occurred, but he had already made a name for himself—a bad name. Handsome, athletic, artistic, and insecure, Nero's legend lives nearly two millennia after his death, but not the way his ego wanted.

Nero reigned in Rome from 54 to 68, just fourteen years. During that time he turned from being one of the most promising emperors into a sadistic dictator in need of constant applause. He was, in the words of one church historian, "A demon in human shape."[1]

The fire of Rome would have a devastating impact on Christians and the fledgling church. To understand the fire of Rome and how it shaped the church, we must first understand the man in the middle of it all: Nero.

Prologue to Infamy

Nero was born on December 15, AD 37, in the Italian coastal city of Antium about thirty-five miles south of Rome. His father was Gnaeus Domitius Ahenobarbus, an unlikable fellow whom the ancient historian Suetonius described as "a man of execrable character in every part of his life." The historian recounts events that show Nero's father as a murderer and a cheat.[2] He was prosecuted for treason, adultery, and incest. The charges were brought shortly before Emperor Tiberius died. The change in leadership allowed him to fall through the cracks. He died of edema when Nero was three.

Nero's mother, Agrippina, had been given in marriage to Nero's forty-five-year-old father when she was only thirteen years old. She was also his second cousin. Agrippina was related to power: the brutal, violent, and probably insane Emperor Caligula was her brother.

In 41, Claudius became emperor. He was a man unlucky in love and marriage. His third wife, Valeria Messalina, was accused of adultery, and Claudius had her executed in 48. She left behind a young son, Britannicus, the heir to Claudius' throne. Soured on marriage, Claudius vowed to never wed again. The vow didn't last.

On New Year's Day of 49, Claudius married the widow Agrippina, who was the daughter of his brother. In other words, Claudius married his niece. She was his fourth wife. Agrippina would wield great influence on the emperor.

43

Agrippina was devious, full of intrigue, and not afraid to take lovers or to conspire to kill. She had an agenda behind marrying the most powerful man in the empire. She had endured ill treatment and had been exiled by another emperor: her brother Caligula. In the world of emperors, intrigue crouched around every corner.

One of her first achievements as wife to Claudius was to convince him to formally adopt her child Nero as his own son, something he did on February 25, AD 50. Next, she persuaded him that Nero would be a better successor than Claudius' own son Britannicus, who was four years younger than Nero. Claudius agreed. Now all that was needed was for Claudius to die. He did so four years later. He was sixty-three years old and had reigned for thirteen years. There is debate about the details of Claudius' death. Most ancient historians say he died after eating poisoned mushrooms, and many point the finger at Agrippina, who had the most to gain by her husband's death.

Nero's climb to power was rocket-like. In 49 he gained a stepfather in Claudius. In 50, he became the adopted son of the emperor. In 53, Nero married Claudius' daughter Octavia, and in 54, he became emperor.

Teenager on the Throne

The sixty-three-year-old Claudius was succeeded by the seventeen-year-old Nero. At least that's how it appears. It might be more accurate to say that the emperor was succeeded by the thirty-nine-year-old Agrippina. Nero's mother could not be empress, not in ancient Rome, but she could pull the strings of an emperor: her son.

Nero was a teenager when he took the throne. The equivalent of a junior in high school ruled the most powerful country in the world—and behind it all was Agrippina. Agrippina was the empire's most powerful "stage mom."

First Years: A Good Start

A teenager with ultimate power and a controlling mother sounds like trouble from the start, but Nero (guided by his tutors Seneca, a

philosopher and teacher, and Burrus, the commander of the Praeto-
rian Guard) gave every indication of being an able and selfless leader.

Nero ended secret trials, gave the Senate more independence,
banned capital punishment (which was later to become one of history's greatest ironies), pleased the people by lowering their taxes,
and allowed slaves to sue unjust owners. He even gave aid to the
Jews, whom Claudius had evicted some years before (yet another
brutal irony).

The following nine years, however, revealed the true nature of the
young man, and it was an ugly sight.

Nero loved to be center stage. He had more interest in performing than in leading. The latter act appealed more to his mother than
him. His thirst for attention and applause was insatiable. He played
the lyre, loved to sing to his dinner guests, drove chariots, and trod
the boards of the stage. The people, however, thought such actions
were beneath those of noble birth or high position. Only lower
class people acted and performed, not government leaders. Nero
didn't care. He longed for—perhaps was addicted to—applause.
Nero needed to be admired.

The days of good Nero lasted five years; the next nine years would
paint him as a monster.

Nero the Menace

During the first years of his reign, Nero ruled justly and with principle, but in his early twenties everything changed. He spread his
wings, casting off the strings his mother and advisors had tied. Something inside Nero could no longer be contained.

Nero was a young man with hidden and unacceptable appetites.
Once entrenched in power, he no longer felt the need to keep those
raging appetites under wraps. He was a man of power, and he stepped
into the same trap that other emperors and men of power before
him had done: he began to believe his own press.

Rumors circulated through Rome that Nero seduced married women
and young boys, and had taken a male lover whom he had castrated

and "married"—a former slave at that. There were also stories that Nero liked to roam the streets at night and murder innocent people.

Nero's life would be cluttered with murder. Less than a year after receiving the throne, while seated at the dining table, he watched his thirteen-year-old stepbrother Britannicus seize, froth at the mouth, fall to the floor, and die. The symptoms match hemlock poisoning. The natural son of Claudius would never be a threat to Nero's position as the head of Rome.

Agrippina, who had schemed and worked to get her son on the throne, became a growing annoyance for Nero. "Stage mother" that she was, she was reluctant to release control. When Nero became more open with his sexual activities, Agrippina complained. Nero had taken Claudia Acte as a mistress, and his mother disapproved (although she had once been a mistress herself).

Stress between mother and son grew until Nero could no longer tolerate the situation. He pushed her from the palace and she took residence in an estate away from Rome. They saw each other infrequently. Still he saw her as a problem and invited her to visit him at a seaside town. It was a ruse. Stories vary about the assassination attempt, but it appears he had a boat rigged with a lead canopy that could be released to crush his mother. Some suggest the boat was designed to sink. The lead covering dropped as planned but Agrippina escaped death because she was seated on a Roman couch, which had curled arms on each end that stopped the fall and kept her from being crushed. She swam to safety.

Safety, however, would be short-lived. Nero took a more direct approach, sending guards to kill her on the pretense that Agrippina had conspired to kill him. When the assassins found her, she motioned to her belly and said, "Smite my womb."[3]

They did.

Romans considered matricide one of the worst of crimes. It was becoming clear that Nero was losing control of himself.

In the years that followed, Nero banished and then killed his wife Octavia. He married Poppaea, but in 62 he killed her by kicking her to death after they argued about the amount of time he spent at the chariot races. She was given a state funeral. She was pregnant, and her death tormented Nero. He later took a male lover whom he called by his wife's name.

His violence extended to the Roman Senate, where he had opponents and critics tortured and killed. Few can look back at Nero and see a hero. It is doubtful that he was insane, but he was paranoid and emotionally needy. Understanding the man allows us to understand the horrible events that followed.

The Spark That Became a Disaster

Movies and some documentaries have skewed our perception of first-century Rome. We conjure images of massive stone buildings, miles of stone aqueducts, grand structures, arenas for sports, expansive mansions. Those images are accurate but incomplete. Rome was a large city with as many as one million people, many of whom lived in wood tenements—tenements and shops that became tinder for one of history's worst fires.

On July 18, AD 64, a fire began in the wood-frame shops southeast of the Great Circus, the chariot racetrack, and spread through much of the city. The fire blazed for six days, destroying ten of Rome's fourteen sections and leveling half of Rome. The fire and subsequent breakouts left most of the city a shapeless, unrecognizable ghost of what it had once been.[4] Gone were many of the temples, works of art, shops, and homes. It was a catastrophe that made the survivors wonder if the city had a future, and if they would have food and shelter in the days ahead.

Rome was a city on its knees.

When the fire broke out, Nero was at the oceanside town of Antium, the place of his birth. He made the thirty-plus mile journey to Rome. There was little he could do but watch the destruction—a destruction that may have originated with him. Ancient historian Cassius Dio reports rumors of men with torches setting the fire.[5]

At first Nero seemed to be helping his citizens by providing food and housing, but he soon gobbled up some of the razed land to build his Golden House, a massive villa that covered 125 acres in the middle of the crowded city. Suetonius wrote, "The courtyard was of such a size that a colossal image of Nero, 120 feet high, stood in it, and so wide that it had a triple colonnade a mile long. There was a pond, like a sea, with buildings representing cities surrounding it; and various landscapes with tilled fields, vineyards, pastures, and woodlands, and great numbers of every kind of domestic and wild animal."[6]

Nero claimed, "It was a dwelling fit for a man."[7]

Building such a massive structure in difficult times and in an area destroyed by a fire that Nero was rumored to have started was becoming too much for citizens to bear. Heated complaints circulated and Nero needed a way out.

The Blame Shifts

He responded by transferring blame. Nero made Christians the scapegoat. Christians were not well loved in Rome. Romans were suspicious of them, and misunderstandings and myths about their practices made them undesirables. Some believed Christians practiced cannibalism because of the language in the Eucharist referring to eating the body and drinking the blood of their Lord. They were also accused of immorality because of their "love feasts." They considered Christians atheists because they rejected polytheism and refused to participate in emperor worship.

The Persecution

There are two ancient accounts of the fire and the persecution of Christians: one by Tacitus in his *Annals* and the other by Suetonius in his *Twelve Caesars*. Later historian Cassius Dio, born in 155, mentions the fire in his *Roman History* but says nothing of the persecution of Christians.

First-century historian Tacitus recorded a popular view:

But not all the relief of men, nor the bounties of the Emperor, nor the propitiation of the gods, could relieve [Nero] from the infamy of being believed to have ordered the conflagration. Therefore, in order to suppress the rumor, Nero falsely charged with the guilt, and punishment with the most exquisite tortures, those persons who, hated for their crimes, were commonly called Christians. The founder of that name, Christus, had been put to death by the procurator of Judea, Pontius Pilate, in the reign of Tiberius; but the pernicious superstition repressed for time, broke out again, not only through Judea, the source of this evil, but also through the city of [Rome], wither all things violent and shameful flow from all quarters, and are encouraged. Accordingly, first only those who confessed. Next, on their information, a vast multitude, were convicted, not so much of the crime of incendiarism as a hatred of the human race. And in their deaths they were made the subject of sport; for they were wrapped in the hides of wild beasts and torn to pieces by dogs, or nailed to crosses, or set on fire, and when day declined, were burned to serve for nocturnal lights. Nero had offered his own gardens for this spectacle, and also exhibited a chariot race on the occasion, now mingling in the crowds in the dress of the charioteer, now actually holding the reins. Once a feeling of compassion arose towards the sufferers, though justly held to be odious, because they seem not to be cut off for the public good, but as victims to the ferocity of one man.[8]

Crucifixions were carried out by the score. Humans were wrapped in animal skins and torn apart by wild dogs. Women were tied to the horns of bulls to reenact a Roman myth. Christians were dipped in flammable material such as wax or oil, tied to stakes, and used as torches. People were invited to see the spectacle. It was entertainment.

Crucifixion was not only a cruel form of execution but also an effective warning. Nero could kill whomever and whenever he wished. Nearly a century before, General Marcus Licinius Crassus had ended the slave revolt of Spartacus by capturing six thousand rebels and crucifying them, displaying them along the Appian Way, spacing the crosses every 120 feet. It served as a deterrent to other slaves who were thinking of revolting. No doubt, Nero treated the Christians the way he did to squash any thoughts of opposing him.

Extent of the Persecution

Knowing what we do of Nero's personality and cruelty, his actions come as no surprise. Christians made perfect sacrifices. No one outside their camp trusted them, understood them, or liked them. That attitude led to the first imperial persecution. Still, so severe was the treatment of the Christians that it sickened many Romans.

Although horrible in every way, the persecution under Nero seems to be confined to Rome. It was not empire-wide, as future persecutions would be. Nonetheless, it set the stage for future persecution and wanton execution. First-century Jewish historian Josephus records the crimes of Nero but does not mention the persecution of Christians in Rome.[9]

Hebrews and 1 Peter refer to the sufferings of Christians and may be a direct reference to the persecution under Nero (1 Pet. 2:12, 19, 20; 3:14–18; 4:12–19; Heb. 10:32–34). Many scholars connect the book of Revelation to the events in Nero's Rome.

Demise of the "Demon"

In AD 65, the year after the fire, Nero made his first public stage performance. That sounds like a small thing, but to Romans it was just short of a crime. Government leaders and members of the upper class did not perform on stage. That was behavior for the lesser people. This need to perform, this hunger to be applauded, led to scandal and plots on his life.

In that same year Nero began to kill anyone suspected of treason. This purging of detractors extended to his former tutor Seneca, who was forced to commit suicide.

Nero's behavior continued to baffle his people. In 66, he took an extended tour of Greece and participated in athletic games and theatrical performances. He "won" every contest, including a chariot race, despite having fallen from the vehicle and failing to finish. The Greeks so wanted to please the emperor that they rescheduled the Olympics so he could participate. Nero's hunger for attention and his love of the arts became more important than governing. Few, however, were willing to confront him.

Death of an "Artist"

At last, the Roman Senate and the people reached a breaking point. Nero had to go. The Senate declared him a public enemy. On June 9, AD 68, Nero was forced to commit suicide. He was thirty-two. He would also suffer the *damnatio memoriae*—all traces of him would be stricken from Roman record. His engraved name would be chiseled out of the marble. Since he was declared an enemy of the state, he would have known this would follow his death. It is possible that he feared being consigned to oblivion as much as he feared death. His last words were, "What an artist dies with me."

Nero would be remembered, but not for his acting, performing, or good looks. His persecution of the Christians and other crimes are what have been remembered through the centuries. Civil war erupted soon after his death.

The Church

The early church was shaped by Nero's persecution. There had always been some hatred, and some in the Holy Land endured hardship, but Nero raised the level of what could be done. The church also learned how deep the world's hatred ran. It would be centuries before Christians could worship openly and freely.

Church leaders made endurance in the faith an important doctrine. Christians had learned that their citizenship was not on this earth but in heaven. The persecution had made that abstract concept concrete. To be a Christian in the first century required not only a heart of faith but also a spine of steel.

The persecution drove many Christians out of Rome and, like the dispersion from Jerusalem and surrounding areas, it spread the faith.

The persecution also separated the merely interested from the truly committed. To remain a Christian in the shadow of Nero's cruelty was an act of great bravery. Those believers were some of the first to shed their blood for their faith. Many more would follow.

The Destruction
of Jerusalem by Titus

(AD 70)

Near the heart of Rome, by the ancient forum, stands a 1,900-year-old arch. It was carved in marble from Mount Pentelicus near Athens. It is over fifty feet high, forty-four feet wide, and over fifteen feet deep. It bears inscriptions and carved artwork, one of particular interest. On one side of the arch is an art panel that is beautiful in appearance but disturbing in its history. In it Roman men, each with a victor's laurel on his head, carry several odd-looking objects. Those items are sacred items taken from the temple in Jerusalem: the Menorah, Table of Shewbread, and Silver Trumpets.

The Arch of Titus was erected around AD 82. It is an honorific arch, meaning it was built to remind future generations of Titus' glorious deeds, including the destruction of Jerusalem and the burning of the temple. The artistic relief displaying the spoils of Jerusalem shows religious items. It was not unusual for ancient conquerors to return home with spoils of war, especially anything taken from a temple. It was a way of saying, "I beat you, your country, and your god."

Romans deified their emperors, and although Titus was emperor for only a couple of years, he received the same treatment. An inscription on the arch reads, "People of Rome to the divine Titus Vespasian Augustus son of Vespasian." The "divine Titus" is best known for being the general who put down a four-year-long Jewish revolt. When the war was finished, over a million people had been killed and one hundred thousand Jews were enslaved.

To the Romans and to the world, this looked like a great victory. To Jews and Christians it was something very different. The fall of Jerusalem in AD 70 is a key moment in history, and the church was right in the middle of it. In fact, they were ahead of the curve.

The Failed Fight for Freedom

There have always been tensions between captors and the people they oppress. The Jews despised their Roman overlords, and the Romans returned the hatred. Jewish animosity was rooted in more than their loss of freedom. The greatest heat of hatred came for religious reasons. They had been conquered by Gentiles. This was not new to Jewish history. The Jews had been in captivity in Egypt, Assyria, and Babylon. But Rome, with all its gods, demanded loyalty to a deified emperor, demanded taxes be paid, and called for offerings to be made on the emperor's behalf.

For the most part, the Jews of Jesus' day tolerated these abuses, but just under the surface boiled a need for revolt. Groups formed, each with its own idea of how to throw off the Roman chains. Romans had been treading their soil since 63 BC. At the time of the First Jewish Revolt, the Jews had been under the heel of Rome for a hundred years. During that time, they faced many indignities.

In AD 39, Emperor Caligula, well down the road to madness, declared himself a god and demanded that his statue be erected in all temples throughout the empire. Only the Jews said no. To the ancient Jews, the temple was God's house and they would not defile it. Infuriated, Caligula vowed to destroy the Jews, and he might have come close to doing so had he not been assassinated in January 41.

Over the next few decades, Romans in Judea insulted Jews in other ways. They even burned a Torah scroll. Romans conquered other lands to gain resources, taxes, and slaves. Roman procurators were responsible for maintaining peace and collecting taxes. In AD 66 the procurator Florus seized silver from the Jewish treasuries, and it was as if he were stealing from God himself.

After eight decades of work, the expansion of the temple grounds begun by Herod the Great came to an end. It was an amazing achievement made possible by thousands of skilled workers, all of whom were suddenly out of work, causing the level of general discontent to rise even higher.

Enough was enough. The hatred that had been simmering in the hearts of the people boiled over. They mocked Florus, who sent soldiers to end the protest. This time, however, the protestors would not be settled. Florus left Jerusalem to return to Caesarea by the sea. He left behind a cohort of soldiers—six hundred men or so. It was a grave mistake. When the embers of hatred and resentment finally ignited into flames of violence, there were too few soldiers to keep peace. It wasn't long before the leaders of the rebellion captured Antonia Fortress and Masada. They even took control of the temple mount. Roman blood ran in the streets, and that was just a trickle of what was to come.

Fires were set to the palaces of Agrippa II, Berenice, and that of the high priest. Fire was also set to the city archives, burning important documents such as debt and tax records. This was no accident.

The conflict spread from Judea in the south to Galilee in the north, and into Samaria. It was no longer a local uprising or a riot. It was war, and if Rome understood anything it understood war.

Two groups, the Sicarri and the Zealots, provided the emotional fuel for the conflict. The Sicarri were a violent group of urban rebels. *Sicarri* translates to English as "dagger-men," a name they earned by carrying concealed daggers and stabbing Romans and Roman sympathizers, including Jews who had grown content with the presence of Rome. Josephus, an ancient historian and a contemporary of the times, mentions them in both his *Antiquities of the Jews* and *War of the Jews.*[1]

Zealots also sought the expulsion of the Roman presence, which they saw as supplanting the role of God. They too could be violent. One of Jesus' disciples is referred to as Simon the Zealot. Zealots hated Roman taxes and tax collectors. The disciple Levi (Matthew) had been such a tax collector, making for an interesting dynamic among the twelve disciples.

It became clear that local Roman forces could not contain the spreading war. In 66 Cestius Gallus, governor of Syria, marched on the area to put down the uprising. It was an optimistic goal and one doomed to failure. The opposition was too strong, and Gallus and his men had to retreat. In the process he lost fifty percent of his army.

In Rome, Nero decided it was time to pull out the stops by sending his general Vespasian. In 67 the powerful military man led the Tenth Roman Legion to the land of the Jews. At the Dead Sea he waged war against the Essenes, a strict religious community that lived apart from the rest of the world. The fate of the monastic community was sealed. They would remain a historical footnote until the discovery of the Dead Sea Scrolls in 1947.

Bit by bit, Vespasian took back the land, and he would have completed the task had things not taken a dramatic turn in Rome. Nero had made a mess of things and fallen out of favor. He was declared an enemy of the state and forced to commit suicide in June 68.

With turmoil in Rome, Vespasian took his time with the reconquest. In 69 the general was declared emperor and returned to Rome to take his throne. He left the battle to his son Titus. Titus took the war to Jerusalem. With four legions of soldiers, he laid siege against the walled city. Siege warfare requires patience. From the Roman point of view, the enemy was trapped inside. It was just a matter of finding or creating a way in, or waiting for everyone to starve. He set siege to the north wall. Three weeks later he had control of the heart of the city. It would take months before the entire city and the temple were his.

In August 70 the temple was looted and burned. Opinions vary about who was responsible for the burning. One report shows Titus' desire to see the temple destroyed "in order that the Jewish and Christian religions might more completely be abolished."[2] We can't be certain of his motivation.

Regardless of who lit the torches, the result was the same: one of the greatest buildings in history was destroyed. Starvation brought an end to those holding out in the city. Some fled to Masada, which would fall in 73 with the death of nine hundred people, probably from suicide. Only two women and five children survived to tell the story.

Four years of battle ended with the destruction of a city and of the great temple. Rome was back in control, but the country it occupied was damaged beyond repair.

The Church Forewarned

The church is often overlooked in the recounting of these events, but it was as much a victim of the conflict as any other group. One difference exists: while the Jews of the day believed they could, and indeed did for a time, expel Rome from their country, the Christians had a different view. They had been told that Jerusalem would fall.

The church was less than forty years old when the rebellion began, but those four decades did not scrub their minds clean of the warning Jesus gave just outside the temple. Mark 13:14–23 records the event:

> But when you see the ABOMINATION OF DESOLATION standing where it should not be (let the reader understand), then those who are in Judea must flee to the mountains. The one who is on the housetop must not go down, or go in to get anything out of his house; and the one who is in the field must not turn back to get his coat. But woe to those who are pregnant and to those who are nursing babies in those days! But pray that it may not happen in the winter. For those days will be a time of tribulation such as has not occurred since the beginning of the creation which God created until now, and never will. Unless the Lord had shortened those days, no life would have been saved; but for the sake of the elect, whom He chose, He shortened the

days. And then if anyone says to you, "Behold, here is the Christ"; or, "Behold, He is there"; do not believe him; for false Christs and false prophets will arise, and will show signs and wonders, in order to lead astray, if possible, the elect. But take heed; behold, I have told you everything in advance.

It is much easier to read these words in the twenty-first century than it was for the disciples to hear them in the first century. Standing next to the massive stones of the temple, its many courts, the ebb and flow of pilgrims moving through the complex, and standing in the knowledge that this structure had been around for five centuries and that it had seen constant renovation over the previous fifty years, a work that was still underway, they must have thought Jesus was speaking allegorically. Certainly, the destruction of the temple was beyond anyone's ability.

Jesus laid out the events like a scriptwriter plotting a movie. The plot points are simple but shocking. There would be false leaders calling themselves the Messiah, and they would have success. A war was coming and nothing could be done to stop it. When the time came they were to flee as quickly as possible. No looking back, no gathering of personal items. Just go, and go now. The hasty exit would be most difficult on pregnant women and mothers of small children.

Forty years later, Jesus' warning rang in the ears of the Christians. While their neighbors held to a belief that victory would be theirs, Christians knew otherwise. Ancient church historian Eusebius states that in 66 the church relocated across the Jordan River in the town of Pella.[3]

The Jewish church continued, but there was fallout. They lost property and, because they fled as Jesus said they should, they were declared traitors and cowards by their countrymen. Animosity continued to rise. Soon they were banned from synagogues. Family turned on family. What had been a separation between traditional Jews and Christian Jews widened into a chasm impossible to span.

The break was permanent.

The church continued to expand beyond its borders. Prompted by the Great Commission (Matt. 28:16–20), persecutions, and further estrangement from its roots in Jewish community life, it continued its global outreach.

The fall of Jerusalem and the repercussions of the Christians' flight before the battle forced the church to form its own identity apart from Judaism. Judaism continued then as it does now to be a vital part of church thinking and theology, but the church ceased to be seen as a Jewish splinter group. The church had its own identity.

6

The Edict of Milan

(313)

There are many great documents in history. Those who live in the United States point to the 1776 Declaration of Independence and 1788 Constitution as being the most important documents in the country's history. Other countries have similar claims on documents that have made them what they are. Perhaps one of the greatest documents in church history is the Edict of Milan, signed by two new emperors: Constantine Augustus and Licinius Augustus. Modern laws are lengthy affairs, often taking scores if not hundreds of pages to enact. By contrast, the Edict of Milan—a law that saved hundreds of thousands of lives—runs only 707 words when translated from Latin to English.

Christians had dealt with persecution off and on for years. They could, in some areas of the Roman Empire, live in relative peace, but in other regions peace was more a dream than a reality. Years earlier, Emperor Diocletian had called for the persecution of Christians. Property was stolen, many endured beatings, and countless numbers were killed. The persecution became so bad in some parts that even pagans who hated the Christians were sickened by what they were seeing. Becoming a Christian was a risky decision, one that affected entire families.

Diocletian

Born in obscurity, Gaius Aurelius Valerius Docletianus, known today as Diocletian, did as many young men did in his day: he joined the military. He quickly showed promise. He was a skillful leader whose abilities landed him in the governor's chair of Moesia (now parts of Bulgaria and Serbia). The empire at the time was hamstrung by competing emperors.

In 282, Carus, a high-ranking soldier and leader, became emperor. Carus liked Diocletian, but the friendship would not last long. Carus was killed in a storm during a campaign against the Persians. Power transferred to two of Carus' sons: Numerian, who ruled in the east, and Carinus, who ruled over the western part of the empire. They too would soon die. Diocletian, almost forty years of age, was named the new emperor. He would remain emperor for two decades (284–305).

He had reason to regret becoming emperor. Rome was in disarray. Frontier land was being lost to non-Romans, and much of the kingdom was near anarchy. He divided the empire into four parts, a tetrarchy, spreading the burden of ruling over diverse people scattered over a million square miles. He restored order, regained lost frontier regions, and built an efficient government. Yet he is most remembered for the persecution of Christians that he instigated.

For most of his reign it seems Diocletian gave little attention to the Christians. Only at the end of his reign did he turn against them. What turned him? First, Christianity was growing at a phenomenal rate. By Diocletian's time it is estimated that 15 percent of the empire's population was Christian, about 75 million people. To some, this made them an empire within an empire. As noted earlier, Christians were also considered atheists because they refused to worship the Roman gods or make the required sacrifices other Romans had to. They were otherwise law-abiding, but they did not mix well with the pagans. There was also a belief that some of Rome's problems were the result of so many people ignoring the gods, and only a return to those gods who had made Rome great would fix the problem. This is something Christians would not do.

In February 303, fire struck Diocletian's palace, not once but twice. As Nero had done almost 250 years before, Diocletian blamed the Christians. They made easy scapegoats.

Diocletian issued three edicts against the Christians. The first (February 23, 303) called for a burning of churches and Scriptures. That summer a second edict was published, calling for the arrest of priests and bishops. The jails were overrun with clergy. In November, that edict was amended: clergy could be released if they would make sacrifices to the Roman gods. Many refused. Finally, in 304, Diocletian called for public sacrifices by all, and for any who refused to be executed.

Eight years of persecution began. Churches, Scriptures, and Christians themselves were destroyed. Murders occurred by the sword, by wild beasts, and many were burned to death. The persecutors took aim at men, women, and children. No one was safe. Some Christians were dragged off to labor in mines, a death sentence in itself. Executioners had to work in shifts.

In May 305 Diocletian had grown ill, and he became the only Roman Emperor to step down from power. The persecutions continued until 311 when Diocletian, near death, called for the end of it, and for Christians to pray for their leaders. Diocletian died on December 3, 311. Some think he may have committed suicide. He was sixty-six years old. His tomb is now part of the Cathedral of Saint Domnius in Split, Croatia.

A Very Different Edict

Christians had been facing persecution of one form or another and in varying degrees for three centuries. In one edict, all that was reversed in the Roman Empire. Flavius Valerius Aurelius Constantinus Augustus—Constantine—put an end to that and overturned Diocletian's previous edicts. And it happened just ten years after Diocletian set out to put an end to Christianity.

Constantine (285–337) was an enigmatic man and the first Christian emperor. The last part of that sentence is debated. Certainly, Constantine did things most Christians would avoid, and no one can tell if his conversion experience was real or just good public relations. Either way, the church benefited. Christians went from being targets to being citizens.

Constantine was declared emperor while his father, Constantius Chlorus, the reigning emperor, lay dying. However, others also claimed the right to the powerful position—at least five others. The privileged child would have to fight for the throne of Rome. But fighting was not a problem for the emperor-to-be. He had led men in battle in Persia and Egypt, gaining the support of thousands of soldiers in the process.

It was during one of the battles for the emperor's chair that one of the strangest stories of church history occurred. Constantine's father, although a pagan, was a monotheist who worshiped the Roman sun god. Although not a Christian, he refused to participate in the persecution. This certainly had some influence on Constantine, but the real turning point came in 312 while Constantine was preparing to do battle with Maxentius, who had claimed the emperor's role since 306. Maxentius prepared to do battle outside the city of Rome and consulted a pagan oracle who assured him that victory would be his.

On the other hand, Constantine had a vision. In the sky he saw two Greek letters: a chi and a rho—similar to an English X and P—the first two letters of the Greek word for Christ. He also saw an inscription: "In this conquer." He took the vision seriously and ordered his men to paint the two letters on their shields. Constantine met Maxentius at the Mulvian Bridge outside of Rome—one armed with the assurance of a pagan oracle and the other with a heavenly vision still vivid in his mind. The battle was a rout. Maxentius and his troops retreated into the Tiber River, where Maxentius drowned.

Constantine was now an undisputed emperor and a professing Christian. Constantine ruled in the west while Licinius, his brother-in-law, ruled in the east. The partnership would last a decade, but ended badly.

"When I, Constantine Augustus, as well as I, Licinius Augustus, fortunately met near Mediolanurn (Milan), and were considering everything that pertained to the public welfare and security, we thought, among other things which we saw would be for the good of many, those regulations pertaining to the reverence of the Divinity ought certainly to be made first,"[1] begins the edict, setting the tone for what was to follow. Part of the motivation, at least as stated in the edict, was the welfare and security of the public, a public who had seen a great deal of violence in general and specifically toward Christians.

The edict overthrew the previous decrees leveled against the Christians and became nothing less than an Emancipation Proclamation for Christians in the Roman Empire. And not just for Christians; the edict allowed a true freedom of all religions. True as that is, the edict mentions Christians, and only Christians, by name—twelve times. No other religion is mentioned. The document clearly has the church in view.

The edict established that individuals had the right to worship without fear of molestation, that worship was a personal choice, and that one religion was not to be favored over another as far as the law was concerned. The edict also did something else: it returned property to Christians and their churches that had been seized, sold, or given as gifts to others. All of that would have to be returned at no cost to the Christians. Those who had received buildings and grounds as gifts would get recompense from the empire for their loss. It is difficult to imagine how all this first sounded, but it was music to the ears of the church.

Historians debate the validity of Constantine's conversion. Some suppose he saw political value in claiming to be a Christian, but there seems to be more depth to him than that. True, he acted in ways that make it impossible to call him a "good Christian." For example, a decade after he ascended to power and named Licinius a co-ruler, the two had a falling out and went to war. Constantine won the day and Licinius lost his life, making Constantine's sister a widow. Constantine was now sole ruler of the empire, and in 324 he made Christianity the official religion of the Roman Empire. In addition to being emperor, Constantine saw himself as having a role to play in the work of the church. At the first church council, a gathering he called for, he announced, "You are bishops whose restriction is within the church, but I also am a Bishop, ordained by God to overlook whatever is external to the church."[2]

Constantine may have been a Christian, but he was also a Roman emperor, and emperors were, with good reason, quick to see conspiracies. Rumors began to spread that his eldest son was having an affair with his stepmother, Constantine's wife. He had both executed. Still, he established freedom of worship, defended the church, returned property to Christians and churches, forced bishops to gather to address a theological problem, aided in the building of new churches, and did much more. He raised the city of Byzantium to be a new Rome, and its name was later changed to Constantinople—Constantine's City.

Although the church would face many problems and new persecutions through the centuries, it would grow into a world power. Once freed from the tyranny of Roman persecution, the church could address new issues such as doctrinal purity. Defining key doctrines would occupy the attention of the church through the ages, resulting in numerous councils and, sadly, great division.

7

The First Council
of Nicaea

(325)

It has long been joked that when you have three Christians in a room, you have five opinions. While it certainly isn't always the case, there have been several moments in church history when it seemed the church could do little but fight. Many of these conflicts, however, were necessary for the formation of a solid set of doctrines that were common to Christians everywhere. Now, about two thousand years after the first church was founded, theological differences remain. Today some denominations baptize infants while others consider the practice unbiblical and restrict themselves to baptizing only those old enough to understand what the practice means (believer's baptism). Some denominations are led by the congregation, while others are more hierarchical. There are those who believe a Christian can lose his or her salvation, while others find that belief unacceptable. The worldwide church has learned to live with such variation.

During the first few centuries the church focused on two primary matters: spreading the gospel and staying alive. Over the centuries the church faced several waves of persecution, beginning with the Jewish leaders in Jerusalem and spreading through the Roman Empire. Still, the importance of sound doctrine was recognized and encouraged. Much of the New Testament consists of letters written to churches to correct false doctrine. On the one hand were the Judaizers, who insisted that all Gentiles must first become Jews before they could be considered Christians. On the other hand were the various flavors of Gnosticism, which taught that a select group of people had a special knowledge, and other ideas in direct contradiction to the teaching of the apostles. The apostle Paul was zealous about maintaining doctrinal purity.

Others would follow the great apostle's footsteps by devoting themselves to teaching and defending a pure doctrine. For eight years prior to the 313 Edict of Milan, which made Christianity legal, the church had worked hard just to stay intact. Twelve years after it became safe to call oneself a Christian, two factions met to hammer out an important bit of doctrine: the true nature of Christ.

Players

A major boxing match of champions would face off in the ring, each believing he was right, each having supporters in the crowd. The match was set to begin in May 325 in the town of Nicaea, now Iznik, Turkey. The man who convened the council was none other than Constantine, the emperor who made freedom of religion the hallmark of the Roman Empire. He considered the verbal war between the two parties to be more dangerous than war. War might take lives, but bad doctrine might take souls. He sent an invitation to 1,800 bishops in the empire, but only a little over three hundred attended the meeting. This meeting, now known as the Council of Nicaea, was the first of the great church councils.

In one corner stood Arius (ca. 250–ca. 336), an elderly church leader from Alexandria, Egypt. He was a popular speaker and had many followers, but his own bishop so disagreed with him that he attempted to have Arius and his views condemned. Arius' many supporters took to the streets to riot in defense of their pastor. Constantine could not allow such disruption in his empire. It was time for the church to settle matters.

Arius attended and made no secret of his belief in the disruptive doctrine. What could he be teaching that would so unsettle all the churches in the Eastern Empire? It could be boiled down to a single question, a question that raised even more disturbing inquiries: Was there ever a time when Jesus wasn't? In other words, does Jesus—like God the Father—have an eternal past? Has Jesus always existed, or was there a moment when he was created? The question had been batted around for a century and a half.

It might seem like a small and probably unknowable question, but it has great ramifications regarding the work of Christ. At its heart is the question of the Trinity. The Trinity has always been a difficult concept to grasp. It has no human equivalent, and there is no metaphor that does the concept justice. Today professional theologians can cite the history of the Trinity's development, and even list Bible chapter and verse supporting the concept, but they still struggle with its mysteries.

The accepted view of the Trinity is that there is one God in three persons. A person is an entity who has three qualities: intellect, emotion, and will (volition). An individual might say, "I think, I feel, and I make decisions about my actions, therefore I am a person distinct from all other persons around me." There are plenty of biblical examples to show that God, Jesus, and the Holy Spirit each have these qualities. They are therefore, by definition, each a distinct person. Left at that point, we might wonder if the doctrine of the Trinity teaches polytheism—in this case, three gods instead of one.

In fact, the Trinity teaches the opposite. Central to the doctrine is the idea that there is one God and one God only, and the three persons of the Godhead (God the Father, God the Son, and God the Holy Spirit), distinct as they are, share the same essence.

Arius taught that the Trinity formed a hierarchy, not a composite of equal persons sharing the same essence. God and only God could be called God. Jesus, although special in every way, was a created being. He has not always been; he came into existence by God's will. To most of the church this was heresy. In Arius' view, which he took from Greek philosophy, God was beyond human knowledge and understanding. Even in the Christian era he remained unknowable. So to Arius, Jesus did not stand on the same footing as God the Father. He was far above man but a level below God. He lacked God's deity.

Arius' teaching was set to music in the form of a hymn that his supporters would sing. He used the song in presenting his case at Nicaea:

> The uncreated God has made the Son
> A beginning of things created,
> And by adoption has God made the Son
> Into an advancement of himself.
> Yet the Son's substance is
> Removed from the substance of the Father:
> The Son is not equal to the Father,
> Nor does he share the same substance.
> God is the all-wise Father,
> And the Son is the teacher of his mysteries.
> The members of the Holy Trinity
> Share unequal glories.[1]

The very concept caused most bishops of the day to gnash their teeth. This was more than just a simple disagreement, more than two men arm wrestling over a fine point of doctrine, more than a couple of lawyers haggling over a fine point of law. The doctrine of salvation, the hope for all humankind, was centered in the notion that God in Christ died for the world. To fragment the Trinity was to remove the basis for the salvation of countless souls. While it might seem that this was nothing more than an intellectual tussle, an effort to prove who was the smartest person in the room, it was much more. Those who opposed Arius were doing their best to keep the church on the proper road without veering off on some side street and wandering away from the truth.

In the other corner of this doctrinal boxing match was the deacon Athanasius, who would one day become the bishop of Alexandria. He felt as strongly about the Trinitarian issue as the apostle Paul felt about the means of salvation and who could be saved. Like many great men, his life would be a roller coaster. Although he had many "highs," he also had many "lows," feeling at one point as though he stood alone against the world. Very few churchgoers today know his name, but their beliefs have been shaped by him. He felt doctrinal purity was important and worth fighting for. One should not simply redefine doctrine to better fit with Greek philosophy, as Arius was attempting to do. Athanasius said, "Those who maintain 'There was a time when the Son was not' rob God of His Word, like plunderers."[2]

Plunderers, that's how he saw Arius and those who wished to change the doctrine of Christ. Athanasius offered a threefold argument. First, Arianism (from Arius) undermined the doctrine of God by assuming the Trinity is not eternal and by creating a new form of polytheism. Second, it rendered liturgical practices such as baptizing in the name of the Father, Son, and Holy Spirit nonsensical. Third, it undermined the Christian idea of Redemption in Christ, "since only if the Mediator was Himself divine could man hope to reestablish fellowship with God."[3]

For Athanasius there were three concepts that needed to be believed. First, Jesus is coequal with God. He is not a level below, he is not less powerful, not less omniscient, not in any way lesser than God the Father. In other words, Jesus does not stand in the number two position.

Second, Jesus is eternal, not just immortal. There is a difference. *Immortal* can refer to someone who is born and lives forever. Part of the doctrine of humankind teaches that every individual has a soul that cannot be destroyed. It lives on forever in the future, but it did not live in the past before the person was born. When a theologian says that God is eternal, it means that he has neither beginning nor end, neither birth nor death. God always was, God is, God will always be. The Trinity teaches the same truth about Jesus: Jesus has always been and always will be.

For the first two propositions to be true, Athanasius argued that Jesus must be *consubstantial* with God, meaning that he shares the same essence. The word *same* is vital to Athanasius' argument. Arius and his supporters would quickly agree that Jesus was "like God" but not the same as God. In making the distinction between the two thoughts, Athanasius and others defending the Trinity used a special Greek word to get their idea across: *homoousios*. The word means "of one substance." The Arians wanted a different word used, a word with one additional letter: *homoiousios*—"similar substance." In some ways it sounds like attorneys arguing over the wording of a contract, but there was much more at stake. The question at the heart of the matter was, "Who and what is Jesus?"

Athanasius and his side won out. The bishops agreed that Arius' teaching was heresy. Only two bishops refused to sign what became known as the Nicene Creed. Those two bishops and Arius were exiled by the command of Emperor Constantine. They may have been sent away, but their belief lingered. Decades later, in 381, another council, this time meeting in Constantinople, reaffirmed the decision made in Nicaea. The Trinity was officially part of church doctrine. Still, the beliefs of Arius remain in some groups to this day.

The Nicene Creed

The Council compiled and distributed the Nicene Creed, a short declaration of belief primarily centered on the hottest issue of the gathering: the Trinity.

> I believe in one God, the Father Almighty, Maker of heaven and earth, and of all things visible and invisible.
>
> And in one Lord Jesus Christ, the only-begotten Son of God, begotten of the Father before all worlds; God of God, Light of Light, very God of very God; begotten, not made, being of one substance with the Father, by whom all things were made.
>
> Who, for us men for our salvation, came down from heaven, and was incarnate by the Holy Spirit of the virgin Mary, and was made man; and was crucified also for us under Pontius Pilate; He suffered

and was buried; and the third day He rose again, according to the Scriptures; and ascended into heaven, and sits on the right hand of the Father; and He shall come again, with glory, to judge the quick and the dead; whose kingdom shall have no end.

And I believe in the Holy Ghost, the Lord and Giver of Life; who proceeds from the Father; who with the Father and the Son together is worshipped and glorified; who spoke by the prophets.

And I believe one holy catholic and apostolic Church. I acknowledge one baptism for the remission of sins; and I look for the resurrection of the dead, and the life of the world to come. Amen.[4]

The decision of the Council of Nicaea regarding the Trinity is found in forty-six words of the Nicene Creed: "And in one Lord Jesus Christ, the only begotten Son of God, begotten of the Father before all worlds; God of God, Light of Light, very God of very God; begotten, not made, being of one substance with the Father, by whom all things were made." Every word was aimed at Arius' heresy.

Other Issues

The Council wrestled with other issues, such as when to celebrate Easter, the correct manner for consecrating bishops, prohibiting bishops from charging interest on money they lend, prohibiting bishops, priests, and other church leaders from moving from church to church, and the role celibacy ought to play with the clergy. The proposed requirement for celibacy in ministers failed.

Having Constantine instigate and attend the council muddied the waters of church and state. Constantine's presence, involvement, and decision to exile Arius laid a foundation for secular leaders influencing church decisions, something that would affect the church in centuries to come.

8

Jerome Completes the Vulgate Translation of the Bible

(405)

Fifteenth-century Venetian artist Giovanni Bellini, in his painting "St. Jerome Reading," depicts an elderly man with a balding head and a white beard that reaches his chest. The man sits on a small boulder. He is painfully thin, barefoot, and wearing only the remains of a tattered white tunic. It is clear he is living alone in a cave. A small city can be seen in the distance, indicating that the subject has separated himself from civilization. In front of the old man is a book set on a rough-hewed stand. The subject seems oblivious to his plight, his near-nakedness, and his emaciated body. Instead he focuses on what is clearly a Bible. Bellini captured the key segment in the life of a man known today as St. Jerome.

Jerome, who for a time in his life could have been easily confused with a homeless man, was born in what is now Ljubljana, Slovenia, in the year 342 and given the name Eusebius Hieronymus Sophroimus. Born into a wealthy family, he was the beneficiary of an excellent education. He remained a man of letters his entire life, traveling to several key cities to increase his knowledge. His higher education began at the age of twelve in Rome. It was during that time that his spiritual life came into existence. At about age nineteen he was baptized and spent the next two decades traveling the empire and studying. It was while he was in Gaul studying theology that he developed an interest in monasticism—the belief that the deeper spiritual life came from withdrawing from society and focusing on prayer and study. His love for monasticism endured throughout his life.

Through his studies he developed a love for the ancient philosophers, especially Cicero. A nightmare would change that infatuation overnight. It was during the season of Lent in 375 that Jerome had a dream that forever changed him. In the dream he stood before the judgment seat of Christ, but instead of receiving praise for his years of sacrifice and learning and for his choice to give up the wealth of his family to pursue spiritual matters, he received harsh condemnation: "You are a follower of Cicero, not Christ." The scathing words struck him to the core. From that moment on he refused to read classical writings.

His love for spiritual matters and monasticism compelled him into the Syrian desert, where he lived as a hermit. It was this time that Bonelli captured in paint. There he spent his days praying, fasting, copying manuscripts, learning Hebrew from Jewish Christians, and enduring cold nights and hot days. He often went without food. Although he chose, for a time, a life of seclusion, his loneliness ate at him. He longed for letters from friends and supporters.

He would not remain in that cave forever. He was, at heart, a scholar of the first class. His was a mind on fire, a mind that needed to learn, to analyze, and to produce worthwhile work. Skilled in languages, he became an able translator. These skills were recognized by Bishop Paulinus of Antioch, who offered to ordain Jerome, but Jerome knew he was not cut out to be a priest. He was largely a loner who was more comfortable with books than with people.

While he had the reputation of being a scholar's scholar, he was also well-known to be ill-tempered, acerbic, and quick to offend and be offended by many. He agreed to the ordination with the proviso that he would not be required to do priestly duties. As with many intellectually gifted individuals, he excelled in some areas and was awkward in others.

Having left the cave, he continued his studies and his work, work that was noticed by Damasus, the bishop of Rome. Damasus called Jerome to be his personal secretary. It was a high-ranking position and one of great honor. It also placed Jerome in the position of being Damasus' successor when the bishop died.

By Jerome's day the church had grown into two directions, forming the eastern and western churches. The western church would become known as the Roman Catholic Church in later years. The bishop of Rome felt that a new Bible translation would go a long way in spreading the gospel and helping to eradicate several problems. There were many translations, but their accuracy was suspect and some even contradicted each other. What was needed was a single, new translation of the Septuagint and the New Testament. The Septuagint is a Greek translation of the Old Testament made by seventy translators in the third and second centuries before Christ. When we read the New Testament and see an Old Testament verse quoted, it is usually drawn from the Septuagint. The Septuagint is often referred to by the Roman numerals indicating seventy: LXX.

Many Latin versions were translations of the Greek, which was itself a translation of ancient Hebrew. The original manuscripts of the Bible were written in three languages. The Old Testament was written primarily in Hebrew, with some Aramaic, and the New Testament was written in Koine Greek. What Damasus wanted was a new Latin version of the Greek Bible. Jerome had a different idea. He wrote:

> If we are to pin our faith to the Latin texts, it is for our opponents to tell us which; for there are almost as many forms of texts as there are copies. If, on the other hand, we are to glean the truth from a

comparison of many, why not go back to the original Greek and correct the mistakes introduced by inaccurate translators, and the blundering alterations of confident but ignorant critics, and, further, all that has been inserted or changed by copyists more asleep than awake?[1]

Jerome's idea showed his genius and his acerbic wit. Comparing one Latin version with another Latin version, then deciding which of the two was more accurate than the other, was tantamount to letting error creep into the new work. Why not start from scratch? Why not, for the Old Testament, go directly to the Hebrew documents and translate from them? That was precisely what Jerome did. He also worked on updating and revising the Latin version of the Greek New Testament.

Damasus died in 384, leaving Jerome without his defender. While this position put him in line as the bishop's successor, it was not to be. He moved to Bethlehem in 386 and continued his work. Jerome would labor for twenty years on the project, as well as writing commentaries and many other works.

His translation from the original languages is called the Latin Vulgate. *Vulgate* means "common," as in everyday language. The work is a tour de force of translation for the time. Today, translators have many manuscripts to work from, computers to aid them, and 1,600 years more practice. Jerome did everything by hand, one word at a time, using little more than the muscle of his mind.

The translation was not universally well-received. Jerome's lack of tact made many enemies. Some of the best-known Catholic thinkers, such as Augustine of Hippo, disliked the Old Testament not because Jerome produced something substandard but because it was based on the original languages and not the Greek Septuagint. The Septuagint had been the go-to foundation for translating. The logic was simple: if it was good enough for the apostles, it is good enough for church leaders four centuries later. For many, the Septuagint was the inspired Scripture, not the Hebrew text it was based upon. That view, in most cases, has been dismissed by modern translators.

Augustine exchanged letters with Jerome. In one written in 403, Augustine said, in part:

> For my part, I would much rather that you would furnish us with a translation of the Greek version of the canonical Scriptures known as the work of the Seventy translators. For if your translation begins to be more generally read in many churches, it will be a grievous thing that, in the reading of Scripture, differences must arise between the Latin Churches and the Greek Churches, especially seeing that the discrepancy is easily condemned in a Latin version by the production of the original in Greek, which is a language very widely known; whereas, if any one has been disturbed by the occurrence of something to which he was not accustomed in the translation taken from the Hebrew, and alleges that the new translation is wrong, it will be found difficult, if not impossible, to get at the Hebrew documents by which the version to which exception is taken may be defended. And when they are obtained, who will submit, to have so many Latin and Greek authorities pronounced to be in the wrong? Besides all this, Jews, if consulted as to the meaning of the Hebrew text, may give a different opinion from yours: in which case it will seem as if your presence were indispensable, as being the only one who could refute their view; and it would be a miracle if one could be found capable of acting as arbiter between you and them.[2]

Augustine, considered one of the greatest minds of the early church, was concerned that the new translation would drive a wedge between the church in the east (mostly Greek-speaking) and the one in the west (mostly Latin-speaking). He also argued that Jerome's work couldn't be widely checked since access to the Hebrew documents was limited. Many would just have to take his word on translation choices. Those who had doubts couldn't argue the fine points because they didn't have the same ammunition.

Jerome did not agree with the fears. He found no merit in the arguments used against him. He held the Scriptures in very high regard and could not imagine a translation made centuries after the original Hebrew work could be superior in inspiration to the originals. Of course, Jerome didn't have the original documents, what theologians call "original autographs." No one had those. Still, he used the best material available in the late second and early third centuries.

Modern translators have agreed with Jerome. True translations should be taken from the original languages, and new revisions should be carefully compared to the best manuscripts. This is not easy. Most modern translations are either based on a document called the Textus Receptus or on Majority Text. *Textus Receptus* is Latin for "received text" and is a collection of several Greek New Testaments. It was the basis for Luther's translation of the New Testament into German, Tyndale's translation into English, and the King James Version of the Bible. The weakness of the Textus Receptus, at least in the eyes of its detractors, is that it is based on six manuscripts, none of them a complete New Testament. Even when put together, they still come up short of a full New Testament.

Majority Text is drawn from a collection of over five thousand New Testament manuscripts.[3] Scholars read from the various texts and choose the wording used in the majority of the documents. Most newer translations are based on Majority Text. Jerome did not have access to the many New Testament manuscripts available today. For the Old Testament, modern translations depend on the Masoretic Text, which dates centuries later than Jerome.

Impact

Jerome's translation is a landmark achievement that influenced not only the church in the West but all of Christianity. Although Protestants would part ways with the Catholic church over 1,100 years later, their commitment to an accurate rendering of the Bible in the common language is connected to what Jerome did. Of course, by the time the Reformation came along, Latin was no longer the common language and the Roman Church had turned against the idea of a readable Bible for everyone.

Jerome's approach served as a template for future translations. His emphasis on returning to the original languages and making notes about choices made have lived long past him.

Even though Protestants may feel no connection to the Latin translation, many of the theological and church terms used every Sunday are rooted in the Latin. *Creation, justification, testament, sanctification, regeneration,* and others come from the Latin.

Great as it was, it would take many years before Jerome's work was fully accepted. It wasn't until the Council of Trent, a series of meetings spread over the years 1545–63, that the Vulgate received official recognition. The translation served as the foundation for the medieval church and held an honored place for over one thousand years.

9

The East-West Schism

(1054)

For much of the world there are two types of Christians: Roman Catholics and Protestants. Often overlooked is the Eastern Orthodox Church, with upwards of three hundred million adherents. It is the second largest Christian church in the world, with the Roman Catholic Church being the largest. In church history it is often referred to as the eastern church or the Greek Orthodox Church—Greek as opposed to Latin. The church can claim a history dating back to the first century, much as the Roman Catholic Church can do. At one time the church in the east and the church in the west were one body, but decades of tension caused what is now called the East-West Schism.

Many of the history books dealing with the causes of the schism point out that the differences between the two groups seem almost trivial by today's standards. Those differences were not trivial in the early years of the second millennium. At the heart of the problem was a struggle for power and the right of the pope to rule over churches in the east, churches that felt they did not need such supervision over their practices and doctrine. To the casual observer these two churches have more similarities than differences. Both are considered "high church" by Protestants and both have a strong hierarchy of leadership.

While first appearances might lead us to think that small matters got out of hand and two powerful but unyielding people went out of their way to offend each other, there is more to the story. The problem was not just the fine points of doctrine, although that played a major role in the division, but the heart of the matter was in their thinking. Those church leaders in the west did not think the same as the church leaders in the east. The Greek church covered much of the land around the eastern Mediterranean Sea and the lands of the western and eastern Black Sea.

Differences

The passing centuries brought about marked differences between the two halves of Christianity. The western church was centered in Rome; the eastern in Constantinople. In 330, Constantine the Great moved the capital of the Roman Empire to the city named after him. In the process his presence elevated the city to heights previously reserved only for Rome, and the church thrived—but with its own identity. The Roman church used Latin as its official language, a decision that led to Jerome's creation of the Latin Vulgate and was supported by western theologians who wrote in Latin. The church in the east was Greek-speaking and it used a Greek translation of the Old Testament and the original Greek of the New Testament.

In the west, clergy were forbidden to marry, but in the east it was encouraged. Celibacy was not practiced in the Greek church. The eastern half of the church had never fully embraced purgatory as taught by the Roman church. Clergy in the west were clean shaven, while their counterparts in the east wore beards. Another sore spot was the official dates of Christmas and Easter. The eastern church follows the Julian calendar, while the Gregorian calendar is used by the west. In the western church Easter can be as early as March 22 and as late as April 25, while in the eastern church it can be between April 4 and May 8, based on the first full moon following the March equinox. Occasionally the dates line up, as in 2014 when eastern and western churches both celebrated Easter on April 20.

Another key difference centered on the use of icons and statues. For centuries, statues and pictures of Christ or biblical stories served as focal points for worshipers. The eastern emperor, Leo III, forbade kneeling before pictures or images. Part of this prohibition was to disarm the claims of Muslims that the church practiced idolatry. Leo III's command in 726 called for the removal of every icon except the cross. The eastern church also removed statues, but iconic pictures remained as a means of education and were to be shown reverence but never worshiped. Worship belonged to God alone. The west saw all such items as symbols of divine reality and kept them in place.

The Final Tear

The fabric of unity that existed between the church in the west and the one in the east had worn thin over the centuries, and it finally tore in 1054. Tugging on each end of the fabric were two men: Michael Cerularius, patriarch of Constantinople, and Pope Leo IX. Cerularius (c. 1000–1059) came from a distinguished family and spent much of his adult life in the politics of the day. In 1040 he was implicated in a plot against Emperor Michael IV. He chose to leave public life for the monastery and soon became the patriarch of Constantinople (1043–59) by appointment of Emperor Constantine IX. He was a strong-willed man and not easily pushed around.

The same can be said of Pope Leo IX (1002–54), who came into office in 1051. He was born to a noble family and held several roles in the Roman church. His papacy returned a sense of purpose and power to the office after a series of ineffective popes. He, like many popes to follow, believed in the supremacy of Rome over all other cities and the superiority of the Latin papacy to those led by other bishops. Many of the early tensions continued to fester. Leo wanted to bring the Greek church under the control of Rome. If Cerularius, as patriarch of Constantinople, would submit to the authority of Rome, then so would his followers and the eastern church as a whole. To bring this about, the pope sent three representatives to meet with Cerularius. One of the representatives was Cardinal Humbert, who began his religious work as a fifteen-year-old boy in a French Benedictine abbey. Leo IX brought him to Rome to become papal secretary.

Cerularius, with another Leo, the bishop of Archrida, wrote a letter critical of the west's faith and practice. In response, Leo IX sent his three-man delegation to Constantinople to settle things. The letters exchanged between the two did nothing to help matters, nor did Leo's choice of Humbert of Silva Candida to lead the delegation. It was an unstoppable force about to meet the immovable object. Neither man was accustomed to yielding to demands.

When the delegation arrived, Cerularius refused to welcome them. He had already closed churches that used Latin in their services, so harsh feelings rested just beneath the surface. The delegation handed a letter to the patriarch and walked off in a manner Cerularius found insulting. The letter, probably written by Humbert, was unfriendly and Cerularius took offense. He refused to deal with the delegation in any way.

Animosity continued to grow until a papal bull was delivered to Cerularius. The delivery was timed to happen just as services in the church of Holy Wisdom in Constantinople were beginning. It was more than a letter. It was a notice of excommunication. Michael Cerularius, leader of the eastern church, and his followers had just been excommunicated. A deacon of the church chased down Humbert and the other two delegates and begged them not to do this, to take the letter back. They refused. The letter fell to the street.

If the act was meant to terrorize Cerularius, it failed. He called a synod and excommunicated Leo IX and his followers. Each side considered the other cut off from the church and from faith. The centuries of tension had reached the breaking point.

In 1089, Pope Urban did his best to mend the tear by revoking the patriarch's excommunication. Cerularius, however, had died thirty years before. The rift has never been fully repaired. The church had subdivided itself, and it remains divided today. Four hundred years later the Muslim Turks conquered Constantinople (1453), and even then some in the Greek church said they preferred the Muslim presence over one by the Roman church. Harsh feelings ran deep.

Church history is one of fragmentation, but at times such division leads to a stronger whole. Doctrinal differences between western and eastern churches still exist, but the same can be said of Protestant groups. It seems an unavoidable human trait that we divide the world into "us" and "them." The church *was* not and *is* not exempt from such thinking. Wherever there are people and organizations, there will be disputes. History has shown that, and the future may prove the point again.

10

Innocent III Expands the Power of the Papacy

(1198)

During a large slice of European history, the Roman Catholic Church was a force to be respected and feared. While the Church could raise armies, its greatest weapon was spiritual leverage, leverage that reached new heights. One pope in particular carried papal authority to its pinnacle.

The Man

Lotario del Conti di Segni was born sometime in 1160 or 1161 in Anagni, Italy, near Rome. His father was a count and his uncle was Pope Clement III. He received the best in education, studying theology in Paris and law in Bologna. He held various offices in the Church and later became a cardinal-priest. His rise was rapid. When Pope Celestine III died on January 8, 1198, Lotario was elected pope the next day. He was only thirty-seven. He took the name Innocent III.

By most descriptions, he was a humble man with great administrative skills and a very high view of the position of pope. He showed his humility by removing excesses surrounding the office. Plates of gold used for dining were removed, and wood plates were used in their place. He brought in humble monks to dine with him rather than royalty and powerful people. He demanded that clergy avoid dressing in fancy garments.

While humble, he could be assertive and showed no hesitancy in confronting kings and princes. As pope, he was a man of great power, and he would increase the power of the papacy during his time in Peter's Seat. He would raise the papacy above every throne in Europe.

For Protestants, this is hard to fathom. It is even more difficult to comprehend for those living in countries where church and state are kept apart by constitutional law. In the formation of the United States, one of the greatest concerns was creating a state in which the church could not overrule the government, and creating a government that could not overrule the freedom of religion. The one could not dictate to the other. But this view of separation of church and state would not take hold for over five more centuries.

In Innocent's time, it was not uncommon for a prince to select the bishop for his region. Innocent would have none of that. Before his tenure was complete, he made it so that only the pope could appoint or remove a bishop from office. This very issue would be fought in full public view.

While Innocent may have been personally humble, he did not see the role of pope in the same light. Popes previous to Innocent often referred to themselves as the "Vicar of Peter." Innocent referred to himself as the "Vicar of Christ." The difference is not as subtle as first seems. The original meaning of "vicar" comes from the Latin *vicarius*, meaning "a substitute." The English word *vicarious* comes from the same root and can mean "acting for another." The Vicar of Peter was someone who was the substitute for (in Catholic thinking) the first pope—Peter. The Vicar of Christ is someone acting on behalf of Christ and serving as Christ's representative on earth.

The successor of Peter is the Vicar of Christ: he has been established as a mediator between God and man, below God but beyond man; less than God but more than man; who shall judge all and be judged by no one.[1]

Innocent believed the pope should not only oversee the Church but the secular world as well. To him, the Church was the ultimate authority on earth, given that role by God, and the leader of that Church was the reigning pope. To Innocent and his supporters, there were two camps in the world—the secular and the spiritual—and both were to be guided by the pope.

Of course, not everyone saw it this way, especially secular rulers like those in France and England. Later kings would claim divine right of their own, stating that they were God's choice for the throne. There would be many classes of thrones.

Innocent drew inspiration from the heavens, explaining to leaders that the pope and his office were like the sun, while leaders of kingdoms were like the moon. The former gave light; the latter only reflected light. Everyone understood this to mean that the pope was the greater light and every other leader a mere reflection of that.

To him, kings held their crown by virtue of God's grace and the pope. This might seem a difficult statement to back up, but Innocent had several weapons at his disposal.

The Times

To understand Innocent's ability to force compliance of powerful leaders—and the ability of the popes who would follow—we need to understand the belief of the day. Over the centuries the Church's view of its place in the world and the power of its sacraments grew. In the decades ahead, some of the sacraments would take on very potent meanings. Unlike the belief in Protestant churches, which wouldn't be defined until four centuries later, the Church held that salvation was not the result of a single act. Today, most Protestants believe that salvation is obtained by faith expressed in a belief in the teaching and nature of Christ. It is, to them, a single act followed by ongoing discipleship. In Catholic thinking, the act of faith is joined by baptism, participating in the Eucharist, and other sacraments. These sacraments aid in the salvation of the people, and grace is received by participating in them. This was a developing belief in Innocent's time. The Council of Trent (1545–63) declared heretical any statement that the sacraments were unnecessary and superfluous.

Church members held tightly to these beliefs, and to be deprived of sacraments was terrifying to them. Also, priests provided many services in their parishes: baptisms, weddings, and more. They did much more than appear in church. Those services were considered vital to the community and to lose them would be a severe blow.

Innocent (and other popes) could use the power of interdiction. An interdict was a prohibition barring ecclesiastical function from a region. The pope could simply tell bishops and priests not to perform some of their duties. He could suspend worship, the Eucharist, and other sacraments. No weddings. No funerals. Seldom were baptism or extreme unction (last rites) withheld. An interdict would quickly turn the people against their king. Innocent used or threatened to use the interdict over eighty times.

An interdict was applied to a region and to the people who lived there. The other weapon at Innocent's disposal—excommunication—was aimed at individuals. Excommunication removes a person from the community, excluding them from participation in Church life. When a person was excommunicated they were deprived of the fellowship of the Church; could not serve as a judge, juror, or attorney; could not be a guardian; and could not enter into a contract. If the person was not rejoined to the Church before death, then they could not be buried in consecrated ground, which often meant being buried apart from family members. If such a person were accidentally buried in the consecrated cemetery, the remains would be removed and destroyed. When a person was excommunicated, a funeral bell was rung, a symbolic book was closed, and a candle was snuffed out as if the person had ceased to exist. The person was completely cut off and not allowed to attend Mass. If they showed up during a service they were to be removed or the Mass stopped.

The interdict and excommunication were serious matters.

The Conflicts

These weapons were used in several important struggles. King John of England had appointed his own bishop to the post of Archbishop of Canterbury. Appointing of bishops and archbishops was the job of the pope. That's how Innocent saw it, so he refused to acknowledge the king's choice. King John refused the refusal. He had made up his mind; Innocent was determined to unmake it. He placed an interdict on England, declared the throne vacant, and excommunicated John. He also invited France to invade, something it would have been happy to do. Pressured by his barons and his people, King John relented, accepted Innocent's choice for bishop, was welcomed back into the Church (for which he paid a good deal of money), and thereby saved his throne.

Innocent held a high biblical and moral tone, not only for the clergy but also for secular leaders. When King Philip Augustus, after the death of his first wife during childbirth, decided he had been "bewitched" into taking Ingeborg, the daughter of Denmark's King Valdemar I, as his second wife, he sought an annulment, placed her in a convent, and married Agnes of Merania. Ingeborg would not go quietly. She appealed to the new Pope Innocent, claiming the marriage had been consummated and that she was still the rightful queen of France. Innocent agreed and ordered Philip to separate from Agnes and take Ingeborg back as his rightful wife. He refused, and in 1199 Innocent placed France under an interdict. Philip relented in public but ignored his promise. Agnes died the following year and Ingeborg returned as queen, but not until 1213. (She outlived her husband by fourteen years.)

The Council

Innocent's willingness to expand papal authority and to confront leaders when necessary were not his only claims to fame. He convoked the Fourth Lateran Council, which met on November 11, 1215, at the Lateran Palace in Rome. The council met for three days and adopted many of Innocent's ideas, ideas that continue to this day. The gathering was attended by seventy-one patriarchs, over four hundred bishops, and nine hundred abbots, and issued seventy papal decrees.

Some of the most important of these decrees made transubstantiation an official doctrine. This doctrine teaches that the elements used in the Eucharist—bread and wine—are transformed into the body and blood of Christ, the objects they represent. This meant that priests held in their hands the literal body and blood of Christ. It also meant that the Eucharist imparted some measure of salvation. To ignore the Eucharist was a spiritually dangerous thing to do. When the Eucharist was denied to those under interdict or those who had been excommunicated, they were being denied access to Christ himself.

Innocent and the council also addressed the need for educated priests. Many priests lacked proper training in theology, something that Innocent could not tolerate. He decreed that every cathedral (the seat of the bishop) was to have a theology teacher to train priests.

Wanting every Christian to make at least a token effort to show his or her faith, he also required everyone to attend confession and receive the Eucharist at least once a year. With the growing power of the pope, it became unwise to be critical of the Church. The state was used to punish heretics and confiscate their property.

Perhaps the most disturbing of the decrees was the one that called for Jews and Muslims to wear distinctive clothing making them easy to identify. Christians were not allowed to conduct business with Jews. The result was the growth of Jewish ghettos.

Innocent was one of the most energetic and able administrators of the Catholic church. For many, he is seen as a composite of humility and great assertiveness. He improved the Church in many ways, but some argue that his choices about increasing the power of the pope and the way the world perceived the position were over the top. The papacy is a controversial topic in the twenty-first century and has been for centuries. The division between Catholic and Protestant churches is not likely to be bridged anytime soon. Still, Innocent III must be recognized as a shaper of the Catholic church. Other popes would follow his example of supreme pontiff, a position that would stand for centuries.

11

Unam Sanctam Proclaims Papal Supremacy

(1302)

There is an old English proverb: "The times change, and we change with them." Most languages have a similar proverb. Those who study change know that the only unchanging thing in the world is change itself. Some resist change; others fail to recognize it and often pay the price. One such person was Benedetto Caetani, better known as Pope Boniface VIII, who served as pope from Christmas Eve 1294 until his death in 1303.

Under Innocent III, papal power over government leaders had grown. A century later, Boniface saw that power stripped away with the rise of a new generation of secular leaders willing to challenge him without hesitation.

Europe was moving to nation-states with strong royal leaders. Two of these leaders in particular undid Boniface and forced him to reply with a document that is considered one of the most powerful and far-reaching as any in church history: the papal bull (letter) *Unam Sanctam*.

The Decline of the Papacy

"Follow the money" is a catchphrase among journalists that came to the forefront of public attention in the movie *All the President's Men.* The principle behind the phrase was just as true seven hundred years ago as it is today. Money was not a problem for Boniface. During the Year of Jubilee he declared in 1300, he brought in enough funds to keep priests busy counting it. Boniface declared forgiveness of sins for those who came to Rome to worship, and many did. Bruce Shelley noted Boniface "had a flair for pomp and circumstance. Several times he appeared before the pilgrims in Imperial robes crying, 'I am Caesar. I am Emperor.' According to reports, his papal crown contained forty-eight rubies, seventy-two sapphires, forty-five emeralds, and sixty-six large pearls."[1]

Across the continent, money troubled the minds of two monarchs: Edward I of England and Philip IV of France (also known as Philip the Fair). The two kings were at loggerheads over property in France that England claimed control over. War is expensive and both sides needed cash. Each developed the same idea: tax the clergy. Priests and monks had been exempt from paying taxes, but that came to an end.

The idea was abhorrent to Boniface. The Church could not be required to pay taxes to secular governments. Governments paid money to the Church, not the other way around. Neither Edward nor Philip cared. In 1296, Boniface issued the bull *Clericis Laicos,* a document that threatened excommunication for any leader who attempted to exact money from churches, priests, or monks. The threat of excommunication extended to the clergy who paid such a tax without the pope's approval. We can't help but feel sorry for the priests and monks caught in the middle.

The threat of damnation didn't carry the same weight it used to. There had been enough abuses and immorality among some of the priests that people had lost much of their respect for the Church. Far removed as Edward of England and Philip of France were, they saw no reason to crumble before the pope. Boniface lacked an army to enforce the document. Still, they had to respond, and respond they did. Edward I decreed that clergy must pay the tax, and if they refused they would sacrifice all legal protection they enjoyed and their properties would be confiscated. Philip simply made it illegal to export gold and jewels from France to Italy. In other words, he cut off one of the Church's revenue streams.

Faced with two kings who refused to be moved by the threat of excommunication, Boniface had to backpedal and state that he didn't want to keep clergy from contributing to a country attempting to defend itself and in dire need. Boniface had backed down—but not for long. There was another round to go.

The response to his Jubilee Year encouraged Boniface. Like some of the pontiffs who preceded him, he believed that the reigning pope had power over both spheres of life: the spiritual and the worldly, the soul and the government. He had an additional circlet—a band around the conical cap called the Papal Tiara—added to indicate his authority over worldly matters as well as spiritual.

Philip and Boniface went toe-to-toe again in 1301 when Philip had one of the pope's legates—a representative of the pope, often a cardinal—arrested for treason. Boniface demanded the man be released and ordered King Philip to travel to Rome to explain himself. Philip was not so inclined, and with the full support of his legislative body, the Estates General, he refused.

Boniface's response was to issue another papal bull, one with extreme claims for the power of popes.

Unam Sanctam

Unam sanctam is Latin for "one holy," that is, one holy church. When translated into English, the *Unam Sanctam* letter is less than one thousand words in length, yet most church historians believe it to be one of the most important documents of the Catholic church, a document that raises the presence and power of the pope to its highest point. The document sets in stone several ideas that had been broached before. Boniface states that there is no salvation outside of the Church *and* outside the pope. The message to Philip and others was simple and direct: "Your salvation rests with me and the Church."

The bull follows a pattern of assertion followed by biblical support. To the Protestant biblical scholar the exegesis (analysis of the words and meaning) is suspect and filled with debatable comparisons and conclusions. Regardless, despite the document's biblical strengths or weaknesses, it did more than any other to elevate papal power. Boniface may have been thinking of the glory days of Innocent III, who had managed to win a conflict with another king, King John of England. If that was his goal, it failed in the short term but changed the Church forever.

The *Unam Sanctam*[2] begins with a powerful first and second sentence:

Statement

Urged by faith, we are obliged to believe and to maintain that the Church is one, holy, catholic, and also apostolic. We believe in her firmly and we confess with simplicity that outside of her there is neither salvation nor the remission of sins.

Assertion

Some concepts of faith are obligatory for everyone. There is an obligation upon all people of faith to believe that there is only one Church, and no other church can be recognized as having come from God; the Church is holy, that is, set apart by God for his service; the Church is "catholic," or universal, and encompasses all Christians; the Church is apostolic, meaning that it traces its roots back to Peter and the other apostles; and there is no salvation or forgiveness of sin for those outside the Church. This last part, while directed to the world, certainly had Philip and other secular leaders in mind. If excommunicated there is no remedy except to come back to the Church. Within the Church is salvation and eternal life; outside the Church is nothing but hopelessness.

Argument

a. Boniface quotes Song of Songs 6:9, "One is my dove, my perfect one. She is the only one, the chosen of her who bore her." He equates this verse with the church, which is called the Bride of Christ. The emphasis is on the word "one," meaning one and only one church.

b. A passage from the New Testament is used as added support: "and she represents one sole mystical body whose Head is Christ and the head of Christ is God (1 Cor. 11:3)." Few would argue with the 1 Corinthians passage, although some might hesitate at its use to bolster the original argument.

From these two passages he states, "In her then is one Lord, one faith, one baptism" (Eph. 4:5).

c. He then equates Noah's ark with the Church.

> There had been at the time of the deluge only one ark of Noah, pre-figuring the one Church, which ark, having been finished to a single cubit, had only one pilot and guide, i.e., Noah, and we read that, outside of this ark, all that subsisted on the earth was destroyed.

Again, the pontiff is attempting to build a biblical case for what comes next. Most Protestant theologians equate Noah's ark with Christ, not any particular church. Boniface saw the ark as symbolizing the Church, in which only those on the inside are saved while those on the outside are destroyed.

Assertion

"*We venerate this Church as one.*" Again, an emphasis on the Roman Catholic Church being the only means of salvation. To support this contention he again draws on Scripture.

Argument

a. First he quotes from Psalm 22:20: "'Deliver, O God, my soul from the sword and my only one from the hand of the dog.' He has prayed for his soul, that is for himself, heart and body; and this body, that is to say, the church." Boniface sees "my only one" as the Church, where Protestants see Psalm 22 as a messianic psalm. In fact, Jesus quotes from this psalm while hanging on the cross (Matt. 27:46).

b. He then makes an example of Jesus' cloak. "He has called one because of the unity of the Spouse, of the faith, of the sacraments, and of the charity of the church. This is the tunic of the Lord, the seamless tunic, which was not rent but which was cast by lot (John 19:23–24)." To Boniface, the Church, like Christ's seamless garment, will not be divided.

Assertion

The Church has a single human leader, with Christ as the spiritual leader. Boniface was sending a reminder that he, and all popes to follow, were the head of the only institution Christ founded. To make his point he makes three assertions.

a. "Therefore, of the one and only Church there is one body and one head, not two heads like a monster; that is, Christ and the Vicar of Christ."

b. "Peter and the successor of Peter, since the Lord speaking to Peter Himself said: 'Feed my sheep' (John 21:17), meaning, my sheep in general, not these, nor those in particular, whence we understand that He entrusted all to him [Peter]."

c. One shepherd and one flock. "Therefore, if the Greeks or others should say that they are not confided to Peter and to his successors, they must confess not being the sheep of Christ, since Our Lord says in John 'there is one sheepfold and one shepherd.'"

Assertion

Church authority is superior to secular authority. Boniface uses allegory to show authority over not only Church matters but over governments as well. In allegory, one thing represents another. For example, many Protestants believe baptism represents the death, burial, and resurrection of Christ and of the believer. Drawing from Luke 22:38, Boniface interprets the swords mentioned and Jesus' comment about two swords being enough to mean that the Church would have authority over both spheres of human existence: the spiritual and the earthly.

> We are informed by the texts of the gospels that in this Church and in its power are two swords; namely, the spiritual and the temporal. For when the Apostles say: "Behold, here are two swords" (Luke 22:38) that is to say, in the church, since the Apostles were speaking, the Lord did not reply that there were too many, but sufficient. Certainly the one who denies that the temporal sword is in the power of Peter has not listened well to the word of the Lord commanding: "Put up thy sword into thy scabbard" (Matt. 26:52). Both, therefore, are in the power of the church, that is to say, the spiritual and the material sword, but the former is to be administered for the church but the latter by the church; the former in the hands of the priest; the latter by the hands of kings and soldiers, but at the will and sufferance of the priest.
>
> However, one sword ought to be subordinated to the other and temporal authority, subjected to spiritual power. For since the Apostle said: "There is no power except from God and the things that are, are ordained of God" (Rom. 13:1–2), but they would not be ordained if one sword were not subordinated to the other and if the inferior one, as it were, were not led upwards by the other.

The last paragraph establishes that the "swords" are not equal. One must be subservient to the other. In Boniface's mind that meant that governments were under the authority of the Church, therefore Philip and Edward should submit to the pope's orders.

Assertion

Subjection to the pope is necessary for salvation. Boniface could not move against the English and French sovereigns with armed forces, but he could threaten their eternal destinies. The world has changed enough that most people today would dismiss such a threat out of hand, but in Boniface's day it carried great weight. Papal power was fading. Still, Boniface raised the threat: "Furthermore, we declare, we proclaim, we define that it is absolutely necessary for salvation that every human creature be subject to the Roman Pontiff."

There it is: no one is saved apart from the Roman Catholic Church and obedience to the Holy Father.

Breaking and Entering

The *Unam Sanctam* made clear that the Church and the pope are supreme on earth and salvation can only be found inside the Roman Catholic Church. The idea persists today.

Philip the Fair was not frightened. The *Unam Sanctam* was an extreme effort born out of political need and a struggle for dominant authority more than a theological precedent. To Philip, one extreme action deserved another. Retaining the services of the lawyer and advisor William de Nogaret, Philip set out to unseat Boniface. Philip and Nogaret charged that the pope was improperly and illegally elected and participated in simony (selling ecclesiastical privileges like pardons), heresy, and even immorality. This they did with the blessing of French churchmen. Nogaret and a team of armed men traveled to Rome to arrest the pope, but Boniface had left the city to summer in his hometown of Anagni. They found him there, broke into his bedroom, and held the sixty-eight-year-old prisoner for several days. He was freed when the citizens of Anagni took it upon themselves to rescue him. We don't know what physical and mental harm were inflicted upon Boniface, but he died several weeks later.

Boniface VIII is remembered for declaring a Year of Jubilee, for attempting to keep power and respect in the office of the pope, for standing up to two kings, and for elevating in the clearest form the idea that salvation rests with the pope and the Roman Catholic Church.

The ideas of *Unam Sanctam* were repeated in *Quanto Conficiamur*, an 1863 encyclical issued by Pope Pius IX (who served as pope for thirty-two years). In the document he comforts priests who were living through difficult political upheaval. Three of the twenty-one paragraphs condemn the growing idea among Catholics that people can be saved apart from the Church and the Roman pontiff (para. 7–9, esp. 8). In his encyclical he refers to Catholic teaching, meaning the ideas of the *Unam Sanctam* put forth 560 years earlier had become official and accepted.

The catalyst for Boniface may have been the rise of powerful kings in the west, a battle he lost, but the lasting impact of the conflict for the Roman Catholic Church is that salvation is found in obedience to the Church and the pope. Some of this would change, but not until the 1962 Vatican II.

Gutenberg Produces the First Printed Bible

(1456)

The British Library houses and maintains over 150 million items, including every publication produced in the United Kingdom and Ireland. This requires 625 kilometers (389 miles) of shelves. Every year they add three million more items, requiring an additional twelve kilometers (7.5 miles) of shelves. According to their website (www.bl.uk), it would take a patron viewing five items a day eighty thousand years to view everything.

The Library of Congress in Washington, DC, holds nearly 35 million books and 117 million non-book items like maps, manuscripts, and audio/video material. Its collection grows by nearly ten thousand items a day.

With the advent of the digital age, many books and magazines are now "printed" for ebook readers and computers. Some consider this the greatest revolution in the written word, but that honor goes to a man we know very little about: Johann Gutenberg (1395–1468).

Gutenberg's name is celebrated around the world. *Time* magazine called him the "Man of the Second Millennium."[1] The Arts and Entertainment Network listed Gutenberg as the most influential person of the second millenium. Asteroid 777 is named after him, and Philippe Manoury wrote an opera about the inventor. There are very few people who can claim such distinguished honors.

Mark Twain said, "What the world is today, good and bad, it owes to Gutenberg. Everything can be traced to this source but we are bound to bring him homage . . . for the bad that his colossal invention has brought about is overshadowed a thousand times by the good with which mankind has been favored."

Martin Luther said of printing, "God's highest and most extreme gift, by which the business of the Gospel is driven forward."

French novelist Victor Hugo gushed about the importance of printing: "The invention of printing is the greatest event in history. It is the mother of revolution. It is the mode of expression of humanity which is totally renewed; it is human thought stripping off one form and donning another."[2]

There are also very few people about whom it can be said, "He (or she) changed everything." It might sound like hyperbole, but this German inventor did, in a very literal way, change everything. He has touched the lives of billions.

A Small-Town Man

Much of Johann Gutenberg's life is a mystery. There is little information about him. He was born in the German town of Mainz to upper-class parents. His father, Friele Gensfleisch zur Laden, was a merchant. His mother, Else Wyrich, was Laden's second wife. He was baptized into the Catholic church, it is assumed, at nearby Saint Christoph. The year of his birth is debated and sources list a range from 1395 to 1400. Most likely he was born a few years before the arrival of the fifteenth century. His early years are absent from the historical record.

As a young man he was admitted to the goldsmith guild, where he learned to work with metals, something that would aid him in his invention. Tension between the guilds and the aristocratic leaders compelled Gutenberg's family to leave Mainz for homes they had outside the city, probably to avoid the taxes levied against the guilds.

It was the custom of the time to take the name of the house as one's surname. The house Johann grew up in was called Gutenberg. Therefore, Johann Gensfleisch zur Laden adopted his mother's name, Gutenberg.

Gutenberg eventually returned to Mainz, but continuing political tensions caused him to sail down the Rhine to Strasbourg, France. It was there he began experimenting with inks and with individual and reusable type. To make a living, he created mirror tokens that pilgrims would carry on their journeys to churches to view relics. It was believed that some of the power of the relics could be captured with the mirrors. But when another round of plague swept through the area, pilgrimages ceased and so did the demand for the metal mirrors. Gutenberg's clientele dried up.

Gutenberg was skilled in several areas and turned his experiments into invention. He had an idea about how to make printing more efficient and cost-effective.

How It Used to Be

Books were few and far between in Gutenberg's day. There were two primary reasons for this. First, reproducing a book was done by hand—a slow and often inaccurate process. To reproduce a Bible could take two years and cost the equivalent of three years' salary for a typical worker. Second, very few people could read, so the demand for books was confined to clergy, scholars, and the upper class. And not only could the average person not read in their own language, but most writing was done in Latin.

But society in Germany and other places of the world was changing. Thanks to the dedicated work of religious groups like the Brethren of the Common Life, who emphasized education as a godly pursuit, literacy was on the rise. Europe was in a pivotal position.

What it needed was a way to share ideas across the continent and through the ages. Gutenberg made that happen.

What was needed was a way to create a printed page quickly and accurately, without variation in the ink, the spacing, or the lettering. Scribes grew tired, worked in awkward positions, and sometimes did their work with insufficient light. A mistake could take hours to repair, if it was fixable at all, or the whole page might even have to be redone.

Printing could be done with letters carved onto a large wood block the size of a page, but a mistake in the carving could be beyond repair. The Chinese had invented movable type centuries before, but the small wood blocks weren't suitable for large print runs and required that new blocks continuously be made.

Gutenberg took a different approach. He knew metal, he knew the goldsmiths' art, and he knew printing.

Innovation and Invention

The metal, movable-type printing press is not one invention but many melded together into a greater whole. Not only did metal type need to be invented, but so did a means of holding it in place. There must also be a means of creating the type in great number. It's not a matter of casting one type for each letter in the alphabet, but hundreds of each letter. Ink, while not a new invention, had to be adjusted to stick to the type then cleanly transfer to the page. Gutenberg experimented with oil-based inks until he had the formula for a substance that would work with his press. Water-based inks, like those used in handwriting, would not adhere to the type. By using an ink that was more like paint, with carbon and graphite, he could apply the ink to the surface of the type and it would adhere until pressed onto the paper.

The "printing press" is called a press because Gutenberg's creation was modeled on a winepress. Large wooden structures had been used for decades to press the juice of the grapes from the fruit. This was done on a device that had a reservoir for the grapes, a wide press above, and a hand-carved worm-screw that was attached to a long handle. By pulling the handle, the screw would turn, driving a wood slab down onto the grapes.

Gutenberg took that principle and used the screw drive mechanism to press the page onto the type evenly and with a uniform amount of pressure that was consistent from page to page. No one knows exactly what the first printing press looked like. No drawings remain, but enough description exists to give us a reasonable idea about its operation.

How was the type created? Herein lies Gutenberg's genius. First he created a metal punch: a metal bar tapered at one end. He sculpted the desired letter into the tapered end until he achieved the perfect representation. This was delicate work, the kind a goldsmith excelled at. This, however, was not the type; it was only the first step to creating the typeface. The punch would then be set on a metal bar and struck with a hammer that left an impression in the bar. This bar is called a matrix, and served as a mold from which hundreds of individual types could be made. A form fit over the matrix, and an alloy of tin and lead was poured through an opening. Moments later, the cast type could be removed, cleaned up, and ready for use. Once enough individual types were created, they could be arranged and used countless times.

Of course, uppercase typefaces had to be created as well as lowercase. Those terms show the influence the printing press had on language. Capital letters, usually called "uppercase," are called such because they were kept in the upper drawer of the composition table. "Lowercase" type elements were kept in the lower case (drawer).

Those looking at the device for the first time would be reminded of a winepress. Just as a winemaker would use a wheel or lever to turn a worm screw so a press would crush grapes piled in a tub below, the printer would turn a similar screw to move a press down upon a piece of paper that had been laid on a block of type. The press would create an even pressure, allowing the inked type below to transfer an image to the paper without smudging. The fact that his press was modeled on a winepress was not wasted on Gutenberg.

Yes, it is a press, certainly, but a press from which shall flow in inexhaustible streams the most abundant and most marvelous liquor that has ever flowed to relieve the thirst of men. Through it, God will spread His word; a spring of pure truth shall flow from it; like a new star it shall scatter the darkness of ignorance, and cause a light heretofore unknown to shine among men.[3]

Gutenberg was an inventor, but it was just as important that he was an innovator. He drew from the ideas of others and synthesized them with his own until he created the first printing method that could produce in a short time what would take years for a scribe to do.

His work was impressive, but it is difficult for scholars to say what Gutenberg printed. His name never appears on any of his printed material. This is understandable. Printers reproduce the work of others, not their own writing. Still, scholars believe they can identify a few of his pieces. Of course, his best-known work is a Bible.

The Gutenberg Bible

One can hardly hear the name of Gutenberg without thinking of the Bible he printed—the first printed Bible. *The Forty-Two Line Bible*, sometimes called the *Mainz Bible*, is the most valuable book in the world and was first printed in 1456. Only about fifty copies exist, and only twenty-one of those are complete.

Gutenberg printed 180 Bibles over a two-year period. The Bible was Jerome's Vulgate—a Latin work. While these were still very expensive and only scholars and priests could read Latin, the door to a freely accessible Bible was kicked open. Martin Luther, who was born shortly after Gutenberg printed his Bibles, would further the Reformation by using the technology to print his "Ninety-Five Theses" into pamphlets and to print his German translation of the Bible, a translation the average German could read. The Reformation was off the launching pad and powered by the Gutenberg press. The irony in this was that Gutenberg saw his printing press as a tool to bring about unity in the church. Instead, it became the wedge that fragmented the Roman church.

He wrote:

> God suffers in the multitude of souls whom His word can not reach. Religious truth is imprisoned in a small number of manuscript books which confine instead of spread the public treasure. Let us break the seal which seals up holy things and give wings to Truth in order that she may win every soul that comes into the world by her word no longer written at great expense by hands easily palsied, but multiplied like the wind by an untiring machine.[4]

Financial Failure

Making printing presses and paying workers was expensive. To deal with debts and financial challenges, Gutenberg borrowed money. One lender was the wealthy banker Johann Fust. Five years after making the loan, Fust demanded repayment. Unable to pay back the money, Gutenberg had to surrender his presses and his business. In 1465 his work was acknowledged, and he was made a gentleman of the court. This provided him with food, clothing, and a stipend. But his presses would remain in the hands of others. He died three years later, the latter part of his life as much of a mystery as his early years.

The Man Who Changed Everything

Gutenberg did more than invent the movable-type press, he changed everything. The printing press allowed for the rise of libraries, the dissemination of new ideas, and the spread of the scientific revolution; kicked off the Reformation; ushered in a new age of communication; laid the foundation for the spread of news; made research more accurate; and, over time, spread ideas around the world.

For the church, the printing press was revolutionary in every sense of the word. Scholarly works could be shared and doctrine codified and spread—but most of all, it put the Bible in the hands of the everyday person. Prior to the mass printing of Bibles, the parishioner had to depend on the priest and church artwork to learn Bible accounts. In many cases, even local priests didn't have Bibles to consult and were often ignorant of its contents.

Outreach efforts of the church increased over the centuries, empowered by the ability to print material in the language of each country where the evangelists served. Translation ministries would arise whose goal was to make the Bible available in every language possible.

To be sure, anti-Christian movements also made use of the printing press. Still, as Mark Twain noted, Gutenberg's invention did far more good than bad. Modern society is based on the written word. The free exchange of ideas led to greater ideas.

New printing techniques would come along, but not for several centuries. Today, printers work at speeds that would amaze Gutenberg, and the digital revolution would be beyond his comprehension. None of that lessens his achievement. *Time* magazine was correct: Johann Gutenberg was the Man of the Second Millennium.

13

The Protestant Reformation

(1517)

It began with a piece of paper tacked to the door of a church. The *tap-tap-tap* of hammer against nail did more than fill the space in front of Wittenburg Church—it echoed through half a millennium and launched a movement that changed the Western world. The hammering was the peal of a bell of revolt, although the man nailing the document to the door wouldn't come to understand that for some time. The tapping would be heard across Western Europe and later across oceans. That simple act did more than alter church life for millions; it bolstered the Renaissance, the Scientific Revolution, business and industrial growth, and more. It would also launch wars.

The colonization of North America began with the Puritans, who left their country to avoid persecution for their faith. In a sense, then, the Reformation was the first step to the founding of the United States. Of those identifying themselves as Christians in the United States, 55 percent are Protestant. Worldwide, close to one billion people claim to belong to one of the many Protestant groups.

The Reformation was a protracted event. It may have begun with a disgruntled monk named Martin Luther in 1517, but it had been fermenting for many years. It would take until the mid-1700s before it could be said to have ended.

There were many Reformers, each motivated by similar reasons, but three come to the forefront as leaders: Martin Luther, Ulrich Zwingli, and John Calvin.

Martin Luther (1483–1546)

For much of his life, Martin Luther was a miserable man. Guilt and fear overshadowed him. No matter how long he confessed—and at times he could confess for up to six hours—he never found peace for his soul.

Martin Ludher (later Luther) was born to Hans, a copper miner, and Margarethe Ludher in Eisleben, Germany, on November 10, 1483. Both parents were harsh disciplinarians, and he was often beaten until blood ran. Hans had ambition for his son and determined that Martin would study law. He attended the University of Erfurt at the age of nineteen, ultimately earning a master's degree in 1505. But on July 2 of that year he experienced a frightening event that changed his plans. While he was returning to the university during a thunderstorm, a bolt of lightning struck near him, knocking him to the ground. Terrified, he screamed, "Help me, Saint Anne. I'll become a monk."

For Luther it was more than a simple exclamation born of momentary terror, it was a pledge. Two weeks later he entered an Augustinian monastery at Erfurt. His father was furious, but Luther's mind was set. He would serve God as a monk.

Monastic life brought him neither joy nor happiness. He afflicted himself for his sins, spent hours in confession, and struggled to find the love of God, but he only saw future retribution for his sin. Guilt dogged his steps no matter how righteously he lived. He hated himself for imagined sins, and no amount of good work alleviated the negative stew of emotion that roiled in him. Fasting, sleeping in the cold, self-flagellation, and hours of prayer only deepened his despair.

Luther was a brilliant man, albeit a troubled one. He had earned his early degrees in the shortest time allowed by the university. He went on to earn a doctorate in theology and was soon invited to teach at a new university in Wittenberg. Ever the diligent student, he became a diligent teacher, learning as much as possible about the subjects he would teach. While working on a series of lectures on the book of Romans, he came upon Romans 1:17 and, like the lightning bolt that set him on a religious course, he was struck with the truth of the passage:

> For I am not ashamed of the gospel, for it is the power of God for salvation to everyone who believes, to the Jew first and also to the Greek. For in it the righteousness of God is revealed from faith to faith; as it is written, "But the righteous man shall live by faith."

Faith over works. To Protestants today it is a common and well-known doctrine, but to Luther it was new and changed everything. For so long he had tried to earn God's love, to be righteous in God's eyes, and here the apostle Paul was teaching that all one needed was faith.

> Night and day I pondered until I saw the connection between the justice of God and the statement that the just shall live by faith. Then I grasped that the justice of God is the justice which through grace and sheer mercy God justifies us through faith. Thereupon I felt myself to be reborn and to have gone through open doors into paradise.[1]

The passage from Romans unlocked the emotional shackles Martin Luther had put upon himself. Once he had challenged the idea of works-based salvation he had been taught and replaced it with a faith-based belief, he began examining other things he had been taught, such as the need for priests, the Mass, praying to saints, purgatory, and indulgences. If, as Martin Luther had come to believe, faith was the key to salvation and the Bible the key to understanding God, then what good were all the trappings of Roman Catholicism?

He was already frustrated with what the Church had become, and even more disenchantment stemmed from a 1510 trip to Rome he made on behalf of his monastery. There he saw misuse of wealth, immoral priests, and a woeful lack of sincere piety. He saw magnificent churches built to a vengeful God. His new insights into Scripture and salvation freed him from a sense of obligation to the Church and opened his soul to a God of love and mercy.

Martin Luther met his breaking point at last when John Tetzel, a Dominican friar, arrived in Wittenburg selling indulgences. For a price, an indulgence could be purchased to help a loved one escape purgatory. The practice was widespread and had evolved into a profitable means to raise money for the Church. In Tetzel's case, he was raising funds to help complete Saint Peter's Basilica in Rome. "As soon as the coin in the coffer rings, the soul from purgatory springs," his slogan ran. Those who feared that a father, mother, or spouse was stuck in purgatory gave money they could little afford with a belief that the grace stored up by the saints might be applied to the account of their dead family member.

It was more than Luther could stand. He could no longer keep quiet. Believing in *sola fide* (the belief that faith and faith alone can bring salvation) and *sola scriptura* (the belief that the Scriptures are all one needs to provide the basis for doctrine and behavior, as opposed to councils and edicts), he chose to challenge the practice of selling indulgences. He composed *Disputation of Martin Luther on the Power and Efficacy of Indulgences*, better known today as Luther's "Ninety-Five Theses," and nailed it to the front door of All Saints' Church in Wittenberg. It was October 31, 1517. This was not an act of rebellion. Posting items on the door, as some do with a school bulletin board, was not unusual. What was rebellious was the direct manner in which he challenged a longstanding belief and practice.

What Luther wanted was a debate on the topic. Breaking from the Catholic church was not on his mind. He, as other Reformers would do, wanted the Church to return to its biblical roots. He longed for reform, not division. But he wouldn't get it.

The Roman church derived its doctrine from several sources: the Bible, papal decrees (the pope speaking *ex cathedra*, "from the seat"), Church councils, and traditions. Martin Luther had just attacked two of those pillars.

Luther was granted his debate in Leipzig and faced off with John Eck, a theologian. The debate lasted eighteen days. "The council may sometimes err," Luther said. "Neither the church nor pope can establish articles of faith. These must come from Scriptures."[2] The Church was not convinced.

To promote his belief, he began writing. Writing would become the outlet of his ministry. Six decades before, Johann Gutenberg had invented a printing press that used movable type. It was the mass media of Luther's day, and he would use it to its highest potential. No Reformer published as much as Luther. From 1518 to 1525 he published more material than the combined output of the next seventeen Reformers. He was a superb writer who could adjust his tone to his audience. He could be studious and rigorous; he could also be entertaining and funny.

Pope Leo X excommunicated Luther in 1520, giving him two months to recant. To Leo and other church leaders, Luther was a heretic, a dangerous thing to be. Heretics were often burned at the stake. Luther was summoned to the German town of Worms to face twenty-one-year-old Emperor Charles V. As Holy Roman Emperor, it was his job to try Luther. At the meeting Luther was given an opportunity to recant, but he was beyond intimidation. "My conscience is captive to the word of God. I will not recant anything, for to go against conscience is neither honest nor safe."[3]

Charles said of Luther, "The devil in the habit of a monk has brought together ancient errors into one stinking puddle, and has invented new ones."[4]

To protect him, Duke Frederick the Wise spirited Luther away to Wartburg Castle, where the former monk lived for ten months. He grew a beard to diminish his chance of being recognized and spent his days translating the Bible into German.

Luther had not set out to start a new church, but one was created anyway. Lutheranism would become the official church of Germany.

The floodgates of the Reformation had been completely opened, and others rose to bring about a change in the church.

Ulrich Zwingli (1484–1531)

Martin Luther lit the fire that would become the Reformation, and that German flame spread over the Alps and into Switzerland. There the son of a town mayor was born in Wildhause, but politics was not in the future of young Ulrich Zwingli. Instead, he set his sights on church work, attending schools in Basel, Bern, and Vienna. In 1506 he earned his master's degree, was ordained, and began serving as a priest in Glarus.

Political alliances allowed members of the Swiss army to be used by other countries or groups. France, the emperor, and even the pope made use of Swiss forces. Zwingli despised the practice and felt it unfair that young men should face injury and death in the service of others. There was little he could do about it other than attempt to meet their spiritual needs. To do this, he twice served as chaplain to the Swiss soldiers sent to fight in other people's wars (1513, 1515).

Zwingli's transformation from priest to Reformer was a slow one. Many priests in his time knew little about the Bible. They had been schooled in Church doctrine and traditions, but biblical interpretation was secondary. Like Luther's, his transformation came from Bible study. Zwingli had developed a love for the Greek Bible and obtained a copy of Erasmus' Greek New Testament, which he studied, teaching himself Greek. The more he read and learned, the more puzzled he became. Many of the practices and rites he had learned in the Roman Catholic Church did not mesh with what he was reading in the New Testament. This created a quandary. Roman Catholicism highly valued the Bible as one source of its doctrine, but not the only source.

What was Zwingli to do? Like Luther, he came to believe that all doctrine and practice could only come from the Bible. Like Luther's *sola scriptura*, if it wasn't supported in the Bible it was to be avoided. This was one area where Zwingli and Luther differed.

Luther believed that whatever the Bible didn't prohibit was allowable. Zwingli went the other direction: what wasn't allowed in Scripture wasn't allowed in life.

A little over a year after Luther tacked his "Ninety-Five Theses" to the door of the Wittenberg church, Zwingli departed from the Roman Catholic practice of priests following a prescribed lectionary. On the first day of 1519, he defied that practice and instead began a series of messages drawn from the Gospel of Matthew. His goal was to allow his congregation to hear the teachings of the New Testament. It seems a simple matter today, but it was an act of defiance in Zwingli's time. There would be more rebellion.

Three years later, in 1522, some of his congregation defied the ban on eating meat during Lent. Zwingli joined them, demonstrating his solidarity by eating a sausage in public. He could find no biblical reason to abstain from eating meat, so he felt free to break the Lenten prohibition. He followed that up with a sermon on freedom.

It might be hard today to imagine this becoming an issue, but it was seen as an act of betrayal. Most modern Western countries have some form of separation of church and state, but that wasn't the case in Zwingli's day. The church and the state were intertwined, and the state was the enforcement arm of the Roman church. Pope Adrian VI called on Zurich to oust Zwingli. Zwingli appeared before city leaders to defend his behavior and teaching. There he presented his "Sixty-Seven Articles" in which he argued that Christ must be at the center of all teaching, rejected the Mass as part of salvation, encouraged Christians to pray to Christ instead of to saints, argued against the celibacy of priests and nuns, and rejected the notion of purgatory. And the city officials chose Zwingli's side.

The following years saw a transformation in Zurich. Once a staunch Catholic city, its clergy began to take spouses, statues and other icons were removed from church buildings, and biblical teaching became the focus of worship services. These and other changes spread to other Swiss cities. Zwingli had done for Switzerland what Luther had done for Germany.

Luther, a former monk, and Zwingli, a former priest, were both driven to make changes based on what they read in the Bible. An observer could be forgiven for thinking Zwingli and Luther were a match for a partnership. Philip of Hesse certainly thought so, and brought the two men together in the city of Marburg in the German state of Hesse. His goal was to get the two to join forces. The question was: Did their doctrine match enough for such a partnership? Fifteen doctrinal items were discussed, and they agreed on fourteen. The fifteenth, however, proved to be a deal-breaker.

Both had departed from the Catholic view of the Eucharist with its belief in transubstantiation—the bread and wine being literally changed to the body and blood of Christ. Zwingli's view that no change took place, that the wine remained wine and the bread remained bread, clashed with Luther's consubstantiation view (Christ's blood mixed with the wine and the body of Christ mingled with the bread). The talks broke down, forever dividing the great Reformers. Luther, who could be critical of other Reformers, is said to have rejoiced when he learned of Zwingli's death.

That death came in 1531, during the Second Kappel War. Tensions between Catholic and Reformed cantons (states) reached a breaking point. The cantons had a great deal of autonomy, and five of the thirteen states declared war on Zurich. The first conflict was decided peacefully, but the second erupted in violence. In a battle that lasted a single hour, five hundred soldiers died, including Zwingli. Not only was he killed, but his body was also dismembered. Two dozen other Protestant ministers also died.

Zwingli had been killed, but the Swiss Reformation continued to flourish.

John Calvin (1509–64)

Martin Luther might be the best-known name from the Reformation, but John Calvin may have had as great an impact, if not greater.

His views on predestination made him a hero to some, while others believed he damaged God's image in the world.

Calvin was born in Noyon, north of Paris, to Gérard Cauvin, a lawyer working for the Church. "Calvin" is the Latinized form of Cauvin. His mother died when Calvin was a young child. As was common for the day, Gérard made decisions about his son's education and future occupation. At first he sent Calvin to Paris when the boy was just fourteen. There he encountered the finest minds of the times. His skill as a writer blossomed, as did his very logical mind. Then things changed. Gérard parted with the Church and decided Calvin would earn more money as a lawyer. Calvin exchanged the study of theology for that of law at the University of Orleans. The change may have made his father happy, but Calvin maintained a love for theology and the classics.

In 1531, Gérard died of cancer. The loss of his father allowed Calvin to return to Paris and resume his earlier studies. He longed for the quiet life of the academic. While at the University of Paris he met and befriended Nicholas Cop, the newly appointed rector at the college. In a November 1533 speech to the university, Cop called for reform in the Catholic church and revealed his sympathy for Martin Luther. It was not well-received. Two days later, under charges of heresy, Cop fled. Calvin, perhaps because he shared the same views or participated in the writing of the speech, fled with him. His exodus led him to Basel, Switzerland.

It was in Zwingli's Switzerland that Calvin began work on one of the greatest theological works in church history: *Institutes of the Christian Religion*. The first edition of the work appeared in March 1536. Calvin was twenty-seven years old. He would continue to work on *Institutes* through much of his adult life.

Calvin determined to travel to Strasbourg but was detoured by war in the area. He planned to spend one night in Geneva, a night that would change his life and change church history. William Farel, a Reformer, heard that the author of *Institutes* was in the city and called on him to try to enlist him in the ongoing Reformation work in the city. Calvin was a shy man who preferred the quiet life of study and writing, but Farel would not be denied. He accused Calvin of being selfish, desiring to promote his own will instead of God's. Calvin succumbed to the pressure. His planned one night in the city turned into a much longer stay.

Calvin, with his education in theology and law, became Professor of Sacred Scripture for the city. Geneva became a blend of church and city government. In his new role, he wrote a confession of faith that all citizens, and those wishing to be citizens, must agree to. He also established rules for excommunication. A question arose about who bore the responsibility for excommunications. It was an important question since one could be expelled for drunkenness, gambling, or dancing. Things didn't go Calvin's way. Victory in the debate went to Calvin's opponents, and soon Calvin was on the run again. He settled in Strasbourg, the city he first wanted to reach when he came to Geneva, and undertook the academic lifestyle he longed for. He studied, wrote, and pastored a church of French refugees. He also married Idelette de Bure.

Geneva changed directions again when supporters of Calvin came back to power and pleaded for his return, and return he did. The city benefited from his spiritual leadership, but enemies remained.

Calvin's theology was deep and controversial, and none more so than his idea of predestination. It is still a much-debated topic among Protestants. Calvin's reading of the Bible led him to believe and teach that God had, in his foreknowledge, determined from the beginning of time who would be saved and who would be condemned. To many it seemed an unfair and harsh doctrine. Those destined to be saved would be, those not chosen would spend eternity in punishment to show the power and glory of God. Then, as now, some rejected the idea out of hand, but the idea was welcomed by others. Several denominations, such as Presbyterian and some Baptists, strictly hold to Calvin's doctrine.

Of all the Reformers, and there were many, these three established what would become the Protestant church. Protestantism is not a uniform system. Some Protestants are Calvinists, many are not; some are closely aligned with Luther, others with one of the other Reformers. These three—a monk, a priest, and a scholar—charted the path that many would follow in the centuries ahead. Their work continues to shape theological thinking.

14

The Scientific
Revolution Begins

(1543)

The tension between science and religion seems to escalate each year. Anti-religionists hunker behind a homemade fortress, chucking rocks at anti-science opponents who are equally armed. At least, that is how some see the division of ideas. But it is an inaccurate and unfair portrayal. Certainly there are those who enjoy tossing rocks instead of ideas, but the division, real as it is, is not so extreme. Christians have not been opposed to scientific advances as their accusers state. While some extreme groups do exist, most churchgoing folk embrace science and technology. When a believer is ill, he or she seeks the care of a doctor, just like the science-lover does. Many individuals trained in the sciences are people of faith. This includes astronomers, biologists, physicists, medical researchers and practitioners, geologists, and members of every other neighborhood of science.

Famed Harvard paleontologist and science historian Stephen Jay Gould (1941–2002) wrote: "But the actual relationship between religion and science is far more complex and varied. Often, religion has actively encouraged science. If there is any consistent enemy of science, it is not religion, but irrationalism."[1] Although an agnostic and a strict evolutionist, Gould understood the role that religion played in the development of science.

This fact is nowhere more evident than during the Scientific Revolution. "Scientific Revolution" is a bit of a misnomer. The word *revolution* conjures images of blood, war, and a quick overthrow of some ruling organization. None of those items apply to the era dubbed the Scientific Revolution. It was not fast, and its timeline is still debated. Most historians set the revolution between 1550 and 1727, filling a period of slightly over 170 years. The first bookend was formed by Polish astronomer Nicholaus Copernicus, who established the mathematical framework indicating a sun-centered solar system instead of the widely held earth-centric idea. The other bookend was formed by British physicist Sir Isaac Newton (1642–1727), who is considered by many to be the greatest of all scientists.

The Intellectual Environment

The European world before the late sixteenth century had been scientifically dormant. The nearly nine centuries of the Middle Ages (500–1350) produced little scientific advance. The dominant intellectual pursuits could be found in the Roman church, which incorporated Greek and Roman philosophy into its thinking, primarily that of Aristotle (384–322 BC). The ancient Greek philosopher wrote on many wide-ranging topics, such as metaphysics, politics, physics, ethics, logic, and what we would today call natural science. He tutored Alexander the Great. Aristotle was revered in the centuries before the Scientific Revolution, and he continues to be admired today.

Respected as Aristotle was, the world had changed in the 1,800 years since he taught. While many see the Scientific Revolution as pushing aside the beliefs of the Catholic church, it also parted company with Aristotle. Of course, on many levels, the two were linked.

121

To turn a cold shoulder to Aristotle was to do the same to the Church, and the reverse was also true.

During that time, and long before, the Church was considered the repository of knowledge. For centuries such a belief made sense. Priests and monks received a better education than most and spent much of their lives in study. But another institution held knowledge and taught it to its students: universities. Universities had been around for centuries. The University of Bologna was founded in 1088, the University of Paris sometime about 1150, and Cambridge in 1209. Young men born to families of means could study in a number of fields.

The Scientific Revolution needed and received two other ingredients that enabled it to move forward.

The Reformation Plowed the Fields

Often overlooked is the role the Reformation played in the Scientific Revolution. Although anti-Catholic sentiments were abundant for many years before, the Reformation took its first major step forward when Martin Luther, a monk disgruntled with the selling of indulgences, composed and nailed his "Ninety-Five Theses" to the door of the church in Wittenberg. That was 1517. In many ways, it was the first shot fired over the bow of the Roman Catholic Church. Luther had no designs to start a separate church. What he and others like him wanted was reform. That didn't work out. Other Reformers met with the same problems.

Theology was not the only thing being reformed. The idea of an individual's right to spiritual discovery was being born. Tyndale's translation of the New Testament into English was published in 1524. Prior to this, worshipers could only listen to Scripture as it was read in church, and that in Latin. Tyndale's belief that everyone should be able to read the Bible in their own language cost him his life. In 1536 he was strangled to death and then burned at the stake. But about the same time, Martin Luther was translating the Bible into German for his people.

What Reformers like Luther, Calvin, Zwingli, and others did was to make questioning church authority viable. It was still dangerous, but they provided an example of challenging the status quo and correcting error. Luther became a Reformer by deep study of Scripture, much like a scientist adds to the body of knowledge through keen observation and experimentation. (The word *scientist* is relatively new. In the days of Galileo and Newton, men of science were called "natural philosophers." *Scientist* doesn't appear in the form used today until the late nineteenth century.) In many ways, Reformers and scientists of the day were cut from the same cloth, each wanting greater understanding and the truth.

Historian William H. McNeil wrote in his *World History*, "Yet it would be wrong to suggest that science supplanted religion. On the contrary, the Reformation age left behind a heightened religious concept in all walks of life."[2] McNeil is right, yet many see the Scientific Revolution as unseating religious thinking and replacing it with something more truthful. Very few, if any, of the individuals we associate with the emergence of modern science would have agreed with that description.

Tools That Opened the Mind

While the Reformation plowed the fields for the Scientific Revolution, it was not itself scientific and never had the advancement of natural philosophy as its goal. Reformers were focused on the soul and the truth of Scripture. For science to make new strides after nearly one thousand years of only minor progress, it needed more help.

Science was doing its work by talking things through with the logic of Aristotle to direct observation and measurement. For measurements to be useful, there needed to be robust and versatile mathematics. Mathematics was not new. Algebra was described in ninth-century Arabia. The idea that the number zero could be used as a placeholder came out of India in the ninth century as well. Math continued to develop over time and reached a stage where many things observed by the scientist could be described by formulae. This required the development of geometry, trigonometry, and calculus. Math enabled scientists to describe their observations in ways other scientists could read and understand.

As indispensable as mathematics was, it was only useful if applied to observation and experiments. To make observation, instruments were needed. Science advanced with the introduction of inventions that made observation possible, and some key instruments came into being during the early decades of modern science. By the middle of the seventeenth century scientists had at their disposal the compound microscope (1590), the telescope (1608), the barometer (1643), the thermometer (1654), and the pendulum clock (1656). Even something as simple as a prism helped Isaac Newton understand light and optics.

When the elements of scientific tools, robust math, a willingness to examine new views, and the inspiration of the Reformers came together to rock the boat of long-held beliefs, the chemistry for a revolution in thinking was complete.

Three Who Made a Difference

Many scientists could be named, but three show how a love for science and faith could change the world. Each of this select group contributed to the Scientific Revolution but also demonstrated deep spiritual interest.

Nicolaus Copernicus (1473–1543)

As mentioned earlier, historians fix the start of the Scientific Revolution with Nicolaus Copernicus, or at least with the publications of his work demonstrating that the earth orbited the sun, and not the reverse as almost everyone believed.

Almost every historical reference to Copernicus lists him as a Polish astronomer. No one can argue against that point. He was certainly that, but he was also much more. Although astronomy was one of his passions, it was not his only one. Copernicus' day job was that of a clergyman. Although not an ordained priest, he spent

124

his adult life working as a canon in the cathedral where his uncle served as bishop. His work included helping the poor and handling the administrative work of the cathedral.

His educational résumé is impressive. He studied at Kraków University, the University at Bologna, and the universities in Padua Ferrara. He spent some time in Rome lecturing on math and astronomy. He was a multifaceted man: mathematician, astronomer, medical doctor, and lawyer (he earned a doctorate in law). He spoke several languages. His was a hungry mind. A man that educated could choose from a wide range of careers. While he could have been a lecturer at one of the universities, or practiced medicine, or served as a lawyer, he chose instead a life in the church.

In the preface to his *On the Revolutions of the Heavenly Spheres*, he wrote, "I regard my research as a loving duty to seek the truth in all things, insofar as God has granted."[3] For him, science was a spiritual pursuit. When he looked at the heavens, when he studied the movements of the planets, he saw the craftsmanship of God. Today he would be called a proponent of intelligent design, the belief that sees design and forethought in the universe instead of the coincidence of random events over time.

Most people of his day believed the earth was the center of the solar system and that the sun and other planets orbited it. Part of this belief was based on logic. The earth was stony, and massive stars and planets were specks of light. Obviously things in the heavens would orbit the heavier object instead of a lighter one. This seems silly today, but there was no scientific evidence to show the sun was over one hundred times larger than the earth. That would come in time. The second basis for the earth-centric belief is a bit of tortured theology. The book of Genesis shows humans being personally created by God, making them the center of the creation week. From that, it was assumed that the earth must also be the center of God's creative act and, therefore, must be the center of the universe.

Copernicus studied charts of the planets' movements and could not make the earth-centered belief work. His math showed the sun to be at the center of the solar system. He wrote *On the Revolutions of the Heavenly Spheres (De Revolutionibus Orbium Coelestium)* but knew its publication would upset the apple cart of current belief and was reluctant to publish. Some feared that if the earth wasn't at the center of things, then it would dilute the view of God as Creator. Copernicus didn't see why that should be. "God is the best and most orderly workman of all," he wrote.[4] For him, his sun-centered, or *heliocentric*, view was proof of creation.

The book was published shortly after Copernicus' death in 1543. Someone, most likely an editor, added a preface saying the book did not teach a different view of the solar system. It did, and anyone reading it would notice. The preface did nothing to ward off condemnation. Copernicus' book was added to the Roman Catholic Church's index of forbidden books. It stayed on the list for two hundred years.

Copernicus was not the first to suggest the heliocentric idea, but he made great strides in proving it with math.

Galileo Galilei (1564–1642)

In the history of science, few names are better known than that of Galileo Galilei. Born in Pisa, Italy, in 1564 to a musician father, he was the eldest of six children. Several of his siblings did not live past infancy. His father died in 1591, leaving Galileo with the responsibility of caring for his sisters and younger brother, which brought financial strain.

Galileo began his studies in a monastery outside of Florence, then attended the University of Pisa where he studied medicine. After a few years, he dropped out of school and supported himself by tutoring. Although he left the university, he continued his studies on his own. His work with challenging mathematical problems earned positive attention for him as well as a teaching position at the university in his hometown.

Like many players in the Scientific Revolution, Galileo began to challenge long-held but unproven beliefs. For example, by using eighteen-hundred-year-old Aristotelian logic, one could easily believe that heavier objects fall faster than lighter ones. Galileo wasn't comfortable with that idea. His biographer Vincenzo Viviani describes how Galileo took balls of various weights to the top of the Tower of Pisa and dropped them, proving that lighter balls fell at the same rate as heavier ones. An experiment like this was repeated by Apollo 15 astronaut David Scott, who simultaneously dropped a hammer and feather. Both hit the moon's surface at the same time. The airless moon provided no resistance to the feather.

Not everyone liked Galileo's conclusions. His fellow teachers turned against him. How could Aristotle be wrong? Galileo had to find teaching work elsewhere. He settled in Padua, which was more open to new ideas.

It was while in Padua that Galileo heard of the telescope that had been invented in the Netherlands. Galileo built a telescope seven times more powerful than what was being made in the Netherlands. He took the idea of a spyglass and made it into a telescope to study the sky. Galileo also invented the geometric compass, the pendulum clock, and one of the earliest thermometers.

With his telescope he was able to document what Copernicus had deduced from his math and observational charts: the earth circles the sun. Encouraged by another great scientist, Johannes Kepler, Galileo published a pamphlet, *The Starry Messenger*. It didn't go over well. His fellow scientists turned against him again and the Church declared his work heretical. The science community then, odd as it sounds today, did not like the observe-and-use-math approach, and the still-predominate Roman Catholic Church didn't like to be contradicted. In defense of his views, Galileo said, "The intention of the Holy Spirit is to teach us how one goes to heaven, not how the heavens go."[5]

Galileo was tried for heresy and the Inquisition ruled against him. He was forbidden from teaching the heliocentric structure of the solar system. Then Maffeo Barberini, a man whom Galileo considered a friend, became pope, taking the name Urban VIII. Galileo appealed to Pope Urban in hopes that the new pontiff would remove the prohibition, but such an action was not easily done. It would mean saying the previous pope and those who had tried Galileo had been wrong. Urban already had enough infighting to deal with.

Lifting the teaching ban on Galileo would make matters worse. Still, a concession was made. Galileo could write a book about the matter if he agreed to portray both theories equally and made no attempt to advance the newer idea of a heliocentric solar system.

Galileo ran with it and penned *Dialogue Concerning the Two Chief World Systems*, finishing the work in 1632. Soon after, it was translated into Latin. But Galileo made a tactical error: he named one of the characters in the dialogue Simplicio—"simpleminded." Galileo may have had Simplicius of Cilicia, a sixth-century man who wrote about Aristotle, in mind. The character argues from Aristotle's point of view. Regardless of what Galileo intended, it came to be believed that Simplicio was a thinly veiled reference to Pope Urban, and Urban was not pleased. The book sold well, but it brought more grief to Galileo. He was summoned to Rome to be investigated again. He was sentenced to life in prison, but that penalty was lifted. Galileo, now an old man, was allowed to live out his days under house arrest, where he worked on his final book: *Discourses and Mathematical Demonstrations Relating to Two New Sciences*. Galileo gradually lost his eyesight to glaucoma, and *Dialogue Concerning the Two Chief World Systems* joined Copernicus' book on the index of forbidden books.

The Catholic church formed a commission in 1981 to evaluate Galileo's trials. Eleven years later, Pope John Paul II said errors had been made. Today, Galileo is respected by the church and the scientific community.

Isaac Newton (1642–1727)

"Newton stands alone. There is no underestimating his influence; there is no evading his authority. In creating the science of rational mechanics, Newton determined the goals of mathematical physics as well as its methods," wrote David Berlinski.[6]

Isaac Newton, born the same year Galileo died, towers above other scientists not only in his day but also in modern times. When his name is spoken it is often with a hushed awe. There have been, and are, many great scientists. The pages of scientific history are lit by such luminaries as Louis Pasteur, Madame Curie, Gregor Mendel, Jonas Salk, and scores of others, but no light shines more brightly than the British physicist Newton. He was a man who worked with such obsession that he often forgot to eat, had few friends, possessed the ability to focus with almost inhuman concentration, and could imagine what no one else at the time could. This combination of traits has led some scholars such as Michael Fitzgerald, Irish psychiatrist and professor of psychiatry at Trinity College, Dublin, to suggest that Newton had Asperger's syndrome, an autism spectrum disorder associated with many geniuses.[7] He may have also suffered from mercury poisoning.

Whatever his challenges, Newton proved to possess a mind like none other. He formulated the law of universal gravitation, described the three laws of motion, invented the reflecting telescope, advanced the field of optics by demonstrating that white light is composed of several colors, developed the particle theory of light, and created the principles of calculus.

Born in Woolsthorp, Lincolnshire, he received his education at Trinity College in Cambridge and would become the Lucasian Professor of Mathematics in 1669. He was not yet thirty years old. He was admitted to the prestigious scientific Royal Society and became its president from 1703 until his death in 1727.

In addition to his zeal for science, he was consumed with the Bible and prophecy. Newton wrote more on such matters than he did on science. As a member of the Church of England, he held, for the most part, to the doctrine of the church. In some areas, like the nature of the Trinity, he differed. For him, science revealed what God has done in creation. Near the end of his famous three-volume work *Philosophiæ Naturalis Principia Mathematica*, he wrote:

> This most beautiful system of the sun, planets and comets, could only proceed from the counsel and domination of an intelligent and powerful Being. . . . He is eternal and infinite, omnipotent and omniscient; that is, his duration reaches from eternity to eternity; his presence from infinity to infinity; he governs all things and knows all things that can be done.[8]

Newton became obsessed with biblical prophecy and end-time thinking. He applied a scientist's way of thinking to reading the Bible and gleaning information. He held the book to be sacred and inspired, feeling it was his job to understand it fully and uncover its secrets. His obsessive behavior drove him to analyze the Bible like none other of his day was willing to do. Still, he was no evangelist, keeping many of his writings secret and burning many documents as he neared death. Many of his insights, ideas, and thoughts went up his chimney.

Still, he is considered the center star in the physics constellation. Only Einstein has come close to eclipsing him.

Many factors, including the Protestant Reformation, empowered the Scientific Revolution. It was a series of events certain to happen as knowledge grew and the means to test ideas as they were posited became available. On some issues, the Roman Catholic Church saw heresy, but it came to recognize the validity of scientific enquiry. In what may be a bit of historical irony, the Vatican runs an observatory in two locations. The first location serves as the headquarters and is located in the pope's summer residence at Castel Gandolfo, Italy. It is one of the world's oldest astronomy institutions. The second location is at the Mount Graham International Observatory near Safford, Arizona, and utilizes the VATT—Vatican Advanced Technology Telescope.

While it can't be said that all the participants in the Scientific Revolution were spiritual people, a great many were. The Scientific Revolution changed the world and the church. Scientists like Newton, Galileo, Francis Bacon, Pascal, Copernicus, and Mendel were men of faith as well as science, and the light they shed on the universe continues to inspire awe.

15

The Council of Trent

(1545)

During the seventeenth century Sir Isaac Newton formulated a set of three laws that are well-known. His third law—sometimes called the law of reaction—is summed up in a single line: "For every action there is an equal but opposite reaction." It is the law that explains why rocket ships fly and why cars can motor down the road.

Strange as it seems, this law of physics also applies to human relationships. One person pushes another; the victim wants to push back. It was no different in the sixteenth century when the Roman Catholic Church, facing innumerable internal and external problems, pushed back against the Protestant Reformation of Martin Luther, John Calvin, and Ulrich Zwingli.

For years many believed the Church needed significant reforming. The tipping point came when a disenchanted monk named Martin Luther nailed his "Ninety-Five Theses" to the door of the chapel in Wittenberg. That simple act was the snowball that began an avalanche, which still rumbles today. Each year saw the rise of more and more Protestants, many who left the Church to join new congregations that offered a simpler and more direct worship experience and greater hope.

To those deeply entrenched in the Roman Catholic Church, these new "upstarts" were doing more than rocking the boat, they were attempting to sink the ship. The Church had been around for many centuries, and making significant changes seemed an impossible task. What was the Roman Catholic Church to do? It did what people and organizations have been doing since the dawn of time. It shoved back.

Pushing back meant answering the Reformers' accusations. One way to do this, as well as deal with some internal problems in the Church, was to convene a council to set hard and fast guidelines about belief. This meant achieving two things. First, those within the Church were aware of lapses of morality in some of its leaders and the loss of zeal for ministering to the souls of its members. In other words, the Reformers were right in one sense: sin and corruption within the Church had to be dealt with. However, that did not mean the Reformers' new doctrine was correct. The Church's problems did not stem from spiritual misunderstanding. It needed to reestablish not only what was good and proper behavior, but also what was correct and acceptable doctrine.

The Council of Trent was the Church's effort to become spiritually shipshape.

The Counter-Reformation

This pushback is called the Counter-Reformation. Part of this effort was to officially address the teaching of the Reformers, point out where they differed from Catholic teaching, and set in stone once and for all what all Christians should believe. At this point those who left the Church were considered heretics, excommunicated, and no longer part of the Church. In some cases armed conflict erupted between the two sides and much of church history is stained with the blood of Christian-on-Christian violence.

The Counter-Reformation covers nearly a century, beginning under the leadership of Pope Pius IV in 1560 and continuing to the culmination of the Thirty Years' War in 1648. Many Catholics consider this period a revival and a return to basic Catholic traditions.

There is always a danger in oversimplifying complex beliefs, but the basic doctrinal issues are easy to define. Salvation in the Roman Catholic model of the day was considered participatory—one needed more than mere faith, one also needed good works. Protestants, however, held that good works had nothing to do with salvation. Good works were an *outcome* of salvation, not a key element necessary to a life in heaven.

Protestants also believed that there was a single source of authority for the Christian: the Bible. They believed that every Christian had the right and the duty to read the Bible for themselves, and to do so in their own language. Roman Catholics did not see it this way. Authority for them came from the Bible, traditions handed down through the centuries, and council rulings on matters of doctrine.

The Reformers, sometimes at great cost to themselves, had been successful in winning converts to their way of thinking. Many priests and nuns left their positions to return to society as laymen and laywomen.

There was more at stake here than good doctrine. The Roman Catholic Church was a large organization, one that needed a great deal of money and constant cash flow to keep working. The more people who left the Church, the fewer the dollars. In some areas where the Reformation blossomed, Church property was lost and landed in Protestant hands. There were also political matters to consider. There was no separation of church and state. Just the opposite. The Church and the state were intertwined like a Gordian Knot. This was the error of the Holy Roman Empire, and the Church and various political entities throughout the land were joined at the hip. To be fair, much of this continued under Protestant hands. For example, John Calvin and his followers were tightly tied to the government of Geneva.

Today, most people see the pope as a purely spiritual leader to one billion people, but in the mid-sixteenth century he was much more. John W. O'Malley sums it up this way:

Complicating matters almost beyond resolution was the fact that the pope was not simply the chief pastor of the church but also a secular prince, ruler of the Papal States, a large territory that comprised about a third of the Italian peninsula and stretched northeast from just south of Rome almost to Venice. It was difficult for everybody including the popes themselves, to keep these two responsibilities distinct—because they were in so many ways not distinct. The successor of St. Peter was in every sense of the word a monarch, with army, navy, prisons, political force, and diplomatic corps. Thus he felt that, like every other monarch, he had to maintain a court of a certain magnificence, which was chronically difficult to finance. The popes needed every source of money they could lay their hands on.[1]

The issues raised by the Protestant Reformation and the Counter-Reformation it produced are still hotly debated today. True, many of the clergy in the Roman Catholic Church of the mid-sixteenth century had grown morally loose. The sale of indulgences was out of control, and many priests and bishops were serving multiple roles to double or triple their income. It was not uncommon for a priest or bishop to have a mistress and have children out of wedlock. This is not to say the Church approved of this. With the exception of a couple of corrupt popes, it did not. These were the very reasons that the Council of Trent came to be.

Trent

When we think of a meeting, we tend to imagine people gathering in a specific location, discussing their business for a set period of time, then returning home. The Council of Trent didn't work that way. In fact, it lasted for eighteen years. This does not mean that the attendees moved into the small town for the better part of two decades. Instead, because of the complexities and extreme nature of the council, they met on three separate occasions.

The town of Trent is situated in a glacial valley near the foothills of the Alps. Today Trent, now Trento, has a population of over

117,000, but at the time the council first met in 1545, the city was little more than a burg. In many ways, Trent was ill-prepared for an influx of guests. Had attendance at the first session not been so low, the little city might have been overtaxed. Of the seven hundred eligible church leaders who could have attended the council, only thirty-four showed for the first meeting. While that may not sound like much, it must be remembered that bishops often traveled with retinues. It was not a matter of each bishop arriving with one or two aides; in some cases they arrived with scores of people. Housing, feeding, stabling horses, and dozens of other challenges fell to the citizens of Trent.

Low attendance was a hallmark of the council. By the third session in 1563, the number had grown to 255 church leaders, not even close to half of those eligible to attend. At times travel could be dangerous, even life-threatening, and travel was made more difficult by tensions in the region and around the empire. Also, some of the bishops simply didn't believe that such a council could be convened and that the idea would ever become reality.

The numbers may not have been impressive, but the council did meet, decisions were made, issues were discussed and fought over, and decrees were issued. In the end, those decisions would stand for four hundred years.

Three Popes

Three popes—Paul III, Julius III, and Pius IV—were involved with the council during its protracted eighteen-year run. No pope visited the council, each letting the convention do its work, but they did stay abreast of the happenings. Messengers traveled from Trent to Rome and back again. If theologians or bishops wanted a papal opinion, they would send a messenger to Rome. The trip took three days each way, so the quickest response took at least a week.

In addition to three popes, the council worked under two emperors: Charles V, who reigned from June 1519 to August 1556, and Ferdinand I, who reigned from 1558 to 1564.

Dealing with a Morally Eroding Church

Pope Paul III was interested in reforming a church that was, in some areas, slipping from its moorings. To understand what reforms were needed, he established a commission to look at the problem and make recommendations. The report they brought was startling as well as discouraging: the clergy had grown worldly, some ranking clergy had bought their positions through bribery, immorality among the clergy was epidemic, the sale of indulgences had become corrupt, and Rome, which should be the world's most holy city, was awash in prostitutes.

The Reformers had been right to object to such sinful practices, and Paul III wanted to bring the church back to its purity and glory. However, abuses by some church leaders did not mean a new doctrine was needed. In those areas, the Reformers were wrong. That had to be made clear.

Pope Paul called for the Council of Trent. He would not see the end of the council as he died in November 1549, four years after the first session began. Still, what he began changed the Roman Catholic Church for centuries, although not to the satisfaction of Protestants, who felt more ostracized than ever before. The practice of selling indulgences was ended and the clergy were called upon to avoid even the smallest of sins.

Taking On the Reformers

Four hundred years later, however, the most talked about aspect of the Council of Trent was its response to Protestant doctrine. Much of the council's work centered on countering the teaching of Martin Luther. While there were many other Protestant groups and leaders, Luther remained the center of the bull's-eye until late in the third session, when some attention was directed to John Calvin. Calvin would, in 1547, publish *Acta Synodi Tridentinae cum Antidoto* (*Acts of the Council of Trent and Antidote*).

Session 1 (1545–47)

The first session dealt with several key doctrines. First, the canon (the accepted books of the Bible) was established. It contained all the books found in today's Protestant Bible but included additional books in the Old Testament: the books of Esdras, Tobias (Tobit), Judith, Rest of Esther (Ester in the Vulgate), Ecclesiasticus, Baruch, and First and Second Maccabees. The list was finalized by an astonishingly tiny margin: twenty-four in favor, fifteen opposed, and sixteen abstentions.[2]

Church tradition was accepted as an authoritative source for doctrine and revelation, something Protestants denied. For Protestants of all stripes, the Bible alone was authoritative. Only what could be supported by biblical texts could be considered binding. Trent disagreed.

Protestants had been reading the Bible in their own language in some countries and drawing their own conclusions. The Council of Trent ruled that only the Latin Vulgate—the translation made by Jerome in the late fourth century—was to be used to establish and support doctrinal belief.

Protestants had railed against the sacramental system of the Roman church, reducing the number of sacraments to two: the Lord's Supper (Eucharist) and baptism. Protestants differed with each other on the nature of these ordinances. Luther, for example, taught consubstantiation, a belief that the body and blood of Christ mingled with the bread and wine. Zwingli rejected both that belief and transubstantiation (the bread and wine transformed into the body and blood of Christ during the Eucharist). Some Protestants baptized infants; others, like the Anabaptists, practiced believer's baptism, in which the person being baptized had to be old enough to make a profession of faith.

Trent reaffirmed the Roman doctrine of seven sacraments: baptism, confirmation, holy Eucharist, penance (confession), last anointing ("last rites"), holy orders, and marriage. Each provided some measure of grace to the recipient, something Protestants, with their emphasis on faith over works, rejected.

The council also reiterated the Catholic stance on justification—the act of being made right with God (to be saved): salvation came from cooperating with the grace of God. Faith alone was not enough.

On an internal Church matter, the council ruled that bishops and priests had to live in their respective dioceses and parishes.

Session 2 (1551–52)

During the second session, the council made clear its rejection of both Zwingli's view of the Eucharist being only symbolic and Luther's idea of consubstantiation. The rite of penance was further defined, and an explanation for last rites was offered.

Military actions in the region forced an early adjournment of the council.

Session 3 (1562–63)

A decade passed between the end of the second session and the beginning of the third when the council was reinstated by Pius IV. Although only 225 delegates attended, it was the best attended of the three sessions. French bishops again stirred up the controversy of a bishop's obligation to live in his see (a bishop's area of responsibility).

It took some time for peace to return to the gathering. Once it did, they wrestled with another Eucharistic matter: Should the chalice be offered to the laity or confined to the priests alone? This they left to the pope.

They also defined Mass as a true sacrifice, not merely a symbolic one. Luther had complained that this was in violation of Hebrews 7:27: "who does not need daily, like those high priests, to offer up sacrifices, first for His own sins and then for the sins of the people, because this He did once for all when He offered up Himself."

Also confirmed were the doctrines on the veneration of saints and the use of icons in church buildings. Protestants stripped icons from the walls of their churches.

The council reaffirmed the doctrine of purgatory. Purgatory was believed to be the place where those who died but needed purification would go before being allowed into heaven. Most people could not lead a life worthy of heaven, but they did not deserve hell. Purgatory was a preparatory place. The living could help those in purgatory along their path by prayer, righteous living, the purchase of indulgences, and alms. Trent made purgatory officially acceptable and insisted it be taught in churches. Protestants denied the existence of purgatory.

A Forever Separation

In every case but one, the Council of Trent ruled against Protestant doctrinal beliefs. Only in admitting that moral corruption had infected the ranks of the clergy and needed to be excised quickly were they in agreement. To that end, the Council of Trent was a success. Bridging the gap to those leaving the Church was never attempted. The parties were just too far apart. To concede to Protestant reasoning meant casting off centuries of tradition and practice, beliefs that were part of the weave of the Roman church, and it just couldn't be done, not by a small number of representatives meeting in the bucolic town of Trent.

The decisions of Trent were published in a series of twelve publications between April 8, 1546, and December 4, 1563. If there had been a bridge spanning the gorge of doctrine separating Protestant from Catholic, it had been set afire and left to burn until fully collapsed. Christianity had fragmented again. The division often turned acrimonious. For some, the pope—any pope—was the antichrist; for others he was the voice of God on earth. To some Catholics, Protestants were wayward and lost children living outside the grace of the Church. Many Catholics were taught that salvation could only be found in the Church, and they were discouraged from attending Protestant worship services and from marrying non-Catholics. Of course, many did so anyway.

For 417 years, the edicts of Trent guided the Roman church. It wasn't until the 1962 meeting of Vatican II that some of these issues were addressed again and a new, more tolerant view of Protestants grew.

Still, it was a long four centuries.

139

16

Smyth Baptizes Himself and Begins the Early Baptists

(1609)

The church has changed much since its founding nearly two thousand years ago. Still, several things have remained the same. One lingering problem is the church's ability to subdivide itself, to fragment from the whole. This began in the first-century church with the rise of Judaizers who wanted all Christians to first be Jews, and with the Gnostics who wanted nothing more than to redefine the nature of Christ and set themselves up as the only trustees of knowledge. Even in established churches, divisions began within decades of a congregation's establishment. Paul had to face such fragmentation in the church at Corinth.

> Now I exhort you, brethren, by the name of our Lord Jesus Christ, that you all agree and that there be no divisions among you, but that you be made complete in the same mind and in the same judgment.

For I have been informed concerning you, my brethren, by Chloe's people, that there are quarrels among you. Now I mean this, that each one of you is saying, "I am of Paul," and "I of Apollos," and "I of Cephas," and "I of Christ." Has Christ been divided? Paul was not crucified for you, was he? Or were you baptized in the name of Paul? (1 Cor. 1:10–15)

Seeing division in the church deeply wounded Paul. Such divisions became a pattern, and the partings were often bitter, including exile and even, in some historical periods of the church, violence and execution. Some hold that division led to denominations and might be beneficial to the overall mission of the church, with Presbyterians reaching people Methodists can't, Methodists reaching those Baptists can't, and so on. This is true, but the fragmentation often came at great sacrifice and pain, and it would take centuries for the various branches of the church to learn to live together.

The birth of what most consider the largest "Protestant" denomination, Baptist, came with pains delivered from without and within. Protestant is in quotes because some Baptist groups do not see themselves as part of the Protestant Reformation but rather a continuation of Baptist-like groups reaching back to the first century. Others hold to a different tradition. Baptist history has been a sore spot in some of the denominations. There are three lines of thought regarding the history of the Baptists.

First is Landmarkism, a belief that there exists an unbroken link to the days of the apostles. The view came to light in the mid-1800s in the American South. When the Southern Baptist Convention passed several resolutions against the idea, adherents split from the SBC to form their own conventions and churches.

Second, the Anabaptist theory, a belief that the Anabaptist movement of the early sixteenth century served as the foundation for what would become the Baptist denomination. Early Baptists, however, while sharing much in common with Anabaptists, also had some differences.

The most accepted view is the English Separatist view. This approach has the best historical evidence, a history that has its beginning in 1609 in a restless minister named John Smyth. Baptists are marked by a fierce independence, not just in the past but continuing to today.

John Smyth

Born around 1570, John Smyth had an early life that is lost to us, but we do pick up his work at Cambridge and Christ's College in England, where he prepared to minister in the Church of England. In 1593 he took his master of arts degree. He became, by a very narrow vote of eight to seven, a preacher in the city of Lincoln on September 27, 1600. It didn't last long. He was dismissed October 13 of that same year. Apparently his criticism of the Anglican church was not shared.

The Anglican church had split from the Roman Catholic Church and, with the Act of Supremacy (November 1534) making King Henry VIII head of the Church of England, expected everyone to be part of the church. The Church of England was no more patient with dissenters than the Roman Catholics had been. Critics complained that the church was too Roman and retained doctrines that the growing Protestant movement was addressing. Within the church were critics who chose to remain in the fellowship and work to purify the doctrine, people we now call Puritans. A second group had come to believe remaining was impossible and left the church to start their own congregations. These were the Separatists.

John Smyth slid along the ranks from Anglican priest to Puritan to Separatist, and would continue to struggle to find a doctrinal home. In Smyth's hometown of Gainsborough on Trent was a new Congregational church. Congregationalists believed the church should be run not by a church or political hierarchy but by the congregation. They practiced a democratic form of church government. Four years after its founding in 1602, the church divided. It was a division of convenience, not of dispute. Richard Clyton led one group. This congregation would become the Pilgrims who eventually crossed the Atlantic to the New World. The second group remained in town, and Smyth became its spiritual leader.

The two congregations were nonconformist and therefore the target of the government. Pressure increased to the point that both moved to the less-threatening environs of Holland. In 1607, the Gainsborough group, led by Smyth and Thomas Helwys, was the first of the two congregations to make the move. Drawing followers from Lincolnshire, Nottinghamshire, and Yorkshire, they settled in Amsterdam. The second congregation—Scrooby Manor Church—arrived in Amsterdam sometime in 1608 and may have joined with a Congregational church. Smyth's group remained separate from the Congregationalists. In 1608, Smyth wrote *The Differences of the Churches of the Separation*, in which he argued that no minister should preach from a manuscript or notes, believing that it could hamper the Holy Spirit. It was a view not shared by many, including other Separatists.

Smyth was a student of the Bible, and like many in the Protestant movement he had come to believe that the Bible had the final word on all matters. If it wasn't in the Bible, then it shouldn't be a practice of the church. One such topic was infant baptism. Roman Catholics and the Church of England baptized infants. Infants were baptized to make sure their souls would be ushered into heaven should they die. In an age when it was common to lose half of one's children at an early age, such a belief was a powerful one to shake. Smyth, however, could find no evidence for the belief that baptism provided any benefit to the child, and could not find a New Testament example of the practice. The only people baptized were people who had made a profession of faith. This would become the idea of "believer's baptism."

This created another problem for Smyth: he had been baptized in the Church of England as an infant. All of his congregation had been too. If there was no biblical basis for infant baptism, then his own baptism was unbiblical. He decided to baptize himself, and forty or so of his flock followed. He baptized himself and the others by affusion. Affusion comes from the Latin *affusio*, meaning "to pour fluid on or over something," in this case, a person. By "re-baptizing" himself and the others, he was doing more than satisfying his view of baptism; he was dismissing the infant baptism that had been practiced for so long. It was 1609 and Baptists were born.

Smyth's spiritual journey was not over. He had a change of heart and began to question the appropriateness of his self-baptism, and came to believe he had made an error. He and some of his followers petitioned to join the Mennonites. It was too much for Thomas Helwys, one of the leaders in Smyth's group. This questioning of the re-baptism he and Smyth had received pushed Helwys to separate from Smyth, excommunicate him, and send a letter to the Mennonites explaining the situation.

Thomas Helwys

Around 1612, Thomas Helwys and a handful of others returned to London to propagate their message of religious freedom. They established a church in Spitalfields in East London. This congregation became the first Baptist church on English soil. Helwys was assertive in his writing. He wrote several works and didn't mince words. In *A Short Declaration of the Mystery of Iniquity*, he stated:

> Let the king judge, is it not most equal that men should choose their religion themselves, seeing they only must stand themselves before the judgment seat of God to answer for themselves. . . . [We] profess and teach that in all earthly things the king's power is to be submitted unto; and in heavenly or spiritual things, if the king or any in authority under him shall exercise power against any they are not to resist by any way or means, although it were in their power, but rather to submit their lives as Christ and his disciples did, and yet keep their consciences to God.[1]

That statement was the first written defense of freedom of religion in English. What got him in trouble was this line in the inscription:

> The King is a mortal man and not God, therefore hath no power over immortal souls of his subjects to make laws and ordinances for them and to set spiritual Lords over them.[2]

He then had the temerity to send the king a copy. As expected, King James I was offended. That line led to Helwys' arrest and imprisonment in Newgate Prison, where he died at the age of forty.

General Baptists and Particular Baptists

The first Baptist churches, created by Smyth and Helwys, came to be called General Baptists. The term refers to the Arminian approach to salvation, a belief that anyone who believes can be saved. In contrast, Particular Baptists stood on the opposite side of the predestination fence, choosing the Calvinist view of predestination—only those selected could become believers.

Baptists, then and now, were fiercely independent. They recognized no hierarchal authority in the church. Power rested with the congregation and with the many, not the few. Each congregation made its own decisions about the work of the church. Outsiders had no authority to dictate doctrine or procedure. Of course, the minister held a great deal of influence, but only as long as the congregation allowed.

It is a bit of historical irony that the first Baptists did not practice the doctrine that is most often associated with the denomination: baptism by immersion. When Smyth baptized himself and his followers, he did so by affusion, pouring water over the candidate. Their primary advance was the idea of believer's baptism. While not unique to Baptists, it became their keystone doctrine. Modes of baptism vary from denomination to denomination. Some practice sprinkling (aspersion); others, like the first Baptists, pour water over the head (affusion); and some practice baptism by immersion, in which the person is plunged beneath the water.

The move from pouring to immersion was a quick and natural progression for Baptists. With the Baptist emphasis on following the New Testament pattern of doctrine, it was only a matter of time before immersion became one of the foundational doctrines for the group. The practice of adult immersion, according to Baptist historian Robert Torbet, was first championed by Leonard Busher, a member of Helwys' church. He did this several decades before it became the practice in Calvinistic Baptist churches.[3]

Most modern Baptist churches require baptism by immersion for someone coming from a denomination that sprinkles or pours, even if that baptism was conducted after they had become a believer.

Baptists Today

Taken as a whole, Baptists form the largest non-Catholic denomination in the world, with one hundred million or so members divided between two hundred conventions. The largest grouping is the Southern Baptist Convention, first organized in 1845. It is comprised of forty-five thousand churches and missions ministering to nearly sixteen million members. Despite its regional name, the denomination has reached far from its southern US roots and into the world. Ever mission-minded, the organization operates mission work domestically through its North American Mission Board and into the world through their International Mission Board, where they have mobilized over five thousand field workers and are ministering to close to 1,100 ethnically or geographically distinct people groups. They also operate six seminaries to train future pastors and missionaries.

While it is the largest of the Baptist groups, Southern Baptists are not alone. Smaller denominations, some holding doctrines unique to them, carry on the work started by Smyth, Helwys, and others. While it might be true that there have been Baptist-like groups from the days of the apostles on down, we can pin the start of the denomination called Baptist to John Smyth in 1609. From Amsterdam and London, the movement spread to the world.

The King James Version Is Published

(1611)

Some names are associated with an important event. Just uttering the name conjures up the occasion. Say Henry Ford and the image of a "horseless carriage" rises in the mind. The names Wilbur and Orville Wright conjure up the first airplane. Hear Edison and we think of the lightbulb. Linking three names, Lee Harvey Oswald, calls to mind something far less pleasant to remember. For most people, "King James" means only one thing: the King James Bible (often called the Authorized Version).

The King James Version (KJV) is the most beloved English translation in the world. While the New International Version of the Bible might sell more these days, it has a long way to go to match the KJV's four-hundred-year record.

The Man behind the Name

While the Bible that bears his name is deeply loved, the people of James' day did not feel so warmly toward the man. Historian Earle Cairns refers to him as "the pudgy, ricket-deformed, vain, garrulous ruler."[1] Bruce Shelley remarked that James "had an inflated view of his own intelligence."[2]

Born June 19, 1566, in Edinburgh Castle, Scotland, to Mary, Queen of Scots, James was destined to rule. A few months after his birth, in February 1567, his father, Lord Darnley, was murdered while recuperating from smallpox (some speculate syphilis) at their estate Kirk o' Field. There had been an explosion in the building a short time before, but his body and that of his valet showed no damage that could be attributed to exploding barrels of gunpowder. James' father had been strangled. Mary was away at a wedding.

Things went from bad to worse for Mary in Scotland. She remarried, and neither the Catholics nor the Protestants thought the marriage was valid. Finally, Mary was forced to abdicate her throne, and James VI became ruler of Scotland. He was one year old. The country was ruled by a string of regents until 1576 when, at the age of ten, he stepped to the forefront. He became ruler-in-fact five years later, in 1581.

In 1587 James' mother Mary was beheaded under the reign of Elizabeth I at Fotheringhay Castle, Northamptonshire, in a gruesome manner. It took three attempts to do the job.

Elizabeth I died in March 1603 with no children to take the throne after her. James, her cousin, was named successor. James VI of Scotland became James I of England, and for the first time united the two kingdoms under a single ruler.

Christianity was a fractured institution in James' day. Roman Catholicism and the Church of England remained at odds. The Church of England had other problems. Many Protestants felt their church was still too much like the Roman church and sought changes. Many were dedicated to purifying it from within. These were the Puritans. Others pulled away, not willing to endure decades more of what they considered unbiblical practices. These were the Separatists.

How the KJV Came to Be

James had no patience with the Roman Catholic Church. At the opening of Parliament in 1604, he said, "I acknowledge the Roman Church to be our mother church, although defiled with some infirmities and corruptions. . . . Let them assure themselves, that, as I am a friend of their persons, if they be good subjects, so am I a vowed enemy, and do denounce mortal war to their errors."[3]

He was no more patient with reformers in the Anglican church. While on his way from Edinburgh to London he was presented with the Millenary Petition, a document outlining grievances Puritan ministers wanted addressed. As many as one thousand Puritan leaders signed the document. Since James had grown up in Scotland with its great Presbyterian influence, the Puritans had hopes that he would be sympathetic to their cause. The opposite was the case.

The Millenary Petition led to the January 1604 Hampton Court Conference with the king, bishops, and Puritans present. The Puritans walked away with very little success. James handled them roughly. Speaking of the Puritans, he said, "I will make them conform themselves, or else I will harry them out of the land, or else do worse."[4] James saw himself above religious parties.

They did have one significant success that shaped the church. John Reynolds, the Puritan president of Corpus Christi College, Oxford, appealed for a new Bible translation that would be acceptable to all. James took to this idea. Two English Bibles were prominent at the time: the Geneva Bible (1560), which James disliked, and the Bishop's Bible (1568). The Bishop's Bible was more acceptable to the Church of England but it didn't catch on with anyone else. A new translation would allow James to replace the two "offending" translations and win support from some of his subjects.

They set a plan in motion. Fifty-four translators were chosen and divided into six groups: two groups in Cambridge would work on the books from 1 Chronicles through Ecclesiastes; two in Oxford were to revise Isaiah through Malachi, the Gospels, the Book of Acts, and Revelation; and two groups at Westminster were to revise Genesis through 2 Kings and Romans through Jude.

The scholars were to begin with the Bishop's Bible and compare it to original texts, choosing to follow the Tyndale, Coverdale, or other translations if they were found to represent the original text better. The first edition of the new Bible was published in 1611 and would undergo many revisions, corrections, and updates.

The end product has endured for over four hundred years, with good reason. The KJV is beautifully rendered and considered a very accurate translation. The seventeenth-century language, however, can be difficult to follow, and some of the terms that were well understood in King James' day are confusing to the contemporary reader. For example, the KJV refers to the Holy Spirit as the Holy Ghost. *Ghost*, in present-day English, refers to the spirit of someone who has died. The Holy Spirit is the third person of the Trinity and as such has never experienced death. Other terms, such as *prevent*, which we understand to mean stopping an action from occurring, were fine choices in the seventeenth century but are misleading today. In 1 Thessalonians 4:15 "prevent" is used for "precede." Very different meanings. Of course, this can be said about any translation, English or otherwise.

There is also some general confusion about the work. Although called the Authorized Bible, it was never authorized by Parliament, perhaps because James dissolved the institution the same year the Bible was published. Nonetheless, it remained the standard text in the Anglican church and elsewhere for 250 years.

Another area of confusion is the common title "King James Version." Scholars have more technical definitions than the general populace. "Version" to a theologian refers to a translation from the original languages to a new language. The Bible was originally written in three languages over a 1,500-year period. The Old Testament is primarily Hebrew with some Aramaic (not to be confused with Arabic), and the New Testament was penned in Koine Greek. Like many modern "translations," the King James was based on previous versions and compared to the original languages. The KJV is therefore a revision, not a translation or version. As Norman Geisler and William Nix noted in their book *From God to Us*, the KJV is neither a version nor authorized.[5] This, however, does not detract from the scholarship, beauty, and lasting influence of the KJV. To some, the King James Bible remains the best of the English Bibles.

The Puritans got the new Bible revision they wanted but very little else. They became outcasts, and some who were Separatists, exasperated with King James and the Anglican church, left England for Holland where they could worship in safety and freedom. As their children grew accustomed to life in Holland they began to forget their roots and the language of their family. This so concerned Pastor John Robinson that he and his followers, unwilling to return to England, followed the lead of an English colony established on the new continent America in 1607. The Puritans had become Pilgrims.

James I died on March 27, 1625, at the age of fifty-eight. In the latter years of his life he suffered from several afflictions: gout, arthritis, and kidney stones. Dysentery finally took his life. He is remembered for many things, but nothing more than the Bible revision that bears his name. Today, the King James Bible continues to win new readers and to impress with its beautiful prose.

18

Bishop Ussher's Chronology

(1650)

A portrait hangs in the National Portrait Gallery in London. Rendered by artist Peter Lely, the subject appears to be staring at the viewer through eyes that seem to be holding back a secret. Dressed in ecclesiastical robes, an Elizabethan collar, and a dark skullcap, his expression is that of a playful man attempting to appear stern. A handsome man with penetrating eyes, full brows, a large nose, and a solid chin draped with a minimal Van Dyke beard, he looks nothing like the buffoon some hold him to be. The subject is perhaps one of the most maligned men in history. Although those in his day held him in the highest regard, he has become a joke to many, and nowadays James Ussher (1581–1656), Irish archbishop of Armagh, professor and twice vice-chancellor of Trinity College, Dublin, and primate of the Irish Anglican Church, is more likely to be ridiculed than praised.

He deserves none of the criticism he has received from contemporary thinkers. He was not a charlatan or a fool as some portray him. Quite the contrary. He was one of the most learned men of his day. Admired by almost everyone, Ussher produced an astonishing volume of work, all the while carrying out his duties to the Irish church. He was a theologian, Bible expert, minister, historian, and gifted linguist. His skills in ancient languages allowed him to work in Latin, Greek, Hebrew, and Aramaic. In an age many centuries before computers, he still managed to produce enough work to fill ten thousand pages of printed text. Today, scholars still admire his work, but beyond the ranks of the academics, only one piece of work is mentioned: Ussher's date for creation.

What's in a Date?

The contemporary church is divided over the date of creation. Young Earth creationists hold to a creation event 6,000 to 10,000 years before the present. (Some go so far as to suggest 20,000 years ago.) Old Earth creationists hold to the current scientific date of 13.8 billion years ago for the universe and 4.5 billion years ago for the formation of the earth. This debate is not likely to be resolved anytime soon. Archbishop Ussher has become the poster child for a recent date of creation: October 23, 4004 BC.

To many, if not most, contemporary people, that date is laughable, but those who snicker do an injustice to Ussher. Ussher was neither the first nor the last to suggest a 4000 BC date for creation. In fact, he was in the dead center of academic understanding in the mid-seventeenth century. There had been approximately two hundred attempts to date creation, and none of them veered far from Ussher's conclusions. Famed astronomer Johannes Kepler (1571–1630), who is revered in scientific circles and whose name has been applied to an asteroid, a crater on the moon, spacecraft, universities, and much more, believed creation occurred in 3992 BC. No scientist is held in higher regard than Sir Isaac Newton, who opened the doors of modern physics and laid the foundation for several fields of science. Like Ussher—like *everyone* of the day—he believed in a young Earth, dating creation to 4000 BC, just four years different from Ussher's date.

Ussher's chronology came out of his work to write a history of the world from creation to 70 AD, the fall of Jerusalem. The work was written in Latin: *Annales veteris Testamenti, a Prima Mundi Origine deducti, una cum Rerum Asiaticarum Aegypticarum Chronico, a temporis historici principio usque ad Maccabaicorum initia producto* (*Annals of the Old Testament, Deduced from the First Origins of the World, the Chronicle of Asiatic and Egyptian Matter Together Produced from the Beginning of Historical Time up to the Beginnings of Maccabees*). Most refer to the book as Ussher's *Annals*. It was a monumental undertaking.

Like all historians of his day, Ussher faced a problem. There was no clear way to date ancient events. He chose to start with the date the Babylonian king Nebuchadnezzar died. He worked backward from there using the Bible, especially the genealogies, until he reached 4004 BC. There was no other reliable source Ussher could use. As a Christian, he believed the Bible to be accurate in all it taught and took the position that the genealogies were there for a reason.

When thinking of dating creation, it must be remembered that the Scientific Revolution was just getting underway. Modern geology would not come to be until James Hutton's publication in 1788 (138 years after Ussher's work) of *Theory of the Earth; or an Investigation of the Laws Observable in the Composition, Dissolution, and Restoration of Land upon the Globe*. Radiometric dating such as Carbon-14 did not come about until 1949, almost three centuries after Ussher's chronology.

Ussher took the matter seriously. The calculations he made fill one hundred pages and take into account what was known of ancient calendars. Many ancients used a 360-day calendar instead of 365 days. Even the latter isn't fully accurate, since a year is 365.26 days long.

The October 23 date puzzles many. Tracing genealogies will not lead to a particular day on the calendar. Ussher derived that date on a set of assumptions. The ancient Jews (and others) began their year in autumn. After consulting astronomy tables, he pegged the autumnal equinox as October 23. On our current calendars the equinox occurs on September 22 or 23. Ussher adjusted for the change in calendars, compensating for the difference between the Gregorian calendar and what the ancients used. Since the ancients began their year with the beginning of autumn, Ussher assumed their new year would fall on the equinox.

Ussher begins his *Annals* with Genesis 1:1: "In the beginning God created the heaven and the earth" (KJV). Then he adds, "The beginning of time, according to our chronology, happened at the start of the evening preceding the twenty-third day of October (on the Julian calendar) 4004 BC."[1]

Dating creation's beginning was an ambitious task and one impossible to prove. It rests on the assumption that the genealogies were complete, containing no gaps. Is that the case? Many have said no. Larry Richards and Lawrence O. Richards remark in *Bible Teacher's Commentary*:

> These attempts at dating assumed that the genealogies of the Bible were complete, and overlooked the Hebrew way of compressing genealogical records. For instance, compare Exodus 6:16–20 where there are only 4 kings between Levi and Moses mentioned with 1 Chronicles 7:20–27 where 17 links are listed between a nephew of Levi (Ephraim) and Joshua. Clearly, the terms "son of" and "beget" are used in Hebrew literature in the sense of "descendant" and "progenitor" rather than of "child" and "parent."[2]

Many Bible commentators call the 4004 BC date doubtful and, of course, the scientific community dismisses it out of hand. One may question Ussher's conclusion, but it is difficult to question his sincerity.

How Did Ussher Become a Household Name?

If there have been two hundred attempts to date creation through biblical analysis, then how did Ussher become the central figure in the controversy? After all, famed scientists like Newton and Kepler did the same work and came up with nearly identical dates. Why don't we speak of the Newtonian creation date or the Kepler chronology? For one important reason: the King James Version popularized Ussher's dates. In many versions of the translation, the KJV included the dates drawn from Ussher. This influence was expanded with the 1917 edition of the *Scofield Reference Bible*, which became popular in the twentieth century. Scofield included Ussher's chronology, introducing the concept to millions of readers.

Of course, neither Ussher nor—250 years later—Scofield intended for the date to be considered part of Scripture, but rather a comment on a passage. When the modern age of geology, archaeology, biology, and related sciences began to teach a much older view of the universe, earth, and humankind, it came into direct conflict with Ussher's system and he became the butt of ridicule, unjustly so. Young Earth creationists have held to the concept espoused by Ussher, although not necessarily the 4004 BC date, putting the two sides at odds. The battle continues to this day.

Archbishop James Ussher was not the foolish cleric as some portray him. He was the proverbial "smartest man in the room." One need not agree with the assumptions he used to date creation to acknowledge his intent, his in-depth work, and his desire to pull together a history spanning nearly 4,100 years.

19

The Great Awakening
in the United States

(1740)

Spontaneous combustion can be a dangerous thing. Oily rags left in a container can self-ignite and cause a fire that spreads through a building, leaving little but ashes. It seems odd that such a thing could happen without some outside force to suddenly spark it all. There's a human analogue to this: almost anything can happen in society when the right ingredients are put together. This happens not only in the physical world but the spiritual as well. The Great Awakening that swept through the American colonies in the mid-1700s is such an example.

The United States is a pluralistic society, drawing people from around the world. It was and remains a melting pot of culture, thinking, and values. It was no different in the decades leading to the Revolutionary War. Walking the streets of the cities in the colonies or working the fields in the rural areas were a mix of people from England, Scotland, France, Germany, Sweden, Holland, and other countries. The churches of the day reflected the countries of the citizens. From England came Roman Catholics and Anglicans, with Anglicanism being the state church for Georgia, Maryland, North Carolina, New York, South Carolina, and Virginia. Also from England came the Puritan Separatists and the Congregationalists, who settled mostly in Massachusetts. From that group came Baptists in Rhode Island and Connecticut. Quakers and Methodists can also trace their roots back to England. Scotland contributed Presbyterianism and the doctrine of Calvin, mostly in Pennsylvania. From France came the Huguenots in South Carolina; from Germany came the Lutherans in Pennsylvania, and more Lutherans in Delaware came from Sweden. Holland added the Dutch Reformed Church and the Mennonites in Pennsylvania.

The doctrines of these churches, while similar, were different enough to create stress. Much preaching of the day was centered on doctrine, making sure the congregation understood and believed the right things. But by the mid-1700s things were beginning to change. The Enlightenment was underway both at home and abroad. Logic was replacing faith. Morals had begun to decline sometime before 1700, influenced by a changing population and an unshakable desire to see a separation between church and state, as well as the rough-and-tumble lifestyle of frontier people.

Faced with this moral decline and a noticeable weakening of the church, many clergymen switched from an emphasis on doctrine, which remained important, to an emphasis on a personal relationship between the individual and God. Even Calvinists, who believed the redeemed were predetermined, began to speak of the duty of the Christian to maintain a proper relationship with God.

Often church revivals begin in times of uncertainty and conflict. People, not just clergy, could see their society was changing. They were accustomed to long sermons on a particular Bible passage and church belief while their souls hungered for something more personal, freeing, and dynamic. Spiritual spontaneous combustion was just around the corner, and it would be led by several church leaders, and two in particular.

Jonathan Edwards—Not for the Faint of Heart

What may be the most famous sermon in the history of preaching was delivered by a narrow-faced man with a receding hairline as he stood in the pulpit of the church in Enfield, Connecticut, on a July day in 1741. A thin, scholarly man, a man many historians consider one of the brightest lights and finest minds of his time, Jonathan Edwards can be considered the catalyst of the Great Awakening. He'd been invited to the church as a guest preacher to share a sermon that had been used to call many back to faith. He stood behind the pulpit in a black robe and lace drop "preaching" bands. Before him the congregation sat in a crowded sanctuary, most of the city of Enfield having turned out to hear the famous preacher. There were some who may have wished they had stayed home. The sermon, "Sinners in the Hands of an Angry God," began with almost an academic tone, but before long the message turned personal. It was not flowery, not warm, not the kind of message to soothe the soul and quiet the mind. Instead the words were hot coals that singed the ears and the hearts of the congregation. Listeners moaned, groaned, pleaded to God for mercy, gripped the backs of the pews, and some even cried out.

We might imagine Edwards marching around the raised lectern shaking his fist and pointing his finger, pounding the pulpit, and raising his voice so loud the windows rattled in sympathy, but we would be wrong. Jonathan Edwards, pastor of the Church of Christ in Northampton, was a refined and disciplined man uncomfortable with emotional outbursts. Instead of prancing about like the stereotypical hellfire-and-brimstone preachers, he remained planted behind the pulpit, his face directed toward his manuscript as he read the words he had written. Calm and avoiding any sign of great emotion, he ran through the sermon—it was enough to frighten everyone within hearing. As he moved into the application portion, the sermon's words became personal and he portrayed the desperate position of the unrepentant sinner. Before he was done, everyone in the room believed they were seconds from eternal damnation. Even now a cold reading of the printed words can move a person. Not even the stilted, formal delivery of the message could quench the impact.

> The bow of God's wrath is bent, and the arrow made ready on the string, and justice bends the arrow at your heart, and strains the bow, and it is nothing but the mere pleasure of God, and that of an angry God, without any promise or obligation at all, that keeps the arrow one moment from being made drunk with your blood.
>
> The God that holds you over the pit of hell, much as one holds a spider, or some loathsome insect over the fire, abhors you, and is dreadfully provoked: his wrath towards you burns like fire; he looks upon you as worthy of nothing else, but to be cast into the fire; he is of purer eyes than to bear to have you in his sight; you are ten thousand times more abominable in his eyes, than the most hateful venomous serpent is in ours. You have offended him infinitely more than ever a stubborn rebel did his prince; and yet it is nothing but his hand that holds you from falling into the fire every moment. . . .
>
> O sinner! Consider the fearful danger you are in: it is a great furnace of wrath, a wide and bottomless pit, full of the fire of wrath, that you are held over in the hand of that God, whose wrath is provoked and incensed as much against you, as against many of the damned in hell. You hang by a slender thread, with the flames of divine wrath flashing about it, and ready every moment to singe it, and burn it asunder; and you have no interest in any Mediator, and nothing to lay hold of to save yourself, nothing to keep off the flames of wrath, nothing of your own, nothing that you ever have done, nothing that you can do, to induce God to spare you one moment.[1]

Chilling.

Edwards was not the kind of man who enjoyed tormenting his parishioners. He was driven by a deep belief that the people in New England were losing their spiritual roots and drifting away. For men like Edwards, such drifting had eternal consequences, consequences he felt responsible to address. He was a man of great discipline who rose every morning at 4:00 and spent thirteen hours a day in study. His was an active mind with multiple interests. He began his studies at Yale University when he was just thirteen and continued on until he had earned his master's degree in theology. He had a fondness for philosophy and later in life the writings of Sir Isaac Newton. But his calling was to church work—something he did until he and his church came to a parting of ways and he moved on to become the third president of Princeton University.

Seeing the waning interest in spiritual matters, he began to pray for what he called the "harvest." He was praying for revival, and that prayer was answered in 1734 as a new spiritual enthusiasm swept through his church. He wrote, "The town seemed to be full of the presence of God. It never was so full of love, so full of joy, and yet so full of distress, as it was then."[2] That revival was the beginning of a movement that would change the American colonies, a movement that would last two decades and would result in new and vibrant churches.

But Jonathan Edwards was not the only one to contribute to the Great Awakening.

George Whitefield

In many ways, George Whitefield was the opposite of Jonathan Edwards. Where Edwards was slim and reserved, Whitefield was round and very much an extrovert who was a pioneer in a new form of preaching. But there was nothing about him to make one think he was a great orator. When he rose to speak he wore his Anglican minister's garb and lace collar. He was a man difficult to take seriously on first impression. Then he began to speak, and when he spoke, loud and disorderly crowds quieted, mouths shut, and ears opened. Before he was done, men and women were brought to tears, their attention hanging on every sentence. He was an enigma who helped launch the Great Awakening in America, yet he was not a colonist. George Whitefield was an English clergyman.

He, along with the Wesleys, was a founder of Methodism. Like Jonathan Edwards, he felt the need to do more than preach about doctrine; he wanted to speak about rebirth. No one worked as long and as hard as Whitefield. He died in 1770 at the age of fifty-five,

161

but before he left this world he had preached over eighteen thousand times, had traveled to the American colonies seven times, and had preached throughout Europe, especially in England and Scotland. It is estimated that over the course of his ministry he had preached to as many as ten million people. This small man with a big voice pioneered mass evangelism and crusade-style preaching.

Whitefield was born in Gloucester, England, to innkeeper parents. His father died when Whitefield was just two. His family lacked the money to pay for his college education, so he worked his way through Pembroke College, Oxford, serving the wealthier students. While in school he developed an interest in theater and learned skills that would later, unknown to him at the time, make him one of the best preachers in history.

It was while in college that he became acquainted with John and Charles Wesley. While he developed an interest in spiritual matters as a young boy, he never formed religious convictions until he began attending the Holy Club, a student-run Christian organization led by the Wesleys. He struggled with his faith and never felt like he was worthy of salvation. He would fast for days and deprive himself of anything and everything that gave him pleasure, but this did not settle his restless soul. A two-month battle with illness caused him to cry out to God in desperation, indicating his heartfelt need by repeating Jesus' words from the cross, "I thirst!" Later he would write, "Soon after this, I found and felt in myself that I was delivered from the burden that has so heavily oppressed me. The spirit of mourning was taken from me, and I knew what it was truly to rejoice in God my Savior; for some time, I could not avoid singing Psalms where ever I was."[3] It was 1735 and he was twenty-one years old.

He was ordained the following year and began preaching, but very few expected much of value from such a young man. It didn't take long for him to prove them wrong, leaving some hearers impressed and some clergy jealous. While he fully acknowledged the importance of doctrine in preaching, he focused on the individual's need to accept salvation. It might sound odd today, but that focus closed the doors of many churches to him. When it became clear that he was no longer welcome to preach *inside* the church, he began preaching *outside* the church, and crowds would gather to hear the strange minister. The system worked well for him. Outside of Bristol, Whitefield gathered the families of coal miners, and he was able to gain the interest of about two hundred people. He continued to preach, and a few weeks later the two hundred had grown to twenty thousand. He'd found not only his God but also his calling.

This endeared him to the people, but it further separated him from the clergy of his day. It was considered unseemly, perhaps even barbaric, to preach outside the walls of the church. No one did that. Later John Wesley would follow Whitefield's example, but he had to battle every church instinct he possessed. Whitefield took to preaching outdoors easily, but John Wesley had to be convinced and prodded.

Whitefield took his preaching to America, traveling from colony to colony, and as he did, crowds gathered. Often the number in the crowds would exceed the population of the town. People traveled on foot, by horse, and by buggy from surrounding regions to hear Whitefield preach. And he preached like no other. His delivery and his voice became the envy of actors everywhere. In an age without electronic amplification, Whitefield could project his voice far enough to be heard by as many as thirty thousand people. The number seems too large to believe. That was true for no less a person than Benjamin Franklin, who had read about the size of the crowds in the newspapers. He doubted the truth of the reports. While listening to Whitefield preach, Franklin, ever the scientist as well as statesman, conducted a small experiment. He described it this way:

> [Whitefield] had a loud and clear voice, and articulated his words and sentences so perfectly, that he might be heard and understood at a great distance, especially as audiences, however numerous, observ'd the most exact silence. He preached one evening from the top of the Court-house steps, which are in the middle of Market-street, and on the west side of Second-street, which crosses it at right angles. Both streets were fill'd with his hearers to a considerable distance. Being among the hindmost in Market-street, I had the curiosity to learn how

far he could be heard, by retiring backwards down the street towards the river; and I found his voice distinct till I came near Front-street, when some noise in that street obscur'd it.[4]

Whitefield and Franklin, although very different men with very different views about spirituality, became friends and corresponded over the years. It was Franklin who printed Whitefield's sermons for others to read. Franklin did not seem to adopt Whitefield's view that everyone needed a spiritual rebirth, but nonetheless, he admired the man greatly.

The success of Whitefield's ministry did not come easily or without opposition. He was not always greeted warmly. Many times people in the crowds would launch stones, vegetables, and even small dead animals at the preacher. Traveling between Europe and America, and then through the colonies, was grueling and took a toll on Whitefield's already precarious health. He often exhibited symptoms of asthma. Still he pressed on. On Sunday, September 30, 1770, while in Newburyport, Massachusetts, after a morning and evening of preaching, Whitefield died. He was just fifty-five years old.

Impact

Historian Bruce L. Shelley wrote, "The Great Awakening knew both the frown and the smile of God. It restored both the tears of repentance to colonial Christianity and the joy of salvation."[5]

The new revivalism changed everything, at least for a time. In New England as many as forty thousand people were added to the church—this in a population of three hundred thousand. Approximately 150 new churches were added in those northern states. Similar numbers can be found throughout the colonies.

In addition to new converts and those recommitting to a spiritual life came more and more men who wanted to dedicate themselves to the ministry. Several colleges—Princeton, King's (now Columbia), and others—started to provide ministers for the great number of new congregations. Others devoted themselves to missionary work among the Native Americans, while some committed themselves to humanitarian endeavors. All of it tied to the revivals of the Great Awakening.

Perhaps the one thing that never changes is the fact that change is always resisted. Today ministers speak of "Old Guard" and "New Guard" to describe the division that seems to come with every new generation of ministers. During the Great Awakening there was a similar division between "Old" and "New." These divisions were sharp and serious. The older faction of clergy liked things the way they were and resented the intrusion of revivalists into established churches and parishes, resisted change, and opposed the idea of licensing and ordaining men who had not been trained for the ministry. The "New Lights" held the opposite view and continued their new work. At times the division was so great that denominations split. Major groups of the Presbyterians in the middle colonies divided in 1741 (but would reunite in 1758), and the Dutch Reformed Church of New Jersey as well as the Baptists in the Southern colonies also underwent temporary separations.

Much of this new spiritual comfort and dedication would be needed in the years ahead to give the people a spiritual foundation to see them through the French and Indian Wars of 1756–63. The Great Awakening may even have played a part in uniting the colonies in the years leading to the Revolutionary War.

20

The Bill of Rights
Is Written

(1789)

In 1620, forty-one English colonists, mostly Puritans from England, signed the Mayflower Compact, the first document of governance in the New World. The first words of that document are, "In the name of God, Amen." The Constitution of the United States begins, "We the people."

From "In the name of God" to "We the people" is quite a change. Granted, 167 years had passed, but other founding documents of the United States mention God. In the Declaration of Independence the word *God* appears in the first paragraph. He is called Creator in the second paragraph and is later referred to as Supreme Judge. There is also the mention of Divine Providence.

The US Constitution, however, has none of that language. God is not mentioned or referred to by any title. The vague word *religion* is used only twice in the great document, and one of those mentions is in the Bill of Rights.

Yet the Constitution and the Bill of Rights, despite their departure from the mention of any deity, had a great influence on the church in America and would serve as an example to other countries in Europe, South America, and in Australia.

Those who peer through the two-plus centuries of history that separate the present from the epicenter of modern democracy often have a very different perception of what the framers intended.

The Constitution

In the summer of 1787, delegates of the original thirteen colonies, now states, met in Independence Hall to create a lasting Constitution for the fledgling nation. Since March 1, 1781, the Articles of Confederation had been the law of the land. It was the first constitution of the United States, but it proved more experiment than solution. Lessons were learned, leading to a new document. It's nice to imagine the best and the brightest leaders of the country, under the leadership of George Washington, gathering to politely discuss monumental issues. It is true that delegates represented some of the best minds in the country, but the meetings were anything but genteel chats. There was bickering, verbal shoving matches, and ideas that seem unthinkable today (such as making the offices of president and senator lifelong positions).

They met behind closed doors (and often closed windows) to hash out how the country would operate. In a stuffy room, fifty-five delegates debated the separation of branches of government, formulas for representation, ways of guaranteeing that smaller states had equal representation, and scores of other touchy issues. They also had a "gentleman's agreement" not to discuss the proceedings and debates and to refrain from publishing their notes and journals for fifty years after the creation of the Constitution. They were not a unified body, but they wanted to appear as such.

When the conference ended, the Constitution had been hammered out, something many considered a miracle, and it was sent to the states for ratification. It was not unanimous. Only thirty-nine of the fifty-five delegates signed the document. Then it was up to the states. Nine of the thirteen states were needed to ratify the Constitution. On March 4, 1789, the new laws went into effect. This did not mean the states were happy. Pennsylvania, Virginia, Massachusetts, New York, and South Carolina had ratified the Constitution but did so with reservation.

There had been a battle between the Federalists, who wanted a strong central government, and the Antifederalists, who worried about states' rights. Also, many were worried about individual freedoms and demanded a Bill of Rights be added to the Constitution.

The Bill of Rights

In 1789, Congress met to discuss a series of "rights" and how they would be added to the Constitution. Fourteen amendments had been suggested, but the Senate reduced that number to twelve. On September 25, 1789, Congress adopted the Bill of Rights and sent it to the states. Three-fourths of the states would have to approve the items before they could become law. Ten of the twelve amendments were ratified. Those ten became known as the Bill of Rights.

For the church, the most important of these was the First Amendment:

> Congress shall make no law respecting an establishment of religion, or prohibiting the free exercise thereof; or abridging the freedom of speech, or of the press; or the right of the people peaceably to assemble, and to petition the government for a redress of grievances.

Just forty-five words in all. The amendment seems simple enough: Congress (the law-making branch of the government) cannot establish a religion or keep an established religion from carrying out its business of worship and education. Even the clauses dealing with freedom of speech, assembly, and the right to petition the government for a redress of grievances seem to apply to religion.

The tendency is to think of the Christian church when reading this amendment, and certainly that is what the framers had in mind, but they chose a more general term: religion. They were avoiding the appearance of favoritism. By the late eighteenth century, the country had grown more pluralistic. There was no official church. The states were home to Anglicans, Congregationalists, Roman Catholics, Baptists, and more.

Why would such an amendment be needed? Many countries, England in particular, had national churches, churches that received preferential treatment. In England, the Church of England reigned supreme. Even Parliament included members of the clergy called the Lords Spiritual. The Puritans had to leave their homes in England to come to America to escape persecution. The Church of England and England were woven together and inseparable.

Much of church history shows the intertwining of church and state. In Geneva during John Calvin's time, the church could sentence someone to death and the state would carry out the execution. At the time of the ratification of the Bill of Rights, many states had state churches. The idea of a strong central government establishing a church made those states nervous. A state like Connecticut, with its officially recognized Congregationalist church, would resist the federal government adopting the Church of England as the nation's church.

At all costs, the federal government had to be kept out of the church business, and the leaders were happy to let that prohibition become law.

The First Amendment, however, applied only to the federal government. James Madison had suggested that the Bill of Rights should apply to the states as much as it did to the federal government. That idea went nowhere—at least back then. The Supreme Court of the United States would apply the First Amendment to all of the states in 1947.

Elements of the First Amendment would be tested at the Supreme Court well over two hundred times. Almost ninety of these were somehow related to religious activities. The remainder have dealt with freedom of speech, press, and assembly.

Defining and debating the application of the First Amendment continues today and will surely continue in the future. The framers of the Bill of Rights could not imagine a digital world connected by the internet. They could never have imagined technology reaching a level where anyone can publish material and make it instantly available almost anywhere in the world.

The Evolving First Amendment

The first sixteen words (and some think the remaining twenty-nine words) of the First Amendment limit the powers of the federal government to start or control religious activity. Those words limit the *federal* government, but not states. Many states kept their "state churches," feeling no compulsion to "disestablish" them. None of the states felt the First Amendment required them to do so. The limitations were placed on the federal government alone. The Congregational church was the official church of Connecticut until 1818, nearly thirty years after the passing of the Bill of Rights. Massachusetts kept the Congregational church as its official church until 1833. Massachusetts required that every man belong to a church. Churches could tax their members.

Other states, however, disestablished official churches before the First Amendment became law. Maryland, a Church of England state, took the step of separation in 1776, and Virginia did the same in 1783.

In some cases, a state might separate its government from a particular church but still make religious requirements for public service. For example, in 1790 New Hampshire no longer considered the Congregational church as the official state church but continued to require that members of the legislature belong to a Protestant church. That ended in 1877.

Thomas Jefferson may be the best-known of the founding fathers. He was the primary writer of the Declaration of Independence, served as ambassador to France, and much more. In March 1801 he became the third president of the United States. He was a complicated man, an inventor, a writer, a farmer, a politician, and a man who, when it came to religious matters, presented a conflicting image. At times he seems every bit the agnostic, going so far as to redact the

Gospels, cutting out every mention and account of the miraculous and leaving only the ethical teachings of Christ. Yet he attended church services and had no hesitancy about speaking of a heavenly God. When Abigail Adams died, Jefferson, who had lost his wife, wrote his friend John Adams a letter of condolence, a letter that contradicts his deist views of a distant, uninvolved God. He wrote:

MONTICELLO, November 13, 1818.
The public papers, my dear friend, announce the fatal event of which your letter of October the 20th had given me ominous foreboding. Tried myself in the school of affliction, by the loss of every form of connection which can rive the human heart, I know well, and feel what you have lost, what you have suffered, are suffering, and have yet to endure. The same trials have taught me that for ills so immeasurable, time and silence are the only medicine. I will not, therefore, by useless condolences, open afresh the sluices of your grief, nor, although mingling sincerely my tears with yours, will I say a word more where words are vain, but that it is of some comfort to us both, that the term is not very distant, at which we are to deposit in the same cerement, our sorrows and suffering bodies, and to ascend in essence to an ecstatic meeting with the friends we have loved and lost, and whom we shall still love and never lose again. God bless you and support you under your heavy affliction.[1]

Whatever his final beliefs were may never be known. It appears he acknowledged the existence of God but not miracles and other events as recorded in the Bible. Still, he was no enemy of the church.

On New Year's Day 1802, Jefferson responded to several Baptist leaders of the Danbury Connecticut Baptist Association. Baptists in Connecticut were a minority compared to the Congregational churches in the state. They said the state's constitution made it so "that Religion is considered as the first object of Legislation." They also wrote, "Sir, we are sensible that the President of the United States is not the National Legislator and also sensible that the national government cannot destroy the laws of each State." What they wanted was freedom from a state-supported church and hoped that

Jefferson would agree, even if he and the national government could not force Connecticut to adopt such an amendment to its constitution (and indeed it would not do so until 1818).

The Danbury Baptist letter shows two important facts about the time. First, that the establishment clause of the First Amendment was seen to apply only to Congress and the federal government, not to the states that continued to support a particular denomination. Second, that denominations outside the preferred church could be considered of secondary importance.

Jefferson's reply may be one of the most historic letters written by a president. It was a thoughtful letter, and the original draft shows the many times he'd write a word or phrase then cross it out to get it just right. After a line or two of niceties Jefferson penned:

> Believing with you that religion is a matter which lies solely between man and his God, that he owes account to none other for his faith or his worship, that the legislative powers of government reach actions only, and not opinions, I contemplate with sovereign reverence that act of the whole American people which declared that their legislature would "make no law respecting an establishment of religion, or prohibiting the free exercise thereof," thus building a wall of separation between Church and State. Adhering to this expression of the supreme will of the nation in behalf of the rights of conscience, I shall see with sincere satisfaction the progress of those sentiments which tend to restore to man all his natural rights, convinced he has no natural right in opposition to his social duties.
>
> I reciprocate your kind prayers for the protection and blessing of the common Father and Creator of man, and tender you for yourselves and your religious association, assurances of my high respect and esteem.[2]

The letter was not a federal document, was not debated by panels of people, and was not ratified by law. It was the sincere response of a president to his constituents in Connecticut, yet seven words would become the law of the land: "thus building a *wall of separation between Church and State*" (emphasis added). There are many today who think the phrase "separation between church and state" appears somewhere in the Bill of Rights or in the Constitution. It doesn't.

What the First Amendment did, and what Jefferson agreed with, was to ban the federal government from creating—establishing—a marriage between the federal government and any religion. It's a one-sided prohibition limiting the state but not limiting the religious group. That, however, was then. The "now" shows a morphing, redefining First Amendment. Jefferson's letter would be forgotten for 150 years, then rise to live in the light once again.

Two Cases

The Supreme Court is charged with interpreting the Constitution in cases brought before it. It is the final arbitrator on what the Constitution means and what the framers intended.

Everson v. Board of Education (1947)

In 1947 a case was brought before the Supreme Court by Arch R. Everson, a taxpayer in New Jersey who objected to the state reimbursing the parents of students who rode public transportation to school. The burr under the saddle was the practice of reimbursing parents whose children went to private, Catholic schools. Everson felt this was a violation of the First Amendment because tax dollars were used to make the reimbursements. The justices ruled against him, stating that enough separation between the religious school and public transportation existed, yet they agreed with the principle complaint of tax money being used to benefit religious schools. In the decision, Justice Hugo Black resurrected Jefferson's words from the letter to the Danbury Baptist Association: "The First Amendment has erected a wall between church and state. That wall must be high and impregnable. We could not approve the slightest breach."[3]

Jefferson's "wall of separation" had moved from opinion about what *federal government* could not do to what *states* could not do.

A letter that had been all but forgotten for a century and a half was now a principle for future First Amendment court cases.

Torcaso v. Watkins (1961)

A second Supreme Court case added weight to the Everson decision. This 1961 case was brought by Roy Torcaso against the state of Maryland. Torcaso claimed he was being denied a commission as a notary public because of his religious beliefs (or lack thereof). Maryland's constitution required those who held public office sign a declaration of belief in a Supreme Being. Article 36 reads:

> That as it is the duty of every man to worship God in such manner as he thinks most acceptable to Him, all persons are equally entitled to protection in their religious liberty; wherefore, no person ought by any law to be molested in his person or estate, on account of his religious persuasion, or profession, or for his religious practice, unless, under the color of religion, he shall disturb the good order, peace or safety of the State, or shall infringe the laws of morality, or injure others in their natural, civil or religious rights; nor ought any person to be compelled to frequent, or maintain, or contribute, unless on contract, to maintain, any place of worship, or any ministry; nor shall any person, otherwise competent, be deemed incompetent as a witness, or juror, on account of his religious belief; *provided, he believes in the existence of God,* and that under His dispensation such person will be held morally accountable for his acts, and be rewarded or punished therefor either in this world or in the world to come. (emphasis added)

As an atheist, Torcaso objected to such a requirement and maintained that Maryland could not require such a declaration without infringing on his First and Fourteenth Amendment rights. A lower court ruled against his claim, and the case went to the Supreme Court. Maryland had been instituting a "religious test." Article VI of the US Constitution forbids such a test as a qualification for holding an office in the federal government. As with the First Amendment, the prohibition applied only to the national government and not to the states. The states could and did do as they saw fit.

That changed when the Supreme Court agreed with Torcaso and ruled that the Maryland constitution required a religious test of service. That was not disputed. The Maryland document makes it clear that it was such a test. What the Supreme Court did through this case is apply another aspect of the US Constitution to the states.

Why All This Is a Good Thing

Dr. Martin E. Marty, church historian and Lutheran minister, in an interview with Bill Moyers, called the separation of church and state (technically "religion" and state) the best thing to happen to the church in the United States.[4]

Most would agree.

Church history indicates that problems arise when church is wedded to state. States represent people of all beliefs. The world has always been pluralistic. Even in the first century, when the church was still new, there were various groups of Jews and differences of opinion among pagans about Greek and Latin gods. The church has a kingdom view; the state has a world view. The two groups can and should work together, but they have never shared identical goals.

The churches in the United States and other countries where freedom of religion is valued have experienced and continue to enjoy unhindered opportunities. Of course, freedom of religion means freedom to not believe. The Constitution enables the atheist as much as the believer. This puts the weight of responsibility for spreading the gospel on the shoulders of the churches. In the early history of the colonies, a man could be arrested for not attending church. While such a rule might assure a full church, it certainly can't guarantee the attendees are faithful adherents.

The First Amendment has protected the church from interference by an ever-changing government. At times, those rights had to be fought for, but the overall benefit has allowed the coexistence of groups as different as Baptists and Roman Catholics, Presbyterians and Lutherans, as well as thousands of independent churches.

The downside is the redefining of the First Amendment in an attempt to keep the church so far from government as to deprive the church of any political influence. Originally, the First Amendment kept the government out of religion, not religion out of government. Many in government understand this. There remains an annual Presidential Prayer Breakfast. Government officials commonly speak of faith, a massive Christmas tree is raised outside the White House—the list of such activities is long. Some resent this, but the practices remain.

Perhaps no better example that God has not been expunged from the US government is the traditional opening of the Supreme Court. When the court convenes at 10:00 a.m., the marshal announces them this way:

> The Honorable, the Chief Justice and the Associate Justices of the Supreme Court of the United States. Oyez! Oyez! Oyez! All persons having business before the Honorable, the Supreme Court of the United States, are admonished to draw near and give their attention, for the Court is now sitting. *God save the United States and this Honorable Court!* (emphasis added)

The First Amendment has freed the church to be the church.

Darwin's *On the Origin of Species* Is Published

(1859)

The theory of evolution is arguably the greatest idea the human mind ever had, and its proposer, Charles Darwin, is among the most influential scientists who ever lived. He changed the way humans view their place in nature. His explanation of the evolutionary process occurring through natural selection forms the basis of modern-day biological sciences, including the applied disciplines of agriculture, medicine, and, most recently, biotechnology.[1]

One might have expected that a theory of such cardinal importance, a theory that literally changed the world, would have been something more than metaphysics, something more than a myth.[2]

These are two very different views of evolution and the man who is known as its father. The second statement is anti-Darwinian, and it may be surprising to learn it was made by an agnostic. Michael Denton, a biochemist, argues against Darwinism without being a creationist. His views highlight the ongoing debate about a theory that changed the world.

Those standing near the bay of Devonport two days after Christmas in 1831 would have seen a common activity: a ship sailing from port. Little did anyone know, the HMS *Beagle* was sailing into history. It would become one of the most famous ships in history, as would the man who walked its decks. Reading the ship's mission would not have impressed anyone. Charles Darwin, the man who changed the thinking of the world, described the beginning of the journey this way:

> After having been twice driven back by heavy south-western gales, Her Majesty's ship *Beagle*, a ten-gun brig, under the command of Captain FitzRoy, RN [Royal Navy], sailed from Devonport on 27 December 1831. The object of the expedition was to complete the survey of Patagonia and Tierra del Fuego, commenced under Captain King in 1826 to 1830; to survey the shores of Chile, Peru, and some islands in the Pacific; and carry a chain of chronometrical measurements round the world.[3]

Darwin was twenty-two years old.

Over the five years of his mission as the *Beagle*'s naturalist, he observed animals and plants in various parts of the world. This raised questions. A theory emerged, a theory he worked on for twenty years. Those ideas were expressed in two books: *On the Origin of Species by Means of Natural Selection or the Preservation of Favoured Races in the Struggle for Life* (1859) and *The Descent of Man, and Selection in Relation to Sex* (1871).

Those books changed everything.

The Man

Charles Robert Darwin was born into a wealthy family on February 12, 1809, in Shrewsbury, Shropshire, England. His maternal grandfather was the famous china maker and abolitionist Josiah Wedgwood. His paternal grandfather was Erasmus Darwin, physician, inventor, poet, and also an abolitionist.

As a young man he had trouble finding his calling. Like his grandfather Erasmus, Darwin considered a medical career and began training at Edinburgh University, then switched schools to study for the ministry at Cambridge. In the end, he chose a career as a naturalist.

During his studies, he came under the influence of Sir Charles Lyell's *Principles of Geology*, published in three volumes from 1830–33. Darwin took Lyell's first volume, given to him by the captain of the *Beagle*, with him when the ship set sail. He picked up the second volume in South America. Lyell promoted the idea of uniformitarianism, the idea that the earth had changed slowly and over great time. The opposite of uniformitarianism is catastrophism, sudden change brought on by an event such as Noah's flood. Lyell had a great influence on Darwin.

By the end of the *Beagle*'s five-year journey, Darwin had the basic idea of evolution by natural selection in mind. That idea became his life's work. He often appeared conflicted. He didn't doubt his theory, just its ability to explain everything he observed. Thanks to his theology studies at Cambridge, he understood Christian doctrine but could not reconcile the cruelty of the animal world with a loving God—nor could he avoid seeing design in the universe. In May 1860 Darwin wrote to American botanist Asa Gray. They were friends, and Gray provided information to Darwin about certain plants. In the letter, Darwin said:

> With respect to the theological view of the question. This is always painful to me. I am bewildered. I had no intention to write atheistically. But I own that I cannot see as plainly as others do, and as I should wish to do, evidence of design and beneficence on all sides of us. There seems to me too much misery in the world. I cannot persuade myself that a beneficent and omnipotent God would have designedly created the Ichneumonidæ with the express intention of their feeding within the living bodies of Caterpillars, or that a cat should play with mice. Not believing this, I see no necessity in

179

the belief that the eye was expressly designed. On the other hand, I cannot anyhow be contented to view this wonderful universe, and especially the nature of man, and to conclude that everything is the result of brute force. I am inclined to look at everything as resulting from designed laws, with the details, whether good or bad, left to the working out of what we may call chance. Not that this notion at all satisfies me. I feel most deeply that the whole subject is too profound for the human intellect. A dog might as well speculate on the mind of Newton. Let each man hope and believe what he can. Certainly I agree with you that my views are not at all necessarily atheistical.[4]

The Idea

Darwin became a hero in the growing scientific movement dealing with origins. He also became a target for scientists who could not accept his ideas and Christians who viewed his work as an effort to undermine biblical doctrine. Regardless, Darwin pressed on, and his views, although altered by contemporary scientists, have become the basis of most thinking on evolution. Combining genetics, first demonstrated by Augustinian monk Gregor Mendel, results in "neo-Darwinism."

Thousands of pages have been written about Darwin and his ideas, but the basic idea is simple. Darwin noted variations within species, most famously the finches of the Galapagos Islands (now known as Darwin finches), whose beaks differed in size from one kind to another. Some birds had larger beaks compared to their counterparts. From this and his many other observations, he formulated an idea that took the world by storm: natural selection. It is impossible to put the concept in a few lines (Darwin's book *Origin* ran five hundred pages), but reduced to a single concept it is this: over time, variations appear within a species; if the variation improves the animal and gives it an advantage, then that trait will be passed on to its offspring. If the change has a negative effect, then the creature will be at a disadvantage and will die off.

In the fifth edition of *Origin*, Darwin added the phrase "survival of the fittest," a term first coined by biologist Herbert Spencer in his

1864 *Principles of Biology*.[5] By mechanistic chance, stronger animals would improve over the ages while the weaker would pass from the scene.

While the idea of evolution did not originate with Darwin, he brought enough evidence to bear that the topic could no longer be treated philosophically. It demanded attention and got it. As the idea became known, a tide of resistance rose, as much from the scientific community as the religious. Darwin was a sensitive man, struggling with health issues at times and with the loss of his young son to scarlet fever. As such, he let his friend Thomas Henry Huxley debate on his behalf, and "Darwin's bulldog" was more than willing to do so.

Public reaction to Darwin's theory was harsh. Cartoons showing Darwin's head on a monkey's body were common. Interestingly, Darwin never claimed man evolved from monkeys. In his *Descent of Man* he argued that humans and apes both evolved from a common ancestor. The public misrepresentation continues today.

None of this was a surprise to Darwin. He expected to be handled roughly. He asked his publisher to send copies to eleven influential scientists, and included with each a letter. He wrote, "How savage you will be, if you read it, and how you will long to crucify me alive!" Still he held some optimism: "I am fully convinced that you will become year after year, less fixed in your belief in the immutability of species."[6]

The Books

Charles Darwin wrote a great deal but is remembered for only two works. These writings and others are available at The Complete Works of Charles Darwin Online.

Writing and publishing *Origin* was a difficult task for Darwin. He was often ill and referred to himself as "living in hell." He had several sources of stress. Alfred Russel Wallace (1823–1913) had been working on a theory of natural selection that closely mirrored Darwin's. Darwin chose to write an abstract that became *On the*

Origin of Species. He had wanted to publish a larger single work, but the pressure was on.

Adding to his concerns was his wife, Emma. She was a devout Unitarian. While Unitarianism did not fit with mainline churches because of its denial of the Trinity, she was still one who believed in a Supreme Being, something that Darwin struggled with. Before they married she expressed her concerns about their differing opinions and wondered if such a marriage would work. All the while Darwin worked on *Origin* and *Descent*, he worried if the books would wound his wife.

Yet he maintained that one belief did not outweigh the other, and stated, "I see no good reason why the views given in this volume should shock the religious feelings of any one."[7]

On the Origin of Species by Means of Natural Selection or the Preservation of Favoured Races in the Struggle for Life was published on November 24, 1859. All 1,250 copies sold out the first day. This number comes from Darwin's diary, and some suspect the number might be inaccurate. But whatever the actual numbers, it sold quickly.

The Descent of Man, and Selection in Relation to Sex was published in February of 1871, twenty-one years after *Origins*, and focused on the evolution of humankind. It was published in two volumes, each about 450 pages. It went into a second printing three weeks later.

Some Shocking Quotes

Darwin's ideas on "survival of the fittest" led to some distasteful conclusions. He expounded on the problem of helping weaker humans survive:

> With savages, the weak in body or mind are soon eliminated; and those that survive commonly exhibit a vigorous state of health. We civilised men, on the other hand, do our utmost to check the process of elimination.... The aid which we feel impelled to give to the helpless is mainly an incidental result of the instinct of sympathy, which was

originally acquired as part of the social instincts, but subsequently rendered, in the manner previously indicated, more tender and more widely diffused. Nor could we check our sympathy, even at the urging of hard reason, without deterioration in the noblest part of our nature. The surgeon may harden himself whilst performing an operation, for he knows that he is acting for the good of his patient; but if we were intentionally to neglect the weak and helpless, it could only be for a contingent benefit, with an overwhelming present evil. We must therefore bear the undoubtedly bad effects of the weak surviving and propagating their kind; but there appears to be at least one check in steady action, namely that the weaker and inferior members of society do not marry so freely as the sound; and this check might be indefinitely increased by the weak in body or mind refraining from marriage, though this is more to be hoped for than expected.[8]

In comparing men to women, he wrote:

The chief distinction in the intellectual powers of the two sexes is shewn by man attaining to a higher eminence, in whatever he takes up, than woman can attain—whether requiring deep thought, reason, or imagination, or merely the use of the senses and hands. If two lists were made of the most eminent men and women in poetry, painting, sculpture, music,—comprising composition and performance, history, science, and philosophy, with half-a-dozen names under each subject, the two lists would not bear comparison. We may also infer, from the law of the deviation of averages, so well illustrated by Mr. Galton, in his work on "Hereditary Genius," that if men are capable of decided eminence over women in many subjects, the average standard of mental power in man must be above that of woman. . . . Thus man has ultimately become superior to woman.[9]

These were common views of the time. Women's right to vote in the United States wasn't guaranteed until the 1920 passing of the Nineteenth Amendment. Women in England did not get the same right to vote as men until the Fifth Reform Act in 1928.

Darwinism has always carried with it the possibility of increased bigotry and justification for misbehavior, but this was not Darwin's

183

goal. Any such idea can be twisted. Famed defense attorney Clarence Darrow used evolution as one of his arguments to keep two young men who brutally murdered a younger man from the death penalty.

History has shown that Darwinism and other variations of evolution have been used to suppress others. Genocide such as that perpetrated against the Tutsi people in Rwanda and exploitation such as the slave trade have been justified and defined by appeals to superiority. Yet Darwin, like his grandfathers, was an abolitionist who hated cruelty. His son William Erasmus Darwin recalled, "The two subjects which moved my father perhaps more deeply than any others were cruelty to animals and slavery. His detestation of both was intense, and his indignation was overpowering in case of any levity or want of feeling on these matters."[10]

What Darwin would not do, others did in his place. Sometimes an idea released is an idea impossible to control.

The Church Response

Darwin's work brought critics from the church and the sciences. It also brought many supporters. The temptation is to think the church responded with a unified front, but it didn't. Most theologians and Bible students were willing to accept evolution for nonhuman creatures. The real rub came with the idea that humankind evolved instead of being the result of God's creative act. Still, devout scientists such as Harvard's Asa Gray (1810–88) and Princeton theologian B. B. Warfield (1851–1921), known for his support of biblical inerrancy, saw no conflict between faith and evolution.

Of course others did, and an anti-Darwinism movement began and grew through the decades. For many, an honest belief in evolution required an honest expression of atheism. After all, Darwin abandoned his faith after deciding that God would not create such cruelty as he saw in the world. He appears to have remained conflicted on some of these issues throughout his life.

There was not, and has not been a unified agreement from Christian leaders about evolution. In the second half of the twentieth century an idea called Young Earth Creationism took hold. Led by credentialed scientists such as Henry Morris (hydrologist), Duane Gish (biochemist), and others, this movement challenged evolution from a scientific perspective and was welcomed by many Christian groups, especially evangelicals and fundamentalists. The best-known group representing this position is the Institute for Creation Research.

But there has remained a lack of unity within the church. Counter to the Young Earth creationists, who hold to a youthful earth of six to ten thousand years of age (some say a little older) and usually a creative week of six twenty-four-hour days, are the Old Earth creationists, who agree with contemporary geologists who date the age of the earth at 4.54 billion years. These are represented by scientists such as Hugh Ross (astronomer) of the group Reasons to Believe.

A third option is theistic evolution. This belief holds that God used evolution to achieve his creative goals. Scientist Francis Collins, founder of BioLogos and its president until he was appointed to the National Institutes of Health, teaches this view. Prior to that, he was the director of the National Human Genome Research Institute. Evangelicals and mainline churches are more comfortable with this position.

Other Christians believe evolution is based on faulty logic, diminishes every human, cheapens life, opens the door for misbehavior, undermines the credibility of the Bible and makes it out to be a book of myths, deprives humankind of hope, dismisses the need for personal salvation, and has a host of other faults.

During the first three decades of the twentieth century of America's history there was great resistance to evolution. Several states held statutes prohibiting teaching the topic, culminating in the Scopes trial in Tennessee. With the First Amendment, which initially applied only to the federal government, now applied to the states, and with creationism being defined as a religious belief, it is now creationism that is kept out of public schools.

When first introduced, Darwinism divided the scientific community, but the greatest division it created was in the church. While creationists of every stripe have challenged evolution, they have spent a great deal of time and effort chastising each other, and doing so in public.

The publication of Darwin's *Origin* and *Descent* changed much of the thinking in the world and thereby changed the church. And Darwin's ideas continue to do so today.

22

The Scofield Reference Bible
Is Published

(1909)

It began with an unexpected visit and a pointed question.

"I've been wanting to ask you a question that I have been afraid to ask, but I'm going to ask now. Why are you not a Christian?"[1]

Thomas S. McPheeters, a St. Louis attorney, asked that question on a September day in 1879. The target of his question was another lawyer, one whose life résumé was filled with ups and downs. At thirty-six, Cyrus Ingerson Scofield had experienced some success but had endured more pain, mostly from his own doing.

The stout, mustachioed Scofield doubted heaven would welcome a man like him. His marriage was in trouble and he had been run out of his position as a US attorney in Kansas. He had served in politics and at twenty-eight years of age had been elected to the Kansas House of Representatives.

Many influential people, those who shape the church by the force of their personality or by some achievement, seem destined to do so from a young age. Others, however, fall headfirst into the class of influencers. Cyrus Ingerson Scofield is one of the latter. For much of his life he seemed destined to anonymity, just one more person who endured decades of tough life. Failed marriage, alcoholism, forced resignation of a prestigious job under a cloud of accusations of misconduct—C. I. Scofield was hardly the kind of man to influence the church. He was not even a believer.

Michigan-born Scofield was the youngest of seven children born to Elias and Abigail Scofield. His mother died shortly after his birth. He grew into a prodigious reader and developed a lawyer's eye for detail, something that would serve him well through the years.

As a young man, Scofield moved south from Michigan to Tennessee, where he lived with relatives. Although born in the North, at the age of seventeen he enlisted in the Confederate Army's Seventh Tennessee Infantry. A year later, after fighting at Sheet Mountain, Seven Pines, and Antietam, he was wounded. Those injuries landed him in a Richmond hospital where he spent a month recuperating. There he petitioned for release from the Army and returned to civilian life. Although he had won his discharge and returned to Lebanon, Tennessee, he was drafted back into service. It proved too much for him, and a short time later he deserted, crossing Union lines. There he took an oath of allegiance to the Union and was allowed to settle in St. Louis.

When McPheeters put the question to him, Scofield was drifting through life, working at the legal profession during the day and watching his family fall apart in the evenings. Scofield had no ready answers and told McPheeters he would think about it. But his colleague would not be put off. He had been sitting on the question for too long to back away from the moment. Before the conversation was over, McPheeters and Scofield knelt in the law office and prayed. Scofield changed. He gave up drinking but was unable to save his marriage. It ended in divorce in 1883. His wife, Leontine Cerre, claimed desertion. They had been separated since 1879.

Soon after his conversion he began working in Christian efforts, such as helping evangelist Dwight L. Moody with his St. Louis campaign and working with the Young Men's Christian Association. He also began to take his personal discipleship seriously and studied under Dr. James Brookes, the influential pastor of Walnut Street Presbyterian Church. There he encountered dispensationalism, the belief that events of the Bible and world can be divided into seven dispensations, each distinct from the one that preceded it and the one that followed. He adopted the belief and it became the core of his doctrine.

In the same year that his divorce was finalized, Scofield was ordained and took his first pulpit in a small Congregationalist church in Dallas, Texas. First Congregational Church was a tiny mission of about a dozen people. Two years later, the number had grown to five hundred congregants. In 1895, Scofield became pastor of Trinitarian Congregational Church in East Northfield, Massachusetts, Dwight Moody's church, and served there until he returned to the Dallas church in 1903. By this time he was hard at work on his most influential project, *The Scofield Reference Bible*. Scofield had become one of the leading defenders of dispensationalism and released a pamphlet titled *Rightly Dividing the Word of Truth* in 1888. He had also started a correspondence course to help Christians around the world study the Bible more deeply. Many of those lessons became part of his reference Bible.

The study and effort to annotate the entire Bible was demanding, and it soon became apparent that doing both the work of a pastor and of a scholar was too much. He resigned from his position at the Dallas church, a church that would later come to bear his name, to focus on completing the reference Bible.

The Unique Nature of *The Scofield Reference Bible*

In 1909, with the help of Oxford University Press, the first edition of *The Scofield Reference Bible* was released. It would be updated in 1917 and again in 1967. It was the first modern reference work blending the text of the Bible with study notes (sometimes called "apparatus") explaining or elaborating on thousands of passages. It was

189

the first modern annotated reference Bible. The closest comparative translation was the 1560 Geneva Bible that included commentary in the margins (the New Testament was released in 1557).

The Bible has always been subject to interpretation. Presbyterians baptize babies and justify the act by appealing to certain biblical passages. Baptists teach "believer's baptism" by immersion and justify the doctrine with a set of different biblical passages. The same can be said of all denominations. The marginal notes in the Geneva Bible were steeped in Calvinism, which the Church of England found too uncomfortable. Especially irritated by some of the reference notes was King James I, the monarch behind the most successful Bible translation of all time, the King James Bible.

Long before he undertook the work that would forever bear his name, Scofield had become a preacher of dispensationalism, so naturally those views made their way into the commentary. While dispensationalism was growing in popularity among conservative Christians and becoming a touchstone for the burgeoning fundamentalist movement in America, it was dismissed by other theologians and denominations. Doctrine has always been the area of hottest friction between Christian belief systems, and Scofield's Bible added a great deal of fuel to the fire.

The Controversies

Dispensationalism is the first thing Bible students and scholars think of when they hear the name Scofield. What is dispensationalism? The simplest definition is that dispensationalism is a way of looking at God's dealings with humankind from the beginning of time until the end of time. A "dispensation" is a system of order, a way of doing things, and is often tied to a period of time or an era. In theology, the term refers to a period when God worked in a particular manner with humankind. In the introductory material to the first edition of *The Scofield Reference Bible*, Scofield, in a note on Genesis 1:28, defined the term this way: "A dispensation is a period of time during which man is tested in respect to his obedience to some specific revelation of the will of God."[2] He then goes into detail, making clear that dispensations are not ways of salvation, but a system to classify how God has worked, the revelation he has given each age, and humankind's handling of that revelation.

The debate over the validity of dispensationalism has been, at times, so active that the rest of Scofield's good work goes unnoticed. The concept did not originate with Scofield or any of his contemporaries (such as the man most associated with the doctrine, John Nelson Darby). Dividing biblical history into defined eras goes back to second-century Irenaeus and fourth-century Augustine of Hippo.

Wrapped up in dispensationalism are several other areas of contention, including the emphasis on historical-grammatical interpretation, sometimes called "literal interpretation," in which the plain, normal meaning of a passage is taken at face value. The interpretation method allows for figures of speech, metaphors, and more, but some have found it too restrictive.

Scofield, along with most dispensationalists, distinguished between the church and Israel. In some theologies, the church has replaced Israel in God's plan. Scofield and others believed the two should be viewed as separate works of God. The age of the church was not to be confused with the age of Israel.

These controversies made and continue to make *The Scofield Reference Bible* the topic of debate. Still, the reference work sold extremely well, surpassing the two million mark by the end of World War II. Oxford University Press continues to print and sell the famous Bible.

Impact

Reference Bibles, often called study Bibles, followed the pattern set down by Scofield. The idea of having a Bible with notes of explanation in the same volume caught on. Today there are scores of study Bibles available that, like the Scofield Bible, appeal to Christians serious about not just reading but understanding the deeper levels of the text. Previously, such students of the Bible had to keep several reference books at hand: a concordance to locate verses, a

Bible dictionary to understand some of the terms, an atlas of the Bible to understand the lands mentioned, and books of doctrine to understand the teaching of the Scripture. Scofield showed that much of that material could be put in line with the text. Notes about a word or verse appeared on the same page as the verse, making Bible study easier.

Of course, Scofield and others who have created study Bibles must decide what is most important to the passage, and these decisions are influenced by the author's interests and doctrinal system. As a dispensationalist, Scofield naturally emphasized the doctrine in his reference Bible. For fundamentalists and similar groups, it was a boon; to non-dispensationalists it was a travesty. Some hailed the Scofield Bible; others denounced it at every turn. This, of course, can be said about any study Bible. The 1611 King James Version came to be because of comments made in the Geneva Bible. It is interesting that Scofield's Bible was based on the King James Version, a translation that was a reaction to the first study Bible.

One does not have to be a dispensationalist to appreciate *The Scofield Reference Bible*. Many non-dispensationalists have found Scofield's other notes to be enlightening. For many, Scofield changed the way people study the Bible.

Technology has made it possible to include a tremendous amount of information in a single volume, making Bible study deeper and richer than ever before. There are study Bibles based on many of the newer translations.

Love it or hate it, *The Scofield Reference Bible* changed the way millions study the Scriptures.

23

The Fundamentals

(1910)

Almost from its inception, the church has struggled to define itself and its place in history. Exactly what should the church look like? How should it operate? Which doctrines are vital and which are secondary? Many councils have convened to wrestle with deep, theological arguments, and theologians have gone to great lengths to refine what is the "right" belief system.

This started in the first century and has yet to cease. The early church first struggled with the question, "Can a Gentile be a Christian?" The answer came quickly and Gentiles were welcomed into the fold. Then a new idea came along. The Judaizers were a group in the first decades of the church who believed Gentiles could belong to the church but only after they converted to Judaism (Acts 15:1, 5; Gal. 2:1–21).

Then came the Gnostics, a group of people who believed they had special knowledge known only to them. Their teaching was divisive and the subject of several New Testament letters, Colossians in particular.

The arguments over correct doctrine have taken many forms, and the church has benefited from some of these. For example, Protestants see the split from the Roman Catholic Church as a good and liberating event. After two thousand years, one might expect that all the rough spots had been worked out, but such is not the case. The church lives in a rapidly changing society. At times it has tried to prevent the changes; at times it has embraced them. At every turn and every change there is tension.

Some church leaders were eager to surrender older beliefs and accept new philosophies; others have done their best to keep the status quo. In the early part of the twentieth century several forces were at work reshaping parts of the Protestant church. One idea in particular frightened conservative Christians: modernism.

Modernism was a movement to reconcile modern thinking with the ancient beliefs of the church. Two of these efforts most bothered conservatives: evolution and German rationalism. The former taught that humankind was the end result of a mindless chain of events in which lower forms of life grew more complex over time, finally giving rise to humankind. Proponents of evolution dismissed the biblical record as myth.

German rationalism questioned the inspiration of the Bible and its teaching. Led primarily by German theologians, ideas previously held as facts were challenged in the light of "scientific" inquiry. To them, Moses could not have written the Torah (Pentateuch). Instead, there were at least four authors, which they dubbed "Jahwist," "Elohist," "Priestly," and "Deuteronomist." This documentary hypothesis is often called JEPD for short. The church had long held to the Jewish belief that Moses was the single author of these first five books of the Bible.

Other books of the Bible were also questioned. Isaiah, it was supposed, had two or three different authors. The prophetic book of Daniel must have been written much later than previously believed and was therefore not prophetic (since it was written after the events).

Between the growing acceptance of evolution and the new liberal approach to biblical studies, it seemed as if the church was being swallowed whole by unbelievers. To evangelical churches, liberals and evolutionists were the new Gnostics, saying, "We know better than you do."

Those who took the Bible at face value could not and would not accept such changes without a fight. Those leaders and their followers became known as fundamentalists.

Books and the Oilman

An unlikely hero rose from the ranks of traditional thinking Christians—unlikely because he was not a theologian or a church leader. He was an oilman. Lyman Stewart (1840–1923) was president of the Union Oil Company. Well thought of and rich, he was a man used to getting things done. This dapper, bearded man was born in Pennsylvania. He worked for his father, who was a tanner, then spent three years in the Sixteenth Pennsylvania Cavalry fighting in the Civil War.

After the war, he turned to oil drilling. After several false starts, he began to make a success of things, especially in California. A merging of companies led to the formation of the Union Oil Company, for which he served as president.

Stewart's work might have been in the oil-bearing ground, but his mind and heart were in heaven. As a Christian philanthropist, he helped start the Bible Institute of Los Angeles, now known as Biola University, and the Union Rescue Mission, also in Los Angeles.

Like many in his day, Stewart began to see modernism as a threat to the future of the church. He feared that the basic doctrines that had been central to the church for two millennia were about to be swept under the rug of modernist thinking, and he wanted to do something to protect the faith.

He decided that church people of all types needed a reminder of the fundamentals of the faith, yet he knew that he was no scholar. He needed help. That help came in the form of A. C. Dixon, pastor of Moody Church in Chicago. Stewart approached Dixon, who had been speaking in his church, and shared his concerns and his dream. Dixon took an immediate liking to the idea.

They selected a panel of men to choose writers and formed the Testimony Publishing Company. With his brother Milton's help, Stewart poured $300,000 into the project. The goal was to publish a series of twelve short books of essays on the fundamentals of the faith. Each booklet would be about 125 pages long. These would be distributed to every pastor, evangelist, missionary, theological student, Sunday school superintendent, and YMCA or YWCA secretary.

The covers of *The Fundamentals* were simple and unadorned. Lyman and Milton's names were not on the cover. In their place was the line, "Compliments of Two Christian Laymen."

Ninety essays were spread over the twelve volumes, covering a wide range of topics from the virgin birth of Christ to academic-sounding titles such as "Holy Scripture and Modern Negations." Three editors oversaw the project. A. C. Dixon oversaw the first five books before moving to London. Lewis Meyer edited the next five before passing away. The famed R. A. Torrey edited the final two. Later, the essays would be compiled into four volumes and rereleased. All totaled, *The Fundamentals* contained the writings of sixty-six authors. Over three million copies of the books were given away in the United States and in England.

The Five Fundamentals

From 1876 to 1897 a group of likeminded Christians gathered at Niagara-on-the-Lake in Ontario to discuss the changing world of Christendom. Led by influential St. Louis Presbyterian pastor and publisher of the magazine *Truth*, James Brookes (the man who discipled C. I. Scofield of *The Scofield Reference Bible* fame), the conference proved pivotal in the fight against modernism. In 1895 the group affirmed the essentials of Christian doctrine. They listed five indispensable doctrines.

1. *The inerrancy of Scripture.* The Bible was to be held as free of error in the "autographs." The term refers to original

documents of the New Testament. They're called autographs because the documents were written in the hand of the biblical author (or his scribe). This allowed for translation errors but also taught that inspiration extended to the words of the text.

2. *The virgin birth of Jesus and his deity.* Modernism denied both of these doctrines since they were miracles. Some modernist teaching presented Jesus as a man deeply in tune with God but with no deity himself.

3. *The necessity of substitutionary atonement.* In theology, substitutionary atonement refers to the work of Christ on the cross: that he willfully became a sacrifice for the sins of the world. Modernists preferred to think of Jesus as a martyr—someone killed for his beliefs. Substitutionary atonement goes much deeper. It is "substitutionary" in that Christ took the place of the sinner. In other words, the perfect took the punishment for the sinful. "Atonement," to most conservative theologians, means Christ's sacrifice was full payment for humanity's sin. It was a payment that satisfied a debt to God.

4. *The bodily resurrection of Christ.* The resurrection is a foundational topic of the New Testament. All of Christianity rests on the resurrection being true. Without it, Jesus ceases being the divine Messiah and becomes just a good man with a new philosophy. Modernists couldn't abide the miracle of the resurrection any more than they could any other miracle.

5. *The bodily return of Christ.* This doctrine was sacrosanct from the earliest days of the church. Modernists who argued against Christ's divinity and resurrection saw no need for a returning Christ. After all, nineteen hundred years had passed without his return. The traditional church continued to look forward to the Second Advent—to Christ's return.

The Presbyterian Church of the USA created "The Doctrinal Deliverance of 1910," a five-point document outlining the "essential and necessary" articles of faith that listed the same five items as the 1895 Niagara meeting.[1] The matter was brought to a head when three men who refused to affirm the virgin birth of Christ were ordained. The document was overturned in 1927 and the Presbyterian denomination split.

These five doctrinal statements would be acceptable to almost any conservative group in any Christian denomination. A Roman Catholic would be as comfortable with these five principles as a Baptist. There is no mention of mode of baptism, the Eucharist/Lord's Supper, church polity, priesthood of the believer, or other doctrines that denominations wrestle over. The people who would have trouble agreeing with these documents were the modernists, which, of course, was the point.

Beyond the Five Fundamentals

The five fundamentals served as the foundation for the growing group of fundamentalists. The word *fundamentalist* was first used by Curtis Lee Laws, editor of *The Watchman-Examiner*, in 1920. He defined a fundamentalist as one "ready to do battle royal for the Fundamentals of the faith."[2]

They had other concerns. The ninety topics of *The Fundamentals* series included essays on "The Fallacies of the Higher Criticism," creation, evolution, science and faith, the Roman Catholic Church (called "Romanism" in the essay), the millennium, and several personal testimonies.

The Fundamentals were written by men with solid academic standing and reputation. While they could not speak for every facet of the church, they could lay out a set of affirmations that most churches could agree to and do so in response to the growing effort to remove the supernatural from the Bible and church life.

It is impossible to judge how successful these efforts were. If the so-called fundamentalists were unable to make converts of the new philosophers and theologians, they and those who followed were at least successful in rallying the faithful around a core set of beliefs—around historic Christian faith.

Early on, fundamentalists withdrew from those with whom they disagreed and encouraged others to do the same. Like the one within the Presbyterian church of the early twentieth century, splits began to take place at both the local church level and in denominations. Two new Baptist denominations came into existence: the General Association of Regular Baptist (1932), and the Conservative Baptist Association of America (1947).

The movement morphed over time, and by the late twentieth century some fundamentalist factions became combative. During the late part of the twentieth century, it was not uncommon to hear adherents to the cause described as "Fighting Fundies." Some considered their approach to the controversy as mean-spirited.

> The harsh spirit of fundamentalism did not always properly adorn the gospel of Christ, and although the statements may or may not have been correct, the attitude in which it was presented was not always favorable, especially when it involved negative statements against fellow believers.[3]

This acerbic approach may have driven more people from the original cause of fundamentalism. Few would argue that it brought peace or reconciliation.

Neo-Fundamentalists

Neo-fundamentalists, the late-twentieth-century outgrowth of the original fundamentalists, withdrew even more, not only separating themselves from non-fundamentalists but refusing to partner with anyone who did not maintain the same degree of separation as they did. Even Billy Graham was ostracized because he did not exclude Roman Catholic participation in his crusades. Billy Graham, a Baptist holding to the same basic doctrine as fundamentalists, considered the group intolerant.

Moody Bible Institute and Dallas Seminary were criticized for allowing certain evangelical speakers on campus. The premier magazine covering Christianity—*Christianity Today*—was shunned.

Other branches of neo-fundamentalism such as the Moral Majority and others arose. The "King James Only" splinter group fostered the belief that divine inspiration extended not just to original biblical manuscripts but to a certain seventeenth-century English translation.

The publishing of *The Fundamentals* series did much to reintroduce the need for sound doctrine. The early movement rekindled the church's mission spirit and its need to have a clear set of doctrinal beliefs. Many Christian colleges and seminaries came from the movement. The church needed a voice to challenge the growing opposition to historic faith.

Fundamentalism is more stew than broth. It isn't uniform across its members. Some decided on a harsh, confrontational approach; others, such as Lyman Stewart, chose to appeal to the intellect.

The final words have not been written on fundamentalism. For now, we look back over the decades and see the good and bad.

24

The Scopes "Monkey Trial"

(1925)

Dayton, Tennessee, was a sleepy hamlet of less than two thousand souls. Like many small towns in the South, it had a "Mayberry" feel. It was not a place for the rich and famous. Instead, hardworking people manned shops or worked the land. Most women felt honored to be called homemakers. Children did what all children in the rural South did: went to school and did their daily chores.

It is easy to imagine the inviting smells of baking bread or pies coming from the open windows of the homes, of seeing people gather at F. E. Robinson's Rexall pharmacy to chat about the weather, the crops, politics, or news about their ever-shrinking town. It was in that pharmacy that a minor conspiracy took place, one that put Dayton on the map and forever fixed its name in the pages of history.

It's been called "The Trial of the Century." Officially, the case was called *The State of Tennessee v. John Thomas Scopes*, but it soon became known as the Scopes Monkey Trial. Ninety years later, people are still talking about it. The events of eight days in July 1925 still stir heated opinion.

Historian Jeffery Moran noted, "Nearly 200 journalists from throughout the United States and abroad filed on the order of 135,000 words daily during the trial."[1] Sociologist Howard Odum suggested that, if compiled, the reporters' combined work would fill three thousand volumes, each three hundred pages long.

It was the first trial to be broadcast over a radio network.

The quiet and sleepy town turned into a circus. So many gathered to watch the proceedings that there was no longer room in the courthouse. People stood outside and listened to the goings-on through open windows. It became difficult to move around. Nearby, an evangelist hawked his latest book, *Hell and the High School*. Near the end of the trial, Judge John T. Raulston moved the proceedings outside. His reason? He feared the floor of the courtroom would collapse under the weight of the observers.

Interest in the case has continued through the decades. Thirty years after the gavel came down for the last time, *Inherit the Wind* by playwrights Jerome Lawrence and Robert Edwin Lee hit the stage. Five years later, in 1960, the movie version played in the nation's theaters. In 2011, the movie *Alleged* took a turn at describing the events of that Tennessee summer.

All of this attention centered not on a major felony but on a misdemeanor, a low-level crime. One of the greatest trials in US history revolved around a misdeed that was only slightly more serious than an infraction. It may be the most important misdemeanor in the United States.

The Scopes trial is well-known but little understood. Some imagine it as a legal test between science and religion. It wasn't. While some of that was certainly evident, and while the defense tried to make academic freedom the central issue, the case was, in the strictest terms, a trial about a teacher willfully and knowingly defying state lawmakers. That decision, however, was the perfect tool to bring to light the changing mores of the American people and others in the Western world.

Changing America

It was the age of jazz. In the cities, short flapper dresses were the rage. The Roaring Twenties, as they became known, came to stand for fun, frolicking, and immorality. For much of the country, especially the rural areas, this party lifestyle was puzzling and immoral.

It was the age of F. Scott Fitzgerald, whose book *The Great Gatsby*, which came out in the same year as the trial, portrayed this lost generation.

It was the age of transformation. Just a few years earlier, World War I ended, a conflict that saw the use of tanks, armed airplanes, trench warfare, chlorine gas used as a weapon, and large ship warfare. By the end of the war, there were nearly ten million dead and over twenty million wounded. The conflict was controversial, with many in the United States opposing it. The effects of the war reverberated through the country for many years after.

It was the age of science. The Western world was enamored with industrialism and science. In late 1859, Charles Darwin published his first book, *On the Origin of Species*. It would, for a time, be the Bible of evolutionary biology and paleontology. Not all scientists of the day agreed with Darwin, but almost all held to some theory of evolution. It would take decades of research and debate before the scientific community came to a consensus. Darwin's second book, *The Descent of Man*, was published in early 1871.

Albert Einstein received the 1922 Nobel Prize for his work on the properties of light. Best known for his Special Theory of Relativity and General Theory of Relativity, he had trouble gaining support for the ideas of space-time and bending light. Proving the principles was difficult. Just creating the experiment took time. British astrophysicist and devout Quaker Arthur Eddington proved Einstein right with a series of photographs of a full eclipse. He had traveled halfway around the world to conduct the experiment. The news of his discovery vindicated Einstein and made the physicist world-famous.

Science was in the news, society and mores were in flux, and for the first time in US history, more people were living in cities than in the country.

No one would have guessed that tiny, insignificant, and rural Dayton, Tennessee, would be the center of attention.

The Four Forces of the Twentieth-Century Church

While it is important to understand the changing face of America in the early 1900s, it is also important to understand the changing shape of the church. Like American society, the church was morphing and not everyone was happy about it. Four forces were shaping the early twentieth-century church: modernism, fundamentalism, the holiness movement, and Pentecostalism. Conflict between the first two created the greatest heat.

Modernism was open to change from outside church walls. It could and did tolerate attacks made by liberal scholars ("liberal" as compared to the fundamentalists). They adopted some of the thinking of liberal theologians who challenged basic doctrine and the inerrancy and infallibility of the Bible. This controversy would affect most of the major Protestant denominations and often led to splits.

In 1922, Harry Emerson Fosdick, a liberal Baptist pastor, took a stand against fundamentalism in a sermon delivered in a New York Presbyterian church. He titled his sermon "Shall the Fundamentalists Win?" The controversy between liberal and conservative factions within denominations led to fractures. For example, in 1936 many conservative Presbyterians split from the denomination to form the Orthodox Presbyterian Church. Denominations were splitting over matters like the historical-critical method of Bible interpretation (often called "higher criticism"). The battle continues today.

Fundamentalists held to five statements that served as a test of belief: (1) the inspiration of the Bible by the Holy Spirit and the Bible's inerrancy (that is, it doesn't contain error in the original writings); (2) the reality of Christ's miracles; (3) the virgin birth of

Jesus; (4) the belief that Christ atoned for our sins (paid the price for our sin and united us with God again); and (5) the reality of Christ's physical resurrection. The conservatives in the church battled to keep these doctrines unaltered and untarnished by modernist thinking. They believed the souls of countless people rested in their success.

The Rise of Antievolutionism

In many areas of the country, evolution was the popular topic among educated people and among the clergy. Evolution, as taught by Darwin and others, did away with God as Creator and slashed the creation accounts from the Bible. To conservative Christians, accepting evolution was the same as denouncing the Bible, at least in part, and if part of the Bible was wrong, how could a person know when it was right?

Little understood among evolutionists was the sacrifice they were asking church people to make. It wasn't a matter of hating science; it never had been. At the heart of the issue was the validity of the Bible. To dispense with the Bible or even portions of it was to reject the faith they had grown up in, the faith of their fathers and mothers, and to be left spiritually twisting in the wind. For those brought up in the Christian faith, the Bible was foundational to life even if they only heard it read from a pulpit. They weren't being asked to modify a belief, they were being summoned to drive a stake through its heart.

Less conservative churches and modernists accommodated the new beliefs by suggesting a new approach to interpreting the Bible—an approach that allowed for evolution. Similarly, many evolutionists went out of their way to accommodate Christians, reframing the debate so both sides could be happy. For example, Paul Amos Moody's textbook *Introduction to Evolution* touches on the sensitive nature of the conflict:

> As children at home and in their churches they learned about how things started; now at college they hear an entirely different story. This is a really unsettling experience when it involves the book that

forms the principal document of our religion. In the light of scientific discoveries must we discard the Bible and with it our religion?

The whole difficulty here lies in the fact that we try to use the Bible in ways for which it was never intended. *It is a book of religion, not a book of science.* . . . Their [the biblical authors] writing stands or falls on the basis of its worth to religion, not of worth to science.[2]

The Scopes trial was not so conciliatory. The defendants saw themselves in a battle against self-chosen ignorance, religious bigotry, and oppression of new ideas. The prosecution worked to enforce a standing law but would also argue for the freedom of the state to dictate what was taught in school—after all, they were the ones who paid for the buildings and teachers.

Political action by antievolutionists did not start in Tennessee. It was the Kentucky General Assembly that, during the winter session of 1921–22, first attempted to outlaw the teaching of evolution. The bill failed in March of 1922. In the first round of voting, the "ayes" and "nays" tied 41–41. The deadlock was broken when legislator Bryce Cundiff cast the needed nay vote. Interestingly, two people who lobbied against the bill were church leaders, including E. Y. Mullins, president of the Southern Baptist Theological Seminary in Louisville.[3]

The razor-edge failure of that bill prompted other states to attempt to do what Kentucky had been unable to do. Within two years of the Scopes trial thirteen states considered antievolution bills.

The Tennessee Law

Where Kentucky had failed, Tennessee succeeded. In January 1925, John Washington Butler introduced the Butler Bill. It passed the Tennessee House of Representatives 71–5. It had more trouble making it through the Tennessee Senate, but still it passed 24–6. Governor Austin Peay signed the bill into law shortly after. Later Peay would say, "Nobody believes that it is going to be an active statute."[4] He was wrong.

The bill:

PUBLIC ACTS
OF THE
STATE OF TENNESSEE
PASSED BY THE
SIXTY - FOURTH GENERAL ASSEMBLY
1925

CHAPTER NO. 27
House Bill No. 185
(By Mr. Butler)

AN ACT prohibiting the teaching of the Evolution Theory in all the Universities, Normals and all other public schools of Tennessee, which are supported in whole or in part by the public school funds of the State, and to provide penalties for the violations thereof.

Section 1. *Be it enacted by the General Assembly of the State of Tennessee*, That it shall be unlawful for any teacher in any of the Universities, Normals and all other public schools of the State which are supported in whole or in part by the public school funds of the State, to teach any theory that denies the story of the Divine Creation of man as taught in the Bible, and to teach instead that man has descended from a lower order of animals.

Section 2. *Be it further enacted*, That any teacher found guilty of the violation of this Act, Shall be guilty of a misdemeanor and upon conviction, shall be fined not less than One Hundred ($100.00) Dollars nor more than Five Hundred ($500.00) Dollars for each offense.

Section 3. *Be it further enacted*, That this Act take effect from and after its passage, the public welfare requiring it.

Passed March 13, 1925

W. F. Barry, Speaker of the House of Representatives
L. D. Hill, Speaker of the Senate

Approved March 21, 1925.
Austin Peay, Governor.

The body of the bill has less than two hundred words. The words written by reporters at the Scopes trial, and by others after the trial, would surpass a million words. The Butler Bill would remain the law in Tennessee until 1967.

The Run-Up to the Trial

The Butler Bill met immediate resistance, especially in the North. There was also resistance in the South. Leaders there felt the southern states still suffered from a poor image after the Civil War and the poverty and trials they endured during Reconstruction. The "war of northern aggression" was still too fresh in southern minds. The last Confederate veteran, Pleasant Crump, died in 1951, twenty-six years after the Scopes trial.

Education nationwide was exploding. In 1920 less than one-third had completed a high school education or greater.[5] In the late nineteenth century less than five percent (20,000) of high-school age people attended secondary schools. By 1920 that number exploded to two million, a tenfold increase.[6] Public education was becoming the norm, and with it came new issues.

By necessary function, teachers became role models and surrogate parents, at least for a large slice of the day. As school populations grew, so did the fear about what was being taught to young minds. Topics such as sex education and patriotism became battlefields. So did the teaching of evolution.

There was a swelling tide of support for freedom of speech in schools and academic freedom (meaning freedom from oversight by those outside the schools and academic leadership). This is no easy issue and continues to be a hot topic. The Scopes trial was less about evolution than about who had the right to decide curriculum.

Enter the American Civil Liberties Union, which saw similarities in the Butler Bill to the Espionage Act and the Sedition Act. Created during the days of war, these acts were designed to rid the land of disloyalty. Demanding loyalty oaths from teachers was, to the mind of the ACLU, overreaching and imposing on individual liberties.

The Butler Bill wore the same clothing as other efforts to control the schools.

What to do about the antievolution bill? To get Tennessee to overturn it would take years and the election of many new legislators. The best approach was to test the bill in court. On May 4, the ACLU ran ads in the major Tennessee newspapers:

> We are looking for a Tennessee teacher who is willing to accept our services in testing this law in the courts. Our lawyers think a friendly test case can be arranged without costing a teacher his or her job.[7]

It was an interesting invitation for business leaders in Dayton to gain publicity. Thirty-one-year-old George W. Rappleyea, a New Yorker who relocated to Dayton and was the manager of nearby mines, saw the ad and an idea was born. Rappleyea was an evolutionist and despised the Tennessee law. He attended a Methodist church, but one with a minister who saw the Bible and evolution as compatible. To Rappleyea, this was an opportunity to bring attention to Dayton.

He needed supporters and found them in Frank E. Robinson's drugstore. Robinson was the head of the Rhea County school board, so he was a natural person to approach. Rappleyea pitched his idea of a test case, one that would catch the eye of every state. Robinson liked it. Joining him was school superintendent Walter White. John Godsey, a local attorney, joined the "boosters." Two city attorneys, Herbert and Sue Hicks, agreed to prosecute the case. Sue Hicks, Herbert's brother (Sue was named after his mother who died giving birth to him) was, ironically, good friends with the man who would be on trial. Scopes would be tried by a friend. Others would join the effort.

They needed a defendant, a teacher who would agree to teach evolution in violation of the law and stand trial for it. The ACLU would pay all the legal fees (all the attorneys refused payment) and the fine when he was found guilty. John Scopes was the perfect pick. Unmarried, boyish, well-liked, with Harry Potter glasses perched on his nose, he was pleasant in appearance and demeanor. He was also likely to move out of Dayton sometime in the near future. In another bit of irony, Scopes was not the biology teacher for the school. He taught math and physics and coached football, but he had been filling in for the principal who normally taught the biology curriculum.

Scopes, who had met with the "boosters" in the store, had a copy of *Civic Biology* by George William Hunter. The textbook contained sections dealing with evolution. He explained that he had retrieved a copy of the book from school storage while he was covering the biology class.

They had their man.

The defense team would grow with the addition of Arthur Garfield Hays, who elbowed his way onto the team. He had run for governor against Governor Peay, who had signed the Butler Bill. He had also lost his teaching position and so had started his own law school.

The group informed the ACLU and the press. The *Banner* wrote:

> J. T. Scopes, head of the science department of the Rhea County high school, was . . . charged with violating the recently enacted law prohibiting the teaching of evolution in the public schools of Tennessee. Prof. Scopes is being prosecuted by George Rappleyea, manager of the Cumberland Coal and Iron Co., who is represented in the prosecution by S.K. Hicks. The defendant will attack the new law on constitutional grounds. The case is brought as a test of the new law. The prosecution is acting under the auspices of the American Civil Liberties [Union] of New York, which, it is said, has offered to defray the expenses of such litigation.[8]

The Associated Press picked up the story, and soon Dayton, Tennessee, was the talk of the nation. There would be another addition to the team that would set the press on fire.

Clarence Darrow

Clarence Seward Darrow was an enigma. Acerbic, pointed, impatient, willing to resort to name-calling in court, he remains the icon for defense attorneys. Once a corporate lawyer, he began to take on lost causes, fighting for those no one else would touch. He fought for labor and for civil rights. There was a ferocity about him and a desire to help the underdog. To many, he is the best defense attorney in US history.

Still, his legal life was not without challenges. Twice he had been accused and tried for jury tampering. He was acquitted in the first case and the second case ended with a hung jury. He was not afraid to take on impossible to win cases. In his most famous case, he defended Nathan Leopold, age nineteen, and Richard Loeb, age eighteen, teenagers from wealthy families who had been arrested for killing fourteen-year-old Bobby Franks for the thrill of it. The "boys," as Darrow called them, pleaded guilty. This took the case out of the hands of the jury and made it a long sentencing hearing. Darrow's closing remarks lasted twelve hours. In those remarks, he laid out a complicated argument showing Leopold and Loeb were the product of society and evolution. He succeeded in saving them from execution, but each was sentenced to life plus ninety-nine years in prison.

After the Leopold and Loeb trial, Darrow announced his intent to retire. But retirement would not come quickly. He had heard of the Scopes trial but had little interest in it until he learned William Jennings Bryan would be aiding the prosecution. Darrow and Bryan had worked together on political and social issues, but Darrow's opinion of Bryan had chilled over time. He considered Bryan too religious for his agnostic blood. He couldn't resist the trial and offered to help the defense team.

> In view of the fact that scientists are so much interested in pursuit of knowledge that they can not make the money that lecturers and Florida real estate agents command, in case you should need us we are willing, without fees or expenses, to help the defense of Professor Scopes.[9]

The "money that lecturers and Florida real estate agents command" crack was aimed at Bryan, who made his living speaking, writing, and investing in Florida real estate. The gloves had come off before Darrow had been invited to the fight.

The defense team was happy to have him and the show he would bring with him. The ACLU, however, was less happy. They feared Darrow's rabid anti-religion stance and razor-sharp attacks might do more harm to the cause than good. They had reason to be worried. Darrow came close to being cited for contempt and had to apologize to the court.

In the Scopes trial, Darrow looked like a man who had seen the rough side of life—a stern brow, a hairline in a permanent march away from his forehead, and eyes that seemed to read everything on a person's mind. Photos of him show a dour man who appeared unable to smile. His body had seen sixty-eight years of life, but his mind was as sharp and pointed as always. He looked every bit the intimidating, fierce defense attorney. Simply standing to speak, he could rivet the attention of every person in the courtroom. Without him the Scopes trial might be nothing more than a footnote in Tennessee legal books.

He was a firecracker looking for a flame. The flame had a name: William Jennings Bryan.

Meet the Prosecution

The prosecution brought lightning of its own. The number of lawyers for the prosecution caused the defense to complain that their chairs were being stolen. Attorney General Tom Stewart handled most of the court work, but all eyes were turned on William Jennings Bryan. A reporter from the *Baltimore Sun* wrote of Bryan, "He is an old man now but that great body of his still is sturdy as an oak. That barrel chest, the sheer build of man make most of those in the courtroom seem puny and undernourished."[10]

At sixty-five, Bryan still struck an impressive figure and could deliver a speech as well as or better than any man of the day. His "Cross of Gold" message is considered one of the best speeches in US history.[11]

He was a man of some girth with a half-halo of hair around his head. He was quick to smile and quicker with a quip. The 1960 movie *Inherit the Wind* portrayed him as clownish at times and prone to playing to the audience. (The characters in the movie, although clearly meant to represent the trial participants, all have different names and do not directly represent the real characters.) The characterization is unfair. Bryan had a fine mind and a zeal for public service. He ran for president of the United States three times and served as Secretary of State for two years in the Woodrow Wilson administration, leaving only after the US entered World War I. He had delivered speeches against the war, saying the country would never enter the fray in Europe while he was Secretary of State. When the country did, he felt duty-bound to resign.

Bryan was an achiever. He helped bring about the direct election of senators to the upper house of Congress by campaigning for the Seventeenth Amendment, which, in 1913, changed the practice of legislators appointing senators to voters selecting their representatives. He also, along with Clarence Darrow, fought for the right of women to vote, a right they were granted in 1920 with the passing of the Nineteenth Amendment. He also fought for prohibition and the Eighteenth Amendment of 1918.

The author of the Butler Bill had consulted Bryan about the measure they were proposing. He supported it but suggested they not levy a fine because it would make martyrs of the teachers. Butler and his supporters ignored the advice and wrote in a minimum fine of $100 and a maximum of $500. While that may not sound like much money, in today's terms the range would be about $1,300 to $6,600.

A Media Event

Every newspaper denounced the trial as a publicity stunt, which, in many ways, it was. No one outside Dayton thought the trial was a good idea. Still, people came in droves. Dayton had the second largest courtroom in the state, but it still was not large enough to hold the growing crowds. It is estimated that over one thousand people squeezed into the room to watch the proceedings. Coupled with temperatures that hovered around 100 degrees, the courtroom was the least comfortable place in the city.

Dayton had only a few hotels, so a committee had been formed to help reporters find lodging in local homes. No one expected this kind of turnout except the "boosters" who orchestrated it all.

The Trial

The trial was overseen by Judge John T. Raulston, a fundamentalist Christian who began each session by having a clergyman lead in prayer, something Darrow would later object to. After threatening to find Darrow in contempt of court, he listened to Darrow's apology, then responded:

> My friends, and Col. Darrow, the Man that I believe came into the world to save man from sin, the Man that died on the cross that man might be redeemed, taught that it was godly to forgive and were it not for the forgiving nature of Himself I would fear for man. The Savior died on the cross pleading with God for the men who crucified Him. I believe in that Christ. I believe in these principles. I accept Col. Darrow's apology. I am sure his remarks were not premeditated. I am sure that if he had had time to have thought and deliberated he would not have spoken those words. He spoke those words, perhaps, just at a moment when he felt that he had suffered perhaps one of the greatest disappointments of his life when the court had held against him. Taking that view of it, I feel that I am justified in speaking for the people of the great state that I represent when I speak as I do to say to him that we forgive him and we forget it and we commend him to go back home and learn in his heart the words of the Man who said: "If you thirst come unto Me and I will give thee life."[12]

It's difficult to imagine a judge speaking this way from the bench today, and while Darrow was glad not to be found in contempt, he certainly must have bristled at the overtly Christian message.

The mechanics consisted first of jury selection, with Darrow doing most of the questioning. All potential jurors were asked if they lived

214

in the area, what they did for work, if they read newspapers and magazines, and if they had read anything about the case or about evolution. A few times Darrow asked if they had heard sermons against evolution. Few had. More shocking, most knew nothing at all about evolution. They had heard of the topic but had never involved themselves in a discussion of the subject.

None of that would matter. While the defense under Darrow fought to have scientists take the stand, they were denied. This became a sore point that illuminated the competing agendas of the legal teams. The Scopes team not only knew they would lose the case, they *wanted* to lose it. A key goal was to take the case to a higher court on appeal where they stood a better chance of getting the Butler Bill declared unconstitutional. Much of their efforts were focused on laying down a case that an appeals court could review and accept. There was no hope or desire to win.

Second, they wanted to use the case to teach the public about evolution and why scientists believed it to be so. They hoped to begin the long process of swaying public opinion. Neither the prosecution nor Judge Raulston were inclined to help them in the process. To them, the trial was a very simple matter: the Tennessee law said no teacher in a publicly funded school could teach that man arose from lower orders of life, or teach anything contrary to the Genesis account of creation. Separation of church and state was not as clearly defined as it is in the twenty-first century.

Darrow and his team worked every angle to make the case more about intellectual and academic freedom, about the country's need to embrace current scientific thought about origins, and they were rebuffed at every turn. The prosecution argued that Scopes knew the law and defied it willfully. There was no requirement for the teacher to embrace the Butler Bill, but a teacher did have to obey it.

This was something Darrow could not tolerate. He, and many like him, believed in the right of the one; Bryan believed in the right of the majority. If the majority said, "No evolution in the classroom," then there would be no evolution in the classroom. Darrow wanted to protect the individual's rights; Bryan wanted to protect the rights of the majority. It was a monumental ideological difference.

Bryan also feared three things about evolution, and these reasons made him so set against it. First, he believed the doctrine of evolution could and did serve as an excuse for war. He needed to look back only a few years to World War I for evidence. Second, it took the heart out of political reform, and Bryan was a reformer at heart. Third, Darwinism did away with God and turned the Bible into a book of myths. Bryan was a man of the Bible and wrote a weekly column about the Holy Book. He feared young people of his day were turning away from their spiritual roots. These concerns arose from parents he met on his speaking tours. So many complained that something was happening to their children when they went off to college. All of this mixed with his belief that employers had certain rights over employees (the opposite of Darrow's belief) and his belief in the power of majority rule to decide what is right for society.

Showdown in Dayton, Tennessee

The one event the Scopes trial is remembered for is the showdown between the agnostic Darrow and the Christian Bryan. The tension between the two had continued to grow throughout the proceedings. Darrow had become frustrated and had taken to calling those who agreed with Bryan "bigots" and "ignoramuses." It was this over-the-top behavior the ACLU had feared.

Darrow then did the unthinkable: he called William Jennings Bryan as an expert witness on the Bible. He ostensibly did this to introduce matters for a court of appeals. Bryan, probably unwisely, went against the objection of prosecutor Stewart and picked up Darrow's gauntlet.

Why would he do this? Bryan had not practiced law in thirty years, but he must have known that as a witness, he would have to be more careful with his words. Everything he said could be challenged. Darrow treated him as a hostile witness. It turned brutal.

Perhaps Bryan's pride got the best of him. Being in front of crowds is what he did. It was on the podium he was most alive. By his own statements we know he wanted to prove that he was not afraid to be examined by the great atheist. Most of all, he stood to defend his faith. Whatever the cause, Bryan took the stand and the tension escalated.

Darrow's approach was to establish Bryan as a Bible expert. Bryan may have believed himself to be such an expert, but the situation called for a biblical apologist, someone trained in the defense of doctrine. Bryan was a great communicator, but he was not properly trained to answer the questions Darrow leveled at him. Interestingly, some of Bryan's answers would put him on the outside of most creationist organizations. For example, he advocated the day-age theory that, while held by many conservative Christians, denies the six twenty-four-hour days of creation in favor of each day representing countless years.

Darrow challenged Bryan on Bishop Ussher's 4004 BC date of creation, the age of the earth, the Tower of Babel, Buddha, Noah's flood, Joshua's long day, Jonah, Eve and the serpent, and more. Bryan made a valiant effort, but spent much of his time avoiding Darrow's traps. The examination ended abruptly when the judge stopped the proceedings for the day.

The next day, Darrow called for a conclusion of the trial, claiming they had no evidence or witness they could bring, and suggested the court get on with finding John T. Scopes guilty.

Which it did.

The fine was the minimum mandated by law. Another trial was held in an appeals court but the conclusion was the same. The Butler Bill remained on the books until 1967.

Bryan and the State of Tennessee had won the case, but they may have lost the battle.

Bryan died in Dayton five days after the trial, most likely from complications from diabetes.

The Outcome for the Church

There are as many opinions about the Scopes trial as there were reporters recording it. For the church, it marked a need to return to the idea of defending the faith and the biblical account—not on simple statements of faith, but on well-reasoned research.

The phrase "The Bible says it and I believe it, and that's good enough for me" might work among church people, but in an increasingly secular society it carries no weight. The church exists in a new era in which atheism is on the rise, and claiming to be an atheist or agnostic is almost chic in some circles. The church has always faced such opinions, but not at the levels being seen in the twenty-first century. Not since the days of the Roman Empire have Christians been dismissed as being unintellectual. Many nowadays think the church's primary focus is to stop progress.

What began in the courtroom in the hamlet of Dayton, Tennessee, would grow from the antievolution movement into the creationist movement. The creationist movement is not unified, but is a mix of Young Earth, Old Earth, Intelligent Design, and other factions. They do share a common goal: to show that the universe and all it contains is the result of the Creator.

25

The Rise of the Neo-Evangelicals

(1943)

The church is not flat. It's lumpy.

If we could look over church history like a commuter looks at the ground from a commercial airliner flying across the country, we would not see a uniform surface. Just as a country has mountains and plains, rivers and lakes, rolling hills and deserts, so the "surface" of the church is varied. There is one church (by theological definition, all the redeemed of the ages) but many different expressions of Christianity. There are approximately sixty varieties of Baptists in the United States alone. That is at least double worldwide.

Over two billion members of the world's population are associated in some way with Christianity. Most fall into one of three categories: Roman Catholic (more than 1 billion adherents), Protestant and Protestant-like groups (800 million), and Orthodox, such as Greek Orthodox and Russian Orthodox (260 million). Each of these categories can be further divided.

Protestants have the greatest variation, dividing themselves into Pentecostals, Charismatics, evangelicals, fundamentalists, Calvinists, and more. Two of the best-known of these groups are evangelicals and fundamentalists. Ironically, those with no church background might, looking at the doctrine of the two groups, think them too similar to call different, yet there are key differences.

What's in a Name?

The rise of evangelicalism happened over centuries, and therefore it is a bit of a stretch to call it an event that shaped the church. But while some events happen in a moment, such as when Martin Luther nailed his "Ninety-Five Theses" to the door of the Wittenberg church, other events are slow to happen, gradually increasing through the decades until their influence is acknowledged. The growth of evangelicalism is one such progressive event. Here, 1943 is chosen because it was in that year that the National Association of Evangelicals was formed, though other significant dates could have been chosen.

What is an evangelical? The term is used frequently, splashed on the pages of magazines, websites, and books. "Evangelical" is attached to dozens of denominations and Christian associations. On June 6, 1958, *Life* called evangelicalism the "third force" in Christianity, standing with Catholicism and Protestantism. *Newsweek* declared 1976 the "Year of the Evangelical" on October 25, 1976. While those dates may seem a long time ago, evangelicalism is much older than that. In the early sixteenth century, Martin Luther used the term *evangelische kirche*, or evangelical church, to describe what would become the Lutheran denomination. In the eighteenth century, the preaching of English evangelists George Whitefield and John Wesley, and American preachers such as Jonathan Edwards, set the foundation for the movement that provided the underpinning for denominations like Methodist and Baptist.

Today we speak of "neo-evangelicalism." *Neo* is a Greek word (*neos*) meaning "new." *Evangelical* is based on *euangelion*, meaning "good message" or "good news." An evangelical is one who believes evangelism, the leading of the lost to salvation, is of primary importance. This is not a goal exclusive to the group, but to evangelicals it is the touchstone of their belief.

Evangelicals have a conservative doctrine. The National Association of Evangelicals lists their beliefs as follows:

1. We believe the Bible to be the inspired, the only infallible, authoritative Word of God.
2. We believe that there is one God, eternally existent in three persons: Father, Son, and Holy Spirit.
3. We believe in the deity of our Lord Jesus Christ, in his virgin birth, in his sinless life, in his miracles, in his vicarious and atoning death through his shed blood, in his bodily resurrection, in his ascension to the right hand of the Father, and in his personal return in power and glory.
4. We believe that for the salvation of lost and sinful people, regeneration by the Holy Spirit is absolutely essential.
5. We believe in the present ministry of the Holy Spirit by whose indwelling the Christian is enabled to live a godly life.
6. We believe in the resurrection of both the saved and the lost; they that are saved unto the resurrection of life and they that are lost unto the resurrection of damnation.
7. We believe in the spiritual unity of believers in our Lord Jesus Christ.[1]

The defining twist is in the last affirmation: "We believe in the spiritual unity of believers in our Lord Jesus Christ." To some, that door is too wide, too open, and too inclusive. During the early 1900s, in response to the inroads made by liberal theology, a branch of Christianity appeared and continued to grow. These fundamentalists held to basically the same set of doctrines as the evangelicals, but more and more they became separatists, pulling back from denominations and groups that didn't hold to the same doctrine. Fundamentalists liked to say they were evangelical (which they were and are) but not *evangelicals*. The feeling was mutual. Evangelicals do not like to be called fundamentalists even if their core beliefs are the same.

Fundamentalists drew circles to keep others out; evangelicals drew circles to keep people in. This meant the evangelicals had to endure differences of opinion, something they did (and do) as long as such belief wasn't counter to the core beliefs about God, Jesus, and the Bible.

Reviewing the doctrinal list above, we see affirmations that almost any church with orthodox beliefs could sign. We also see that some areas are unmentioned or undefined. For example, there is no mention of the Lord's Supper/Eucharist. Baptists believe that the bread and wine (grape juice) elements are just that: bread and grape juice. Lutherans believe in consubstantiation, that the blood of Christ literally mingles with the wine and the body of Christ is present in the bread. This is a middle position between Roman Catholics, who believe the elements are transformed into the body and blood of Christ, and Protestants, who think such a transformation is unbiblical. To the evangelical mind, the difference should be acknowledged but not raised to a level that breaks fellowship.

Evangelicals strive for unity among believers. They see friends where some fundamentalists see heretics.

This chapter began by describing the church as being lumpy, not smooth and uniform. When discussing groups like evangelicals and fundamentalists, it is easy to paint with too broad a brush. Fundamentalists and evangelicals are also "lumpy" groups; that is, they are not in full agreement with themselves. As seen in the chapter on fundamentalism, the group has achieved many good things since its rise in the early twentieth century. Still, it must be acknowledged that some have taken a harsh approach to other church groups.

A New Beginning

The contemporary evangelical finds his or her roots in the days around and following World War II, with the formation of the National Association of Evangelicals. In April 1942, 147 people gathered in St. Louis with the goal of reviving and redirecting evangelical

Christianity in the United States. Since the early part of the century, with the growing encroachment of liberalism in the church and in the years following the Scopes trial in Tennessee, conservative Christianity seemed on the way out. To many, the church was a detrimental holdover from the past, hindering thought and reason. The publication of *The Fundamentals* series had been helpful in defining what conservative Christians believed and also gave a sense of unity to those fighting modernism, but to many it seemed a lost cause. Conservative doctrine was circling the drain.

Those who held to historic, biblical doctrine were not ready to abandon ship. The preliminary meeting in St. Louis was an attempt to chart a new course. Much of the problem was a lack of community. Those conservatives who locked horns with the modernists did so on their own. There was no cohesive, directed action. There were many soldiers but no army.

In 1943, what would become the National Association of Evangelicals (NAE) met in Chicago for a constitutional convention. The group of 147 who had met a year earlier had grown to over one thousand people from nearly fifty denominations. Those denominations, when added together, represent approximately fifteen million parishioners.[2] The NAE was born.

Dr. Harold John Ockenga, pastor, academic, and a leading proponent of evangelicalism, challenged the group to focus on creating a consolidated witness for Christ rather than focusing on denominational differences. The NAE did just that. By 1960, thirty-two denominations held NAE membership.

The rise of the neo-evangelicals did not come about without some challenge. The same year the NAE was formed, the Federal Council of Churches (later called the National Council of Churches) campaigned for legislation that would take evangelical speakers off the radio. They convinced NBC, CBS, and the Mutual Broadcasting System to remove every evangelical broadcaster from the air, confining them to independent stations only. The idea behind this was to allow only "responsible"—by which they meant mainline—religious broadcasters on the air. Some of the evangelical broadcasters had millions of listeners, and *The Lutheran Hour* received more mail than the famous *Amos 'n Andy* show.[3]

In response, church leaders and 150 evangelical broadcasters formed the National Religious Broadcasters. Beginning in 1944, the group fought the unfair and discriminatory practice, and in 1949 it convinced new network ABC to reverse the ban. Other networks followed ABC's lead.

In 1957, the NAE formed a committee to consider the need of a new Bible translation, partly in response to the Federal Council of Churches' release of the Revised Standard Version. The New Testament had been published in 1946, followed by the complete Bible in 1952. The RSV proved to be controversial, and evangelicals were uncomfortable with some of the translation choices. The NAE's translation, the New International Version, became one of the bestselling Bibles of all time. The translation was a result of several groups forming a self-governing committee in 1965. Creating a new and accurate translation is a slow process, but the NIV Bible finally appeared in 1978. Over 450 million units have been sold worldwide.[4]

Neo-Evangelical

In 1948, Harold John Ockenga, then pastor of Park St. Congregational Church in Boston, spoke at Fuller Theological Seminary in Pasadena. In his address he coined the term *neo-evangelical* and defined them as individuals moving away from three groups. First, neo-evangelicals break with neo-orthodoxy. Critics of neo-orthodoxy find nothing orthodox in their teaching, especially with its diluted view of scriptural authority. Evangelicals emphasize the Bible as being infallible, inspired, and the authoritative Word of God. The Evangelical Theological Society (ETS), formed in 1949 to foster evangelical scholarship, goes a step further with its affirmation: "The Bible alone, and the Bible in its entirety, is the Word of God written and is therefore inerrant in the autographs."[5] *Inerrant* is a stronger word than *infallible*. The former means the Bible *contains* no error;

224

the latter that the Bible *teaches* no error. There are variations of meaning, depending on who is doing the defining.

Ockenga went on to say, second, that neo-evangelicals break away from modernist (liberals) who alter or dilute the historical understanding of Bible teaching. Third, neo-evangelicals break away from the fundamentalists who choose seclusion over inclusion. Fundamentalists were seen then, and many still see them this way, as people who used the Bible as an excuse to exclude others: the doctrine *and all of the doctrine* must match, or no fellowship. Over time, some segments turned against seminaries and colleges; some, against this trend, went on to found fundamentalist colleges and seminaries. For Ockenga and other neo-evangelicals, there must be a social aspect to the gospel, not just a personal one. In his 1958 sermon "The New Evangelicals," he describes a purely social gospel as being truncated, and a purely personal gospel as equally truncated. To him, for the gospel to be the gospel, it needed both aspects. The fundamentalists of his day embraced the personal gospel but eschewed the wider application. His was a workable description of neo-evangelicals, one that is still useful.

On paper, the doctrine of fundamentalists and evangelicals looks nearly identical. It is in the expression of that doctrine that they differ. Evangelicals have drawn a larger circle, welcoming groups that would seem liberal to fundamentalists. One such area is the arena of science. Most Christian denominations have little trouble with science except where it asserts the Bible to be myth or inaccurate, such as in the creation account. Most fundamentalists either hold to the Gap Theory, which teaches that there is a creative gap between Genesis 1:1 and Genesis 1:2 (the length of this gap is unknown but is long enough to cover the apparent old age of the earth), or hold to a literal creative week of six twenty-four-hour days. Some evangelicals hold to the same belief, while others make room for the day-age interpretation (each day of the creation week is measured in millions of years) or theistic evolution (the idea that evolution is true and was guided by God). For the evangelical these are not tests of fellowship but matters of interpretation.

An evangelical can be Lutheran, Baptist, Methodist, or any of many other denominations. What matters to the evangelical is the holding of the Scriptures in high regard and the continuation of historic doctrine, evangelism, and addressing social concerns.

Whether evangelicals are too inclusive is for the individual to decide. Regardless, *Life* magazine was right to call the movement the third force of Christianity.

26

The Dead Sea Scrolls
Discovered

(1947)

In a 1947 event that has an eerie parallel to Jesus' parable about the shepherd who leaves his ninety-nine sheep to search for one stray (Matt. 18:12–14), a Ta'amireh shepherd searches the dry, barren slopes and cliffs near the Dead Sea at nearly 1,400 feet below sea level. He searches a crevice in a rocky hillside and sees a cave. Hundreds of such caves can be found in the area. The Bedouin pauses, then idly throws a rock through the opening. To his surprise he hears the sound of a shattering clay pot.

That sound leads to one of the greatest archaeological finds in history. The shepherd enters the cave and finds the broken pot—and scrolls. Those scrolls would become the most talked-about documents in the world.

Because of where the items were found, the documents became known as the Dead Sea Scrolls, the subject of fascination for archaeologists and Jewish and Christian theologians. The story of their find, purchase, and examination is the stuff of adventure novels. Harold Scanlin describes it this way in his *Dead Sea Scrolls & Modern Translations of the Old Testament*:

> Secret agents using assumed names, clandestine meetings under cover of night behind enemy lines, switching cabs to avoid being followed—these sound like things in a spy novel, but they all happened in conjunction with the discovery, sale, and publication of the Dead Sea Scrolls.[1]

In his diary, Hebrew University Professor Eliezer Lipa Sukenik recorded his reaction to opening one of the scrolls:

> My hands shook as I started to unwrap one of them. I read a few sentences. It was written in beautiful biblical Hebrew. The language was like that of the Psalms, but the text was unknown to me. I looked and looked, and I suddenly had the feeling that I was privileged by destiny to gaze upon a Hebrew Scroll which had not been read for more than 2,000 years.[2]

The news of the find circled the world, and those documents, and others soon to be found, would be the center of admiration, accusation, conspiracy, supposition, and fear. What could cause such a response? What could conjure such intrigue? For the church and for Judaism much was at stake. Many of the Dead Sea Scrolls were ancient biblical texts, documents a thousand years older than any previously known. What if they contradicted the Old Testament already in hand?

Such speculation rose quickly. Humankind loves a conspiracy, and several circulated around the Dead Sea Scrolls. If they contradicted the Bible, would the scholars make that fact known, or would they be forced to cover it up?

It would be decades before the manuscripts would be published, conjuring up more controversy, accusations, and theories of conspiracy. The first manuscripts, and the others found over the next nine years, were difficult to work with. Only a few were complete scrolls and much of the material had degraded into irregular-shaped fragments. There were thousands of pieces, none of which looked like another. Many of the scrolls were not biblical, meaning the scholars were reading material new to them and therefore difficult to identify. Even a few words of a Bible text can be matched with the book it belongs to, but nonbiblical phrases were nearly impossible to relate to similar fragments. It was like working a jigsaw puzzle in which every piece has a unique shape. No wonder it took decades to make all the material available.

All this was set in a land of conflict. In the late 1940s, Israel and surrounding lands were unsettled at best and warring at worst. The 1948–49 War of Independence cost Israel approximately 4,000 soldiers and 2,500 civilians—not the best environment for biblical archaeology. Four of the first seven scrolls came into the possession of Archbishop Samuel, leader of the Syrian Orthodox Monastery of St. Mark in Jerusalem. During the turbulent times of 1949, the archbishop smuggled his four scrolls out of the country, transferring them to a Syrian church in New Jersey.

In 1954, Archbishop Samuel ran an ad in the *Wall Street Journal* offering to sell the four scrolls. The ad read:

The Four Dead Sea Scrolls
Biblical Manuscripts dating back to at least 200 BC, are for sale. This would be an ideal gift to an educational or religious institution by an individual or group. Box F 206, *The Wall Street Journal*.

Yigael Yadin, through a middleman, bought the scrolls for the State of Israel, and in 1955 relocated them to Hebrew University, where they were joined to three other scrolls already there.

The search for more scrolls led to the discovery of several largely complete scrolls and thousands of additional fragments. Together they represent over nine hundred different texts. The texts were written in Hebrew, Aramaic, and Greek. While many of the texts are nonbiblical (such as commentaries on Old Testament books)—that is, they don't correspond to any Bible book—there is enough material to represent every book in the Old Testament except Esther.

Essenes and Qumran

The Holy Land is a varied land with mountains, shorelines, significant inland lakes, and one of the most famous rivers in the world. It is this river, the two-hundred-mile-long Jordan, that empties into the Dead Sea. The trip from hilltop Jerusalem to the Dead Sea requires a descent of nearly five thousand feet. Its position at 1,400 feet below sea level has left the land stark, desolate, and very dry. It was in this hostile environment that a group of monastic Jews set up home: a religious community just thirteen miles from Jerusalem. Unhappy with the way the temple in Jerusalem was being run and unable to tolerate Roman rule with its secular worldview, the group established a community of faith and discipline. These are the Essenes.

The Essenes are not mentioned in the New Testament, although other Jewish groups like the Pharisees and Sadducees are. The Essenes were apocalyptic in their beliefs, certain that the end of the present evil age was at hand. When Rome destroyed Jerusalem and subdued surrounding areas, they must have felt the day had come.

As a group, they held books of Scripture in high regard and felt a need to protect the documents. At some point, likely when word of the Jewish rebellion against Rome and the advancing Roman army reached them, the group hid their precious scrolls. The scrolls included copies of the Hebrew Bible (Old Testament), commentaries, and material about community life. All of these were written before 70 AD—some even two centuries earlier.

The Essenes, in their zeal to protect the holy books, hid the scrolls in clay jars and placed them in various natural caves. They would not be recovered for over 1,900 years.

Scholars examined the documents in an effort to date them, and used several approaches to fix a date of writing. Archaeological dating uses history and the environment the scrolls were found in. The crucial event was the destruction of Jerusalem in 70 AD. Paleography is the study of ancient manuscripts and dating them based on handwriting. While paleography cannot pinpoint a date, it can often narrow the window. For example, eighteenth-century American

English wrote the letter "s" in two ways. At the beginning or end of a sentence the "s" looks like modern English, but if the letter appears within the word it looks like an "f." So congress was written as "congrefs."

Researchers also used radiocarbon dating, but in the 1940s and 1950s this process required so much material to be removed and destroyed in the testing process that only associated material, such as wrappings around the scrolls, could be tested. Decades later the technique had been improved enough that small corners of fourteen scrolls could be removed and dated. The process confirmed dates from the third century BC to the first century AD.

Why Does Any of This Matter?

The Bible is central to the church. While the key documents for church life and doctrine are found in New Testament books, the Old Testament is just as valuable. It holds the story of God's work with his chosen people, the establishing of covenants, God's moral law and the Ten Commandments, prophecies of the first coming of Christ, and much more. To some the Bible is a sword, with the New Testament being the blade and the Old Testament the hilt.

Attacks on the Christian faith have often been aimed at the Bible. Proving the Bible to be inaccurate would make the church's view of God, miracles, origins, morality, and everything else suspect. If the Old Testament was unreliable, then the same might be assumed for the New Testament. After all, Jesus quoted from the Old Testament. Most of the New Testament books cite Old Testament passages. The New Testament is built on the framework of the Old.

Modern translations of the Old Testament were based on ancient documents, but very few of them were younger than one thousand years after the Old Testament period. It was easy to claim that the Masoretic Text compiled by scribes had to contain error, since they were copied so many centuries after the originals, but the Masorites were as scrupulous a bunch as has ever been. They were more than human copy machines; they were keepers of the Word.

Ancient Hebrew had no vowels, so pronunciation varied. The Masorites created a system of "vowel points," small dots indicating what vowel sound should be used. They were also meticulous in their copy work, testing each document by a system of word counting and letter counting. They knew exactly what letter must appear in the middle of the page. If the scribe had skipped a letter, then the center letter would be wrong and the document would be destroyed and a new copy made. Their amount of discipline and focus is remarkable. Still, they were making their copies about a thousand years after the last Old Testament book had been written. When the Dead Sea Scrolls were discovered many feared that the Hebrew text that had been used for so long might be shown to be suspect and riddled with error.

But in the end, the Dead Sea Scrolls proved the Masoretic Text was accurate to a nearly impossible degree. There were minor variations, often dealing with spelling choices, but nothing that touched on history or doctrine. The Old Testament translations remained unscathed.

It might be inaccurate to say the Dead Sea Scrolls shaped the church, but it is accurate to claim they kept the shape of the Bible from which the church teaches. Those who expected dramatic changes to the Old Testament were disappointed. Although modern translations have incorporated some of the variant readings from the Dead Sea Scrolls, the previous versions were accurate, valuable, and trustworthy.

The Dead Sea Scrolls show that the ancient Jews of Qumran held the same Old Testament books as sacred. The scrolls included every book currently in the Old Testament except Esther—that's thirty-eight of thirty-nine books (as counted in Protestant Bibles). They also indicated the same reverence for the same Old Testament books.

A young shepherd searching for a lost goat tossed a rock into a cave and made one of the greatest archaeological discoveries of all time. Thanks to the diligent work of scholars, we have some of the oldest copies of the ancient biblical text—a text that continues to touch lives.

27

The Jesus Movement

(1960–70s)

The cover of the June 21, 1971, *Time* magazine was eye-catching, almost impossible to overlook. Printed with psychedelic red and yellow, the cover featured a purple-hued Jesus with long hair, full beard, and piercing eyes that made readers wonder if they were looking at the cover or if the cover was looking at them. This iconic drawing of Jesus set in fluorescent colors was the perfect representation of one of the most unique Christian movements in America, one that also extended to other countries.

The Jesus Movement rose organically from the troubled soil of the late 1960s and continued through the 1970s. The world was an uneasy place, rocking on the threshold between anarchy and extreme patriotism. Baby Boomers, those born between 1946 and 1964, were the largest generational group the country had seen. They were born into a morphing, drifting, uncertain society. Their parents were war survivors. Some had served during World War II and come home to a hero's welcome but, like all veterans of war, carried psychological and emotional wounds inflicted by what they saw and did.

Many sought a quiet and productive life in the burgeoning suburbs. A small house with a picket fence in a nice neighborhood was everyone's dream. But World War II was followed by the Korean conflict. Korea was different from the previous war. It lacked the evil face of a Hitler or Mussolini. The enemy was an idea—a social, economic, political concept called communism.

Historians date the Cold War from 1947 to 1991, and it brought with it a constant fear. Baby Boomers grew up practicing "duck and cover" drills, hiding beneath fragile school desks in a belief that doing so might save them during a nuclear attack. Civil defense sirens would wail in an effort to prepare the country for an attack, and in doing so marred the psyches of millions. For thirteen days in October 1962, the world held its breath as two men, American President John F. Kennedy and Nikita Khrushchev of the Soviet Union, stood nose-to-nose as the world teetered on the crumbling edge of nuclear war. At issue was the presence of nuclear-capable missiles in Cuba, just a few miles off the Florida coast. This standoff became an emblem for fear in the United States. The sense of security was shattered. The knowledge that nuclear-tipped missiles could be nested so close created an era of fear.

That fear multiplied in November 1963 when one of the most powerful men in the world would be gunned down in front of thousands. JFK was shot as he rode in a motorcade through the streets of Dallas and passed the Texas School Book Depository on Dealey Plaza. Photos and film allowed the tragedy to be replayed countless times. The image of a blood-splattered Jackie Kennedy holding her dead husband as the president's limo sped away was tattooed on the minds of anyone old enough to know what happened that November day.

Something else died with the president: a sense of hope and a belief that good wins out. Presidents had been assassinated before, but not in the memory of Baby Boomers or their parents. And earlier assassinations had not been televised.

In 1965 US combat troops were committed to yet another war (although US involvement in Vietnam had been underway since the early 1960s). If the Korean conflict was difficult for Americans to understand, then Vietnam was mind-boggling. Many understood the desire to halt the advance of communism but questioned US involvement in another military conflict, one in which almost sixty thousand American military members would lose their lives. Vietnam became the first conflict in which the horrors of war were played on the evening news. Not even black-and-white televisions could tone down the violence of a gun battle or the sight of wounded soldiers being carried away by fellow combatants. Television did what no newspaper could: it made war real enough to be felt by families in their living rooms.

Two more assassinations stunned the country, especially Baby Boomers, some of whom were now young adults: Martin Luther King Jr., civil rights leader, was shot on April 4, 1968; Robert Kennedy was felled on June 6 of the same year while campaigning in Los Angeles, California. To many Baby Boomers these two men were bright lights in an ever-darkening future. To lose both so close together shattered what optimism they may have had left. Soldiers were dying on distant Asian soil, a president had been assassinated, his brother was mowed down a few years later, and a minister was shot while standing on the balcony of his hotel room in Memphis, Tennessee—all the details were available on the nightly news. Baby Boomers took such images to bed with them each night. And there were more soul-shredding images yet to be seen.

Race riots marred the 1960s and early 1970s, reaching from Chicago to San Francisco to Milwaukee to Los Angeles. In 1970, Kent State University saw four of its students killed by members of the Ohio National Guard. Nine others were wounded. The protest and the shooting filled the television screens of the country and the world. Watching police in the South unleashing attack dogs on black protestors and National Guard soldiers opening fire on college students increased the corporate angst. Innocence and optimism were not the only victims of the 1960s and early 1970s: trust had also been crippled. If the government couldn't keep others from pointing missiles at large cities or extricate itself from a war overseas; couldn't protect a president, a presidential candidate, or a nonviolent civil rights leader; if it could not stop race riots or bring about racial equality in all its states, then how could it be trusted?

Many, feeling powerless to make change, changed themselves into what they believed was the opposite of current society. They replaced conflict with free love.

A Different Kind of Hippie

America had gone from a multifaceted society to a fragmented mix of groups suspicious of each other. From this roiling cauldron of social stress rose a group of religious conservatives who looked very much like the hedonistic hippies. Their hair was long and their dress countercultural; they hung out in groups, started communes, and cared little for material possessions. Faith, Bible reading, a dependence on the Holy Spirit, and a stalwart desire to help others were the treasures they held dear. Many had come from the drug culture and had found that Timothy Leary's "Turn on, tune in, drop out" slogan failed to bring them happiness or meaning. The meditation practiced by the Beatles in the late '60s offered nothing substantial. They longed not just for freedom, but for purpose.

> The beginnings of the Jesus People movement can be traced to the San Francisco Bay area, where in 1965 a group of young bohemian converts began to gather within John MacDonald's First Baptist Church in Mill Valley, California.[1]

In 1967 as many as one hundred thousand people met in the Haight-Ashbury district of San Francisco. The young people in John MacDonald's Baptist church convinced him there was an opportunity to address the spiritual needs of the growing hippie movement. Mac-Donald enlisted the help of other Baptist leaders in the Bay area, and they established the Living Room Coffeehouse in Haight-Ashbury.

Ken Philpott, a student at Golden Gate Seminary, did the same with the Soul Inn Coffeehouse in Lincoln Park Baptist Church. Thousands passed through these establishments, encountering the message of Christ presented by people who cared for them and, very often, looked like them.

For many, the mistrust of organizations of all types—big business, government, military, banks—also extended to the established church. The oldest of the Baby Boomers were now in their early twenties and were disenchanted with normal life. Those brought up in the church found their local congregations boring and out of touch with the world and with their needs. They hungered for a more visceral faith, one less interested in buildings and programs and more focused on personal worship.

The last third of the twentieth century had arrived, man was on his way to the moon, and technology was advancing at a mind-numbing rate, but the Jesus People longed for simplicity in faith. It can be argued that they created a first-century style church in the middle of the twentieth century. Many lived in group homes and evangelized everyone from business executives to drug-addled down-and-outers living on the street. Thousands embraced the message of Christ and would in later years become church leaders.

The June 21, 1971, issue of *Time* put the movement on the map (as did *Life* magazine on June 30, 1972). *Time* reported:

> Jesus is alive and well and living in the radical spiritual fervor of a growing number of young Americans who have proclaimed an extraordinary religious revolution in his name. Their message: the Bible is true, miracles happen, God really did so love the world that he gave it his only begotten son.

Jesus People were radical in their appearance and their approach to society, but their doctrine would fit within most evangelical and charismatic churches. In that sense, they were traditionalists. Like first-century Christians, they spread the gospel wherever they went and took in the outcasts of society. In many ways, *they* were outcasts.

"Jesus Freaks" entered the American vocabulary, and the name was embraced. The term "Christian" was first coined in Antioch during the first century and was intended to be derisive, but it became a badge of honor (Acts 11:26). So it was with "Jesus Freaks." Those in the movement understood *freak* to mean someone extraordinarily committed to a belief or cause, and therefore found the phrase to be an accurate description.

While the Jesus Movement may have been rooted in the San Francisco Bay area, it flourished across the country and spread to Europe. As Larry Eskridge noted, "Similar manifestations of the hippieized Christianity popped up in the next two years—in Oregon, Seattle, Spokane, Fort Lauderdale, Detroit, Milwaukee, upstate New York, seemingly anywhere that the counterculture and evangelical Christianity might rub shoulders."[2]

Southern California became home to a Jesus People hotspot stretching from Santa Barbara to San Diego. The movement blossomed in Costa Mesa, a suburban area south of Los Angeles, with Chuck Smith (1927–2013) planting his small Calvary Chapel of twenty-five people. Jesus People found a home with the small church, which grew quickly. Baptisms often occurred on a beach, at times with hundreds baptized at a time. That one church would be the first of hundreds of congregations around the world to come out of the Jesus Movement—and it still draws twenty-five thousand people each week.

The high-water mark for the Jesus Movement was the Campus Crusade event EXPLO '72 held in Dallas, Texas. Over eighty thousand people attended the week-long event. The enormous turnout was evidence of the Jesus Movement's reach. Faith was not an "old person's" choice—Christ was relevant and real to young people.

New Church Music

Music was important to those in the movement. Rock, pop, and folk music were deeply rooted in the Jesus People, who took secular styles of music and added Christ-honoring lyrics. This made worship more attractive to those outside the faith and gave an empowering means of expression to those on the inside. The movement had an effect on top-notch musicians who, in turn, influenced the movement. Music luminaries such as Dion Di Mucci (Dion, Dion & the Belmonts), Barry McGuire (The New Christy Minstrels), and Paul Stookey (Peter, Paul, and Mary) were touched by Jesus music and in turn influenced the Jesus music of the day. Contemporary music exploded with groups and individuals dedicated to Christian music: Petra, Resurrection Band, Second Chapter of Acts, Randy Stonehill, and others led the way. Such music gradually made its way into the worship services of traditional churches—sometimes over great resistance. Despite that resistance, new Christian music remains a vital part of many church experiences today and is recognized in the larger music scene as a viable genre. Today it is a multimillion dollar industry.

Seeker-Sensitive Churches

While churches have always had the goal of evangelizing and growing their membership, the approach settled into a "here-we-are-come-do-it-our-way" pattern. While there have been many new evangelistic programs designed to reach the unchurched, the church itself changed very little. From the early '50s on, society began to change. The median age of the US population began to decline with the advent of the Baby Boomer generation. Over seventy-six million children were born during the years between 1946 and 1964. These children grew up in a different world from their parents and cultivated an independent way of thinking, a strong sense of rebellion, and an insatiable desire for something they couldn't define.

The Jesus Movement showed the power of reaching people where they were. Instead of asking people to change before coming to church, they accepted people as they were and where they were, not condoning sin but believing that it was God who made the change. Change came through discipleship, which had less to do with programs and more to do with relationships.

Some churches saw the power of the concept and began changing the way they did worship. Contemporary music replaced decades-old (and often centuries-old) music; pastors "dressed down," foregoing suits and ties for jeans and casual shirts. There was less preaching and more teaching. Sermons became "messages," and pastors took to the podium (pulpits passed from the scene in many congregations) to share, not proclaim.

Those looking for a place to worship began approaching the process like shoppers in the mall, sampling one church after another until they found one that fit them. Seekers started to like upbeat music, computer projection systems, and messages that told them how to be happy. Many churches refused to adapt, clinging to the ways they were used to, and were passed over. Many seeker-sensitive churches grew into megachurches with weekly attendance in the tens of thousands.

The Jesus Movement had much to do with seeker-focused ministry. They worked the streets of metropolitan areas, providing food and helping addicts leave behind the drugs that were pushing them to early graves. They saw a need and took Jesus to it. The difference might seem subtle, but it changed the face of contemporary church life around much of the world.

Sailing over the Horizon

The Jesus Movement lasted only a decade. Except for a flash of attention given to it by the media in the early years of the 1970s, Jesus People went largely unnoticed in their beginning and in the end. As they aged, the many leaders of the group turned to the additional responsibilities of family, and some shifted from street to church work. The principles remained the same, but the world changed beneath them. While the days of the "one way" hand sign, Jesus slogans on T-shirts, and communal housing may have passed, the influence of the Jesus People lingers.

28

Vatican II

(1962)

Large naval vessels are impressive. Aircraft carriers are stunning examples of human engineering and science. But as sleek and as powerful as they are, they are difficult to turn quickly. The maneuver in which the ship is turned 180 degrees is called a tactical diameter. A large vessel like a carrier needs about four times its length to make such a U-turn. A thousand-foot ship needs 4,500 feet to make the turn. And in most cases, the larger something is, the more space and time it takes to turn.

The same can also be said for large organizations. The larger and the older an organization is, the more resistant it is to change. The Roman Catholic Church is the largest denomination in Christendom, with over one billion adherents. That means one in seven people consider themselves Roman Catholic. There are about two billion Christians worldwide. Half of those are Roman Catholic.[1]

Such an ancient denomination is steeped in centuries of tradition and history. Over time, the organization of the Church and its doctrine grew more complicated and intricate. In many ways, the

Roman Catholic Church is a very large ship, one that is difficult to alter course. Changing direction is startling and infrequent.

Yet changes to long-established traditions have happened, most recently in the period of time from 1962 to 1965. This event is often called Vatican II.

A New Pope with a New Idea

Angelo Giuseppe Roncalli (1881–1963) became a priest in March 1904 and served the Church until his death almost sixty years later. He served in a variety of positions and through difficult times, including two World Wars. During World War II he worked with the Jewish underground, helping Jews escape the Nazis. Many Jews held him in high regard for the aid he rendered during the war years while in Turkey. His heart for the endangered and lost stayed with him through his life. Even after becoming pope, he would leave Vatican grounds to visit jails and orphanages.

When eighty-two-year-old Pope Pius XII died of heart failure on October 9, 1958, the process of selecting his replacement began. They selected Roncalli, who became the head of the Church on October 28, 1958, and took the name Pope John XXIII. He hit the ground running, something many Church leaders found surprising. Many believed John would be a bookmark, a placeholder as pope. He had other ideas. Less than three months into the job, he announced his intent to call an ecumenical council. Such councils were not simple meetings. The First Vatican Council had been held in 1868, nearly a century before John XXIII's leadership, and the Council of Trent took place in 1545–63, over three centuries before that.

Unlike previous councils, Vatican II was not called to battle Protestants or define doctrine. John had a different concept in mind: *aggiornamento*. The term means "to bring up to date." In his convocation address, given in January 1959, he said,

> This will be a demonstration of the church, always living and always young, that feels the rhythm of time, that in every century beautifies

herself with new splendor, radiates new light, achieves new conquests, all the while remaining identical to herself, faithful to the divine image impressed on her face by her divine Bridegroom, who loves her and protects her, Christ Jesus.[2]

John's goal was to change the Church in such a way that it could meet twentieth-century needs and do so not out of condemnation but concern. In his opening address to the council he said,

The Church has always opposed these errors. Frequently she has condemned them with the greatest severity. Nowadays however, the Spouse of Christ prefers to make use of the medicine of mercy rather than that of severity. She considers that she meets the needs of the present day by demonstrating the validity of her teaching rather than by condemnations.[3]

The phrase "medicine of mercy rather than that of severity" set the tone for the meeting. Pope John XXIII wanted changes that would lead to a softening of the Catholic church's image in the world. But like a large ship, the "tactical diameter" of the Roman Catholic Church was substantial. It was one thing to call for a council, it was quite another to make Church leaders agree.

The gathering began in October 1962 with great fanfare. Over 2,500 of the eligible hierarchy (cardinals, bishops, and abbots) came to Rome, making it the largest council in the history of Roman Catholicism. Only seven hundred or so had attended the First Vatican Council and less than three hundred had attended the sixteenth-century Council of Trent.

Vatican II was not a single meeting. The first gathering of October 1962 was followed by three additional meetings in the fall of consecutive years, ending in 1965. There was no unity at the meetings. As with all large organizations there were conservatives and progressives. The conservatives wanted to keep things as they had been for centuries; the progressives wanted change. This surprised no one.

John did little to interact with or guide the group. He watched most of the proceedings over closed-circuit television, seldom interfering or mediating. The council would decide what it would decide. No doubt, John believed God would achieve his goals through the gathered Church leaders.

The pope would not see the results of the council. He died on June 3, 1963, from problems related to stomach cancer. He was eighty-one years old. Pope John XXIII would be remembered for many things, including his offer to mediate between President John F. Kennedy and Nikita Khrushchev during the Cuban Missile Crisis. *Time* magazine named him Man of the Year in 1962. Vatican II, however, would, in the minds of his supporters, be his greatest victory.

John was followed by Pope Pius XII, who oversaw the remaining work of the council.

Issues and Changes

Vatican II addressed several areas of importance that changed the modern Roman Catholic Church and opened the doors to greater dialogue. In some cases, council opinions changed the way Catholics viewed themselves and others.

Worship

The *Constitution on the Sacred Liturgy (Sacrosanctum Concilium)* was approved in the 1963 meeting with the overwhelming support of 2,147 favorable votes to 4 votes against. With the exception of certain Latin rites, the Mass could now be said in the common language of the people in each local church instead of Latin only. For a church with a billion adherents spread around the world, this was a major change. Allowing the congregation to hear the liturgy in their own language helped them feel more a part of the services and the Church.

The Last Supper (Eucharist) remained central to public worship, but faithful non-clergy could be directly involved. The wall separating priest from parishioner had been lowered.

Bible

Parishioners were encouraged to read the Bible for themselves. While this may seem a natural right, such as it is in Protestant life, up until now it was not encouraged in the Catholic church. Indeed, much of the impetus of the Protestant Reformation came from individuals reading the Bible. Lutherans, Mennonites, and other denominations came into being because their founders first challenged the Church for holding doctrine not found in the Bible. There are many historical events showing the Roman church's efforts to stop the translation of the Bible into the common language.

The *Dogmatic Constitution on Divine Revelation* (*Dei Verbum*, November 18, 1965) passed by 2,300 votes to only a handful of negative votes. Doctrinal authority in the Roman Catholic Church was based on the Bible, tradition/councils, and papal decrees. Vatican II put a new emphasis on the Scriptures but restated the force of sacred tradition. The council reaffirmed the inspiration of the Scriptures.

Other

The decisions of the Vatican II council cover a wide range of topics and do so in depth. Some of the other changes include the idea that all Christians have a calling from God, not just priests. Vatican I taught that only the pope was considered the successor of the apostles. Until Vatican II, he held a special position. That position has remained unchanged. The pope was and remains, in Catholic thinking, the head of the Church, but under the new thinking bishops shared in that apostolic succession.

For many centuries, Roman Catholics viewed their church as the only true expression of Christianity and taught that there was no salvation outside the Church. Catholics were forbidden to attend Protestant churches. Vatican II changed that. Non-Catholics were now called "separated brethren." The word *Christian* no longer meant only Catholic. Catholics were encouraged to pray with Protestants and participate in ecumenical efforts. Much of this result can be traced to Pope John XXIII, who was known to befriend those outside the Catholic church. When a group of Jews visited him after he had become pope, he greeted them, "I am Joseph, your brother." Participating with Protestants and Orthodox churches in ecumenical efforts was encouraged.

Mixed Response

A person changes when it hurts too much to stay the same. This axiom can also be applied to any organization, even one as large as the Roman Catholic Church. Another axiom states that forced change is always resisted. Pope John XXIII's inspiration was a church that looked out to the world instead of looking in on itself. He and others saw a morphing world with materialism and atheism on the rise and no increase in spiritual growth. The troubled world of the '50s and '60s gave every indication of turning its back on Christianity in general and on the Roman Catholic Church in particular. While turning a blind eye was easier, it was not something Pope John XXIII could do nor, in his opinion, something the Church should do. The Church needed to face the new world. The society in which Vatican II existed was very different from that of Vatican I a century before, and unbelievably different from that of the Council of Trent in the sixteenth century.

Like the Apollo spacecraft sailing to the moon, the Roman church needed several midcourse corrections to hit the target. Pope John XXIII recognized that and convened the Second Vatican Council. However, not everyone saw him as a visionary or saw the Vatican II changes as something to be embraced. Some thought they went too far; others thought they didn't go far enough. Birth control remained forbidden, divorce was not allowed, and some felt the power of the papacy had been watered down.

From 1962 to 1974 the Church saw an exodus of priests, monks, and nuns. During that time the number of students in US seminaries decreased by almost a third. From 1966 to 1972, roughly eight thousand priests left the ministry.

At the same time, some churches around the world experienced growth and parishioners felt more a part of the church they attended.

Regardless of where one stands on Vatican II or Catholicism, Vatican II must be acknowledged as one of the most significant changes to any denomination.

29

The Rise
of the Christian Right
Confrontational Christianity

(1979)

For every opinion there is someone somewhere who will take the opposite position. Being contrary is part of human nature. History is certainly filled with evidence of one group willing to battle all others over a view, an opinion, a doctrine, or a perceived set of rights. This is especially true in church history, which can be portrayed as an unending series of conflicts—conflicts with those outside the ranks and many within them. Popes have faced off against kings, Protestants have challenged the views of other Protestants, and large denominations have split over what seem to outsiders as minor issues.

It is common to hear, "I don't talk about religion or politics." The statement is an attempt to avoid an argument, but the two often meet in the arena. In a country like the United States, where freedom of speech is a beloved right and protected by law, conflict is certain. US politics have been contrary from the founding of the country, with groups identifying with those like themselves and battling those who were not.

Through much of American church history the church kept its distance from specific politics and policies except where they directly affected the church. Exceptions can be found, but the two worlds seldom knocked heads. Comfortable with First Amendment protection from federal government interference, and with plenty of work to do in their parishes, clergy were focused on ministry. Still, the church had great influence on the Founding Fathers and the formation of the new country. Society and the government were supportive of churches, or at least tolerant.

Until recent decades, children in school learned that the United States was founded on Christian principles. To a large extent that is true, but the Founding Fathers, who held a variety of religious views, made it clear that they were not creating a congregation but a country. Still, Baby Boomers and those who preceded them grew up believing the church shouldn't be challenged. The generation before the Baby Boomers and the older Boomers grew up with prayer in school.

Societies, however, are not fixed and unchanging. Time brings new ideas and a new sense of the individual. As society moved through the rebellion of the '60s and '70s into the commercialism of the "Me-Generation," new paradigms came to the forefront. The idea that men were defined by the jobs they held and women defined by the number of children they had was morphing into something new. Economics had pressed many of the women who gave birth to the Baby Boomer generation into the working world, something made acceptable by the number of women who had worked in factories during World War II. Women no longer had to view their future solely as housewives and mothers. While some churches debated if it was appropriate for women to wear slacks to church, society was busy redefining family and women's rights.

More and more, the church was seen as out of date and out of touch. Although most people would not recognize the word or the trend, society was being secularized. Where the church called for the sacrificial worship of God, society made the individual the center of thinking. For some, science was becoming (and did become) the new church.

The civil rights movement proved that change could come by passive resistance, marches, and public gatherings. The country learned that such activities could make a change in law and attitudes. Between 1950 and 1999 there were over forty marches on Washington, DC, covering everything from civil rights to farm policy to nuclear disarmament. Crowds numbered as high as five hundred thousand (March for Women's Lives, April 1989). Each march was evidence of the belief that rights could be demanded.

Some conservative churches were unsettled by the pending changes. It would be a mistake to assume that churches were opposed to change. Indeed, they embraced the need for civil rights, but some of the social changes struck at foundational beliefs—not foundational to the church but to the country.

Matches Set to Kindling

Several issues launched many churches into the fight: abortion, feminism, and gay rights—all seen as undermining family values. In 1973, the US Supreme Court ruled in favor of Norma ("Roe") McCorvey (who would later change her stance and become a Roman Catholic), indicating that women had a right to privacy regarding reproductive issues and making abortion legal. Roman Catholics, whose doctrine forbid birth control, found the decision appalling, as did Protestants who believed that life begins at conception. To conservative churches, abortion was not a right but the ending of a life, something that could not be rationalized away. To do nothing was to grant passive consent to infanticide. Opponents, of course, framed the issue differently, but never in a way that convinced pro-lifers that a human wasn't being destroyed. The belief that lives were at stake propelled the church into the public arena.

Women's rights became a hot-button issue for some who feared that the role of mother was being degraded and children were suffering for it. Also at risk was the "ideal" family with the husband as the head, the mother as the heart, and the children as the objects of love and attention. The future of the country was dependent upon the next generation, so a lack of constant parental guidance not only hurt the family but undermined the future of a nation.

Also, a movement in gay communities surfaced in the early '70s. A 1978 proposition that would have kept homosexuals from teaching in public schools failed, giving the antigay movement a significant defeat, strengthening the gay rights movement, and compelling pro-family proponents to greater action.

To conservative church leaders, the very fiber of what made the United States great was being frayed. They were not content to proclaim opinions from the pulpit. Direct action, in their minds, was required.

The Moral Majority

To answer these issues and others, Jerry Falwell (1933–2007), pastor of the Thomas Road Baptist Church, founded the Moral Majority in 1979. He became a catalyst for action and a lightning rod for criticism. He was a controversial leader who was loved by his supporters and despised by his detractors.

Falwell stood on a platform of the biblical concept of family and the idea that America was and should remain a Christian nation. He opposed homosexuality, abortion, and humanism. To him and others, the country was about to succumb to humanism, a belief that Falwell and his followers claimed emphasized human intellect over faith.

The Moral Majority did not work alone. They received support from other organizations like the Christian Voice, Concerned Women for America, and others. To manage their mission, they created several institutions through which to do their work: Moral Majority, Inc., was the lobbying arm working at local, state, and national levels; the Moral Majority Foundation provided education to ministers on political matters; the Moral Majority Legal Defense Fund handled legal matters and served as the opponent to the American Civil

Liberties Union; and the Moral Majority Political Action Committee supported candidates.

Conservative Christians—the Religious Right—stepped to the forefront, but not without controversy. Jerry Falwell made proclamations that even many of his supporters had trouble swallowing. In a 1976 sermon he said, "The idea that religion and politics don't mix was invented by the Devil to keep Christians from running their own country."[1] He also proclaimed, "AIDS is not just God's punishment for homosexuals, it is God's punishment for the society that tolerates homosexuals."[2]

While the goals of the Moral Majority and similar groups might have had biblical motives, they often fell into actions and words that presented an unexpected view of the church and some of its leaders. They not only backed some candidates but attacked others, even those who might have been called "brother" in different circumstances. Jimmy Carter, the thirty-ninth president of the United States, became such a target. He wrote:

> Another serious problem we could not overcome was the bitter attacks on me from the conservative religious and political groups. They accused me of being "soft on Communism," betraying America by "giving away the Panama Canal," subverting the teaching of children by organizing a new Department of Education, encouraging abortion and homosexuality, trying to destroy families by supporting the Equal Rights Amendment, and lowering America's guard against the Soviet threat by negotiating the SALT treaty. I had had some problems with these groups in 1976, and as soon as it became clear that I would be renominated, they came back in full cry. The Reverend Jerry Falwell, the leader of Moral Majority, was one of the worst, in that he had a large audience and was quite careless with the truth.[3]

Non-church people and "liberal" churches saw such groups as damaging the image of the church and the work of Christ. Supporters saw people taking a stand for godliness and the family. If nothing else, Falwell and others pushed their agenda to the front of the political discussions.

The debate over abortion and gay rights was lively and often bitter. The conservative movement, both politically and ecclesiastically, grew in prominence and influence. Nonetheless, women's rights, abortion, and gay rights all made strides forward and came to be thought of as unbeatable. The group, after a decade of activity, dissolved in 1989. The battle for the American mind over these issues continues, but many of the approaches have become less acerbic.

The concerns about the secularization of America proved accurate. Secularization is a movement to restrict or obliterate religious influence. The church was losing its influence. Worse, much of society was becoming "Christophobic." The numbers of people stating they had no religious affiliation grew to one in five, and one in three for adults under thirty. The divorce rate among Christians was less than non-Christians but still high. Pastors were often considered purveyors of hate speech.

A Different Approach

Faith, in the mind of most, is one topic among many. Historically, knowledge of the Bible was much higher, Christian service was seen as a lifetime pursuit, and the church was central to family life. Church was a place of community, but in the late twentieth century a change occurred. Individuals pulled away from groups. Futurist Faith Popcorn identified and named the phenomenon: cocooning. In her 1991 book *The Popcorn Report* she discussed the individual's withdrawal into a technology cocoon.[4] While people still go out to eat, catch a movie, travel, and more, there remains a tendency to maintain a degree of separation from others. Social media has not put an end to the need for human contact, but it has supplanted the process. In this decade texting has come close to replacing phone calls.

People want their own home, and members of the family want their own rooms, televisions, computers, phones, and more. Friends still meet for dinner, but the desire for such social events has declined.

In church terms it means church is the place you go for encourage-ment but not necessarily something you belong to. Many still join churches, but the meaning of such has changed. Church-hopping is common. When a person speaks of "my church," they mean the church they are attending at the moment. Choosing a church often has more to do with child care than with a faith journey.

In the midst of growing secularism and Christophobia in the seventies, a new type of church began and has continued to grow in the following decades. This group has charted a different course from the confrontational church. They are seeker-friendly churches, often starting only after a marketing survey of the community has been done and the service and ministries have been customized to meet the desires of the community. They are friendly, adaptable, upbeat, welcoming, and offer an "experience" rather than a typical worship service. While it might seem a business approach rather than a spiritual one, these churches often have strong evangelical messages and solid discipleship training. Others, however, have softened the message and come close to being self-help seminars.

The rise of the megachurch allows individuals to attend church but still remain anonymous. In most cases, this is not the fault of the church but the result of a social, generational shift. One can hardly blame contemporary churches for trying new things. They are trying to win an audience that is heavily influenced against Christianity by school, television, movies, documentaries, and more. Society has changed sufficiently that it is easy to find someone for whom going to church is unique. Biblical knowledge is almost nonexistent outside the walls of the church and thin even among churchgoers.

Only 5 to 10 percent of people in Europe attend church on a regular basis. In the US the numbers are much higher but declining. In an interesting twist, churches established by missionaries decades or even centuries before have become the fastest growing in the world. From Korea to South America, churches are blossoming, many sending missionaries back to the countries that evangelized them.

The church has seldom been quiet. From Peter, who pointed his finger at the religious leaders for their role in the crucifixion of Christ, to today's nonprofit organizations like Focus on the Family's lobby CitizenLink, Christians continue to confront the society in which they live. At times this has been done with great bitterness, at other times with a grace born of strength. In the process, churches have had to decide what their role is as an organization in confronting what they see as a dangerous shift in thinking and the devaluing of faith, family, and the individual. This decision impacts the way the church does its ministry.

There is no unity among the church at large. Conservatives have banded together and other Christian groups have clustered on the other side of the political and social fence, each casting suspicious glances at the other. At times, it is unpleasant to see, but it is not new, nor—if history is any guide—will it end anytime soon.

30

The Rise of New Atheism

(Present)

In late June 2013, a Montana judge ruled against a case filed by
the Freedom From Religion Foundation, which complained about
a statue of Jesus at a ski resort. It was not, however, a victory for
religious freedom. "The statue's secular and irreverent use far outweigh the few religious uses it has served," US District Judge Dana
Christensen said. "Typical observers of the statue are more interested
in giving it a high five or adorning it in ski gear than sitting before
it in prayer."[1] The statue has stood on its concrete pedestal since its
dedication by the Knights of Columbus in 1954.

In 2009, a US District Court Judge denied an atheist's request
that any reference to God in President Barack Obama's swearing-in
ceremony be barred. The "so help me God" remained. There was
also an attempt to delete the invocation and benediction from the
ceremonies.

The number of cases grows, and grows more bitter with time.
One victory for the atheists came when the four-thousand-member
American Atheists unveiled a monument to atheism at the Bradford

County courthouse near Jacksonville, Florida, a move meant to counterbalance the presence of a pair of stone tablets inscribed with the Ten Commandments. The monument, a granite pillar and bench emblazoned with "American Atheists" on the front edge of the bench, contains secular quotes from American Founding Fathers.[2]

The publishing industry, which often follows trends, saw the rise of bestselling books penned by proud atheists such as Richard Dawkins, Christopher Hitchens, and others. Some of these books have spent many months on the *New York Times* bestseller list.

With the advances in communication, it might seem like such disbelief is new. But atheism is far from new. The psalmist spoke of it three thousand years ago: "The fool has said in his heart, 'There is no God'" (Ps. 14:1). Atheism is an ancient belief system, and the church has been encountering it for millennia—and not just the church, but every established religion. What has changed is the level of hatred coming from some of these non-theists. The movement for atheism has morphed from poking fun at religious people to hateful attacks. It is this, not just the fact that there are those who choose not to believe in any god, that the church is facing and will face in the decades ahead.

According to a Pew Research Center study, the number of people claiming to be atheists in the United States is steadily growing, from 1.6 percent in 2007 to 2.4 percent in 2012. Agnostics saw a bump in their numbers from 2.1 percent to 3.3 percent over the same span. The largest increase is in the unaffiliated group—people who have no religious affiliation—which rose from 11.6 percent to 13.9 percent.[3]

A Word about Terms

Atheist comes from a compound of two Greek words: *a* (no, or without) and *theos*, the word for God, hence, "no-God." This might seem like common knowledge, but according to the Pew survey, the definition is not clear in the minds of some responding to the poll.

> Estimating the number of atheists in the U.S. is complex. Some adults
> who describe themselves as atheists also say they do believe in God or

a universal spirit. At the same time, some people who identify with a religion (e.g., say they are Protestant, Catholic or Jewish) say they do not believe in God.[4]

With such disparity in understanding, it is difficult to come up with hard and fast numbers. Nonetheless, the number of people describing themselves as atheists is on the rise. Incidentally, atheists tend to be male (67 percent) and young (38 percent are in the 18–29 age group).[5]

A "non-theist" is a person who has decided no God exists but is not an activist about the topic. An "anti-theist" not only doesn't believe in God but doesn't want anyone else to do so either.

Agnostic, like atheist, comes from a compound of Greek words: *a* (no, or without) and *gnosis* (knowledge). Agnostics claim to not know if there is a God or claim that God is unknowable. They do not believe a person can know with certainty that either the theist view or the atheist view is correct.

"Nones" is a fairly recent term used to describe those who choose not to affiliate with any religion. They may deny being atheist or agnostic, but religion plays no role in their life or their thinking. They are, philosophically, theological free-floaters. It is said that there are two kinds of atheists: those who state there is no God and those who live as if there is no God. The spiritual has no role in their life. They may have grown up in churches or synagogues or mosques, but their present life is void of such things.

Atheist "Denominations"

The church has denominations to help us distinguish one group from another. Atheists can be divided in a similar way. Often what distinguishes atheists from each other is their motivation.

The Intellectuals. This brand of atheist takes the intellectual approach to propagating atheism or refuting religious claims. They are motivated by knowledge and evidence. They are likely to see themselves as too intelligent or too educated for religion.

The Aggressive. These are the "evangelicals" of the atheist movement, intent on winning people to their side as well as stomping down the rights of others, such as fighting against the placement of a nativity scene in public view.

The Quiet Ones. These are the opposite of the aggressive atheists. While they might share the same goals as the other groups, they are not set on confrontation. They've made their decision about the existence of God but have little interest in winning converts to their side.

The Activists. These are people motivated by some cause to confront something they see as a slight against them, such as prayer in the Supreme Court or a list of the Ten Commandments in a school, or are moved by a social or political cause such as homosexual rights, abortion, or another contentious issue.

The Nones. "Nones" is a coined term for those who choose to have no affiliation with a religious group. They are not necessarily atheists in their philosophy, but they no longer have anything to do with any religious group. This group is also known as "the unaffiliated."

There are scores of ways to categorize atheists and agnostics, and there are many more ways to classify Christians. There is no cookie-cutter atheist any more than there is a cookie-cutter Christian. There are, however, trends to be observed. Christians continue to endure the prejudice that comes from stereotyping. The church is learning that stereotyping atheists is also counterproductive.

An Ongoing Event

While the ranks of atheism show only some growth, their presence and the press they receive has exploded. During the late twentieth century, "coming out" as an atheist seemed almost fashionable. This came mostly from the ranks of scientists, including popularizers of science such as Carl Sagan, who had no hesitancy in letting his atheism be known through his writings. For example, in his book *Broca's Brain: Reflections on the Romance of Science*, Sagan pens a chapter called "A Sunday Sermon" in which he takes several whacks at the idea of God and the superiority of science.

"Religion has been scarred in its confrontation with science, and many people—but by no means all—are reluctant to accept a body of theological belief that is too obviously in conflict with what else we know."[6]

While there have been conflicts between science and religion, faith has played an important role in advancing learning. There are many myths about conflicts between science and faith. *Galileo Goes to Jail and Other Myths about Science and Religion* dispels many of the myths. Of the twenty-five contributors to the work, half self-identify as atheists or agnostics.[7] They recognize that many of the "science vs. religion" tales we hear are either myths or have been incompletely told.

"As we learn more and more about the universe, there seems less and less for God to do."[8] Sagan's line might well be a mantra for other atheists. Sagan spoke forthrightly and in a tone one would expect from a favorite uncle. Many greatly admired Carl Sagan, his commitment to science, and his ability to communicate on television, in documentaries, and through his books. Unlike other atheists who would later stand in his shadow, he was able to speak against faith without being acerbic or using it as a means of drawing attention to himself. This does not mean he is correct about the non-existence of God. The "A Sunday Sermon" chapter, while an interesting read and a well-delivered polemic, has arguments that could be easily dismantled by a second-year seminary student.

Late in the twentieth century it became popular for atheists to go on the attack. Science journals began to take on Christians, usually over the teaching of creationism in schools. It is here we see the crux of tension: the church was becoming more vocal as school systems were becoming more secular. Schools, especially the high school level and down, reflect society. As society has become more and more secular, so have the schools. State-sanctioned prayer in school ended after two US Supreme Court decisions—*Engel v. Vitale* (1962) and *Abington School District v. Schempp* (1963). While today many Christians would agree that required prayer in a pluralistic school is unwise, it was a watershed event.

Another log in the fire burning between atheists and the church is the rise of creationism and the antievolution movement. The former came to prominence in 1970, when Henry Morris established the Institute for Creation Research. The hydrologist and other scientists who believed in Young Earth Creationism entered into debate with evolutionists. The real spark of animosity came with the publication of *Scientific Creationism,* a book intended to provide teachers with the material for the teaching of biblical creation.[9] The book denied evolution, something scientists were not willing to let pass easily. Court battles ensued over teaching creationism in schools. The hard-fought battles were long and bitter and continue to this day. For many, especially the atheists, such things were best left to scientists and the church should just step back—notwithstanding that many scientists were Christians with valid PhDs from reputable secular universities.

The Intelligent Design movement, a scientific approach to interpreting data in science, caused an even greater furor. While not the same as creationism, the view does advocate the need for a designer to explain the complexity of nature. It does not offer opinions about the designer, only that observation indicates an intricacy that cannot be explained by mechanistic evolution. But for science in general and atheists in particular, this is too close to "God-talk."

Not every issue between Christians and atheists has orbited science. In 1973, *Roe v. Wade* opened the doors to legal abortion, and later court cases would extend those legal claims. In America, the Me-Generation was catching on as Baby Boomers became more self-focused. The '80s heightened this propensity toward self-indulgence. Personal "rights" became the rallying cry for those who wanted greater personal freedom. Abortion on-demand became a form of birth control, women's rights dominated the news, and a sense of entitlement swept the country. Christianity teaches restraint, responsibility, and accountability, and some (but certainly not all) of the new attitudes ran contrary to that. Many much-needed reforms came through these decades; still, starting in the late '60s and continuing forward, pushing against authority became expected.

The response to the tragedy of AIDS, first observed in 1981, may have also contributed to disenchantment with the church. Many conservative groups pronounced the epidemic as God's judgment on homosexuals, since so many of the first cases came from the gay community. Some in the church offered hatred and an "it's your own fault" rhetoric, while others saw an opportunity to show the mercy of Christ. The former group got all the press. Again, people began to see the church as judgmental and cruel. Those outside the church knew little about those within the church who were aiding the sick.

Against this pressure rose groups such as the Moral Majority and a swing toward more conservative values. For some, having the church battling evolution, advocating for prayer in school, picketing abortion clinics (and sometimes worse), challenging the moral slide that began in the '60s and grew with each decade, and delivering messages from the pulpit and at rallies calling for a return to decency was too much. For those people, it was easier to ignore or reject God.

This is not likely to change anytime soon. The rise of New Atheism is multifaceted in its cause, was to be expected, and has perhaps been poorly dealt with by the church. Not everyone who left the church turned to atheism, but many adopted an agnostic lifestyle. In a strange twist (but one which may have been true throughout church history), atheists sit in the pews of many churches. They may do so for family reasons, tradition, or simply because they enjoy the fellowship. There may even be some atheists in the pulpit. For example, Jerry DeWitt, a former Bible-Belt preacher, gave up his pulpit to embrace atheism.[10] While this may sound strange and even tragic, it is not new. The church has always had a back door. Even Jesus saw defection in the crowds that followed him. "As a result of this many of His disciples withdrew and were not walking with Him anymore" (John 6:66). "Disciples" in this passage does not refer to the Twelve but to the larger body of Jesus' followers.

The gospel has always been divisive. Paul wrote to the church in Corinth that the preaching of Christ crucified and resurrected is a stumbling block to Jews and foolishness to Gentiles (1 Cor. 1:23). To many atheists, the gospel message just doesn't make sense. In the last half of the twentieth century and in the early years of the twenty-first, some atheists have taken the offensive, working to mitigate religious expression in public venues and government or to strip away such rights altogether. The Freedom From Religion Foundation is a nonprofit organization comprised of nineteen thousand members. American Atheists, which started in 1963, is an activist group that is the visible face of the movement that undertakes reactive and proactive efforts to propagate the ideals of atheism and to sponge away any real or imagined ties between religion and government.

Conclusion

Atheism is an ancient belief system that has taken different forms through the centuries. In a free society, one in which freedom of speech is allowed and encouraged, atheism, religion, and everything in between will find ways to win converts. New Atheists are more direct in their opinions, and some are more militant in getting the attention of others around them.

The rise of New Atheism was an event that happened not in a moment or a day but over an extended time. The church has dealt with atheism since its inception and will continue to do so in the future. Disbelief in the world has forced the church to learn how to defend its principles and doctrines. There exists within the church an entire discipline of apologetics. *Apologetics* comes from a legal term meaning "to give a reasonable defense." Colleges and seminaries offer classes and even graduate degrees in apologetics. Atheism not only forces the church to know *what* it believes but *why* it believes it—especially in the twenty-first century.

This challenge from the New Atheists may make the church stronger and more nimble. The church has always done its best under duress. Good can come from bad, and, as on the day of Pentecost, the timid and weak can be made bold and strong. On that first-century day, suddenly empowered by the Holy Spirit, the early church leaders stood boldly before the same people who had called for Christ's crucifixion and engaged them with the truth of the gospel. The need to do the same in our century remains.

Event by event, the church continues to be shaped.

Notes

Chapter 2 The Conversion of Paul

1. Bruce L. Shelley, *Church History in Plain Language*, 4th ed. (Nashville: Thomas Nelson, 2013), 21.
2. William Shakespeare, *Twelfth Night*, Act II, scene 5, line 157.

Chapter 3 Gentiles and Judaism

1. "Global Christianity: A Report on the Size and Distribution of the World's Christian Population," Pew Research Religion & Public Life Project, December 19, 2011, http://www.pewforum.org/2011/12/19/global-christianity-exec/.

Chapter 4 When Rome Burned

1. Philip Schaff and David Schely Schaff, *History of the Christian Church*, vol. 1 (New York: C. Scribner's Sons, 1910), 379.
2. Suetonius, "Nero," *The Lives of the Twelve Caesars*, trans. J. C. Rolfe (Cambridge, MA: Harvard University Press, 1979), V.
3. Cornelius Tacitus, *The Annals of Imperial Rome*, Great Books of the Western World, vol. 15, trans. Alfred John Church and William Jackson Brodribb (Chicago: Brittanica, 1988), 185.
4. Ibid., 167.
5. Cassius Dio, *Roman History LXII*, 16–17.
6. As quoted in *The Oxford History of the Biblical World*, ed. Michael Coogan (New York: Oxford University Press, 1998), 536.
7. Suetonius, "Nero," XXXI.
8. Tacitus, *Annals*, 168.
9. Josephus, *Antiquities of the Jews*, 20.8.2–3. From *The Works of Josephus*, trans. William Whiston (Lynn, MA: Hendrickson, 1980), 421.

Chapter 5 The Destruction of Jerusalem by Titus

1. Josephus, *Antiquities*, 18.1.1, 20.9.3 for example.
2. F. F. Bruce, *The Spreading Flame: The Rise and Progress of Christianity from Its First Beginnings to the Conversion of the English* (Grand Rapids: Eerdmans, 1958), 156.
3. Eusebius, *The Church History*, III.5.

Notes

Chapter 6 The Edict of Milan

1. Robert F. Lay, *Readings in Historical Theology: Primary Sources of the Christian Faith* (Grand Rapids: Kregel Academic, 2009), 136–37.
2. Eusebius, *The Life of Constantine*, trans. Averil Cameron and Stuart G. Hall (Oxford: Oxford University Press, 1999), 161.

Chapter 7 The First Council of Nicaea

1. As quoted in Robert Payne, *The Holy Fire: The Story of the Fathers of the Eastern Church* (Crestwood, NY: St. Vladimir's Seminary Press, 1980), 82–83.
2. Ibid., 107.
3. Based on J. N. D. Kelly, *Early Christian Doctrines*, rev. ed. (New York: Harper & Row, 1978), 233.
4. Shelley, *Church History in Plain Language*, 109.

Chapter 8 Jerome Completes the Vulgate Translation of the Bible

1. Jerome, *Address to Pope Damasus*, AD 383, as quoted in Stefan Rebenich, *Jerome* (New York: Routledge, 2013), 32–33.
2. Philip Schaff, ed., *A Select Library of Nicene and Post-Nicene Fathers of the Christian Church* (New York: Christian Literature Company, 1892), 327.
3. David S. Dockery, *Christian Scripture* (Nashville: Broadman & Holman, 1995), 80.

Chapter 10 Innocent III Expands the Power of the Papacy

1. As quoted in Shelley, *Church History in Plain Language*, 194.

Chapter 11 *Unam Sanctam* Proclaims Papal Supremacy

1. Shelley, *Church History in Plain Language*, 225.
2. All English quotations from the *Unam Sanctam* are from Charles A. Coulombe, *Vicars of Christ: A History of the Popes* (New York: Citadel Press Books, 2003), 452–53.

Chapter 12 Gutenberg Produces the First Printed Bible

1. Paul Gray, "15th Century: Johann Gutenberg," *Time*, December 31, 1999.
2. Quotations from Diana Childress, *Johannes Gutenberg and the Printing Press* (Minneapolis: Twenty-First Century Books, 2002), 122.
3. As quoted in Gene Fedele, *Heroes of Faith* (Gainesville, FL: Bridge Logos, 2003), 97.
4. William Joseph Federer, ed., *America's God and Country: Encyclopedia of Quotations* (St. Louis: AmeriSearch, 2000), 270.

Chapter 13 The Protestant Reformation

1. Shelley, *Church History in Plain Language*, 249.
2. Ibid.
3. J. James Dixon Douglas, Philip Wesley Comfort, and Donald R. Mitchell, *Who's Who in Christian History* (Wheaton: Tyndale, 1992), 434.
4. Shelley, *Church History in Plain Language*, 254.

Notes

Chapter 14 The Scientific Revolution Begins

1. Stephen Jay Gould, *Ever Since Darwin: Reflections in Natural History* (New York: W. W. Norton, 1977), 141.
2. William H. McNeil, *A World History* (New York: Oxford University Press, 1971), 318–19.
3. Nicolaus Copernicus, "Preface and Dedication to Pope Paul III," *On the Revolutions of the Heavenly Spheres*, ed. Stephen Hawking, trans. Charles Glen Wallis (Philadelphia: Running Press, 2002), 2.
4. Ibid., 4.
5. Galileo, "Letter to Grand Duchess Christina, 1615," as quoted in James Hannam, *The Genesis of Science: How the Christian Middle Ages Launched the Scientific Revolution* (Washington, DC: Regnery, 2011), 321.
6. David Berlinski, *Newton's Gift* (New York: Simon & Schuster, 2000), 15.
7. Nick Fleming, "Albert Einstein 'found genius through autism,'" *The Telegraph*, February 21, 2008.
8. Isaac Newton, *Philosophiæ Naturalis Principia Mathematica*, ed. Stephen W. Hawking (Philadelphia: Running Press, 2005), 426–27.

Chapter 15 The Council of Trent

1. John W. O'Malley, *Trent: What Happened at the Council* (Cambridge: Harvard University Press, 2013), 7.
2. Bruce M. Metzger, *The Canon of the New Testament: Its Origin, Development and Significance* (New York: Oxford University Press, 1997), 246.

Chapter 16 Smyth Baptizes Himself and Begins the Early Baptists

1. Robert G. Torbet, *The History of the Baptists* (Philadelphia: Judson Press, 1950), 67.
2. Ibid. Modernized by author.
3. Ibid., 68.

Chapter 17 The King James Version Is Published

1. Earle E. Cairns, *Christianity Through the Centuries* (Grand Rapids: Zondervan, 1981), 339.
2. Shelley, *Church History in Plain Language*, 307.
3. J. R. Tanner, *Constitutional Documents of the Reign of James I* (Cambridge: Cambridge University Press, 1961), 30.
4. Magnus Magnusson, *Scotland: The Story of a Nation* (New York: Grove Press, 2000), 412.
5. Norman L. Geisler and William E. Nix, *From God to Us* (Chicago: Moody Press, 1974), 188.

Chapter 18 Bishop Ussher's Chronology

1. James Ussher, *The Annals of the World*, ed. Larry Pierce and Marion Pierce (Green Forest, AR: Master Books, 2003), 18.
2. Larry Richards and Lawrence O. Richards, *Bible Teacher's Commentary* (Colorado Springs: David C. Cook, 2002), 24.

Chapter 19 The Great Awakening in the United States

1. John E. Smith, Harry S. Stout, and Kenneth P. Minkema, eds., *A Jonathan Edwards Reader* (New Haven: Yale University Press, 1995), 89.

Notes

2. Jonathan Edwards, *The Works of President Edwards in Four Volumes*, vol. 4 (New York: Leavitt, Trow & Company, 1844), 235.

3. George Whitefield, "A Short Account of God's Dealings with George Whitefield," *George Whitefield's Journals* (repr., Mulberry, IN: Sovereign Grace Publishers, 2000), 17.

4. Benjamin Franklin, *The Autobiography of Benjamin Franklin*, ed. Leonard Woods Labaree (New Haven: Yale University Press, 1964), 175.

5. Shelley, *Church History in Plain Language* , 361.

Chapter 20 The Bill of Rights Is Written

1. Thomas Jefferson, *The Memoirs, Correspondence and Private Papers of Thomas Jefferson*, vol. 4, ed. Thomas Jefferson Randolph (London: Henry Colburn and Richard Bentley, 1829), 317–18.

2. Thomas Jefferson, "Jefferson's Letter to the Danbury Baptists," Library of Congress, accessed June 17, 2014, http://www.loc.gov/loc/lcib/9806/danpre.html.

3. Hugo Black, "Everson v. Board of Education of the Township of Ewing," Corning University Law School, accessed June 17, 2014, http://www.law.cornell.edu/supremecourt/text/330/1#writing-USSC_CR_0330_0001_ZO.

4. Martin E. Marty and Bill Moyers, "God and the Constitution," *In Search of the Constitution*, episode 6, segment 1 (Acorn Media, 1987).

Chapter 21 Darwin's *On the Origin of Species* Is Published

1. Tim M. Berra, *Charles Darwin: A Concise Story of an Extraordinary Man* (Baltimore: Johns Hopkins University Press, 2009), 1.

2. Michael Denton, *Evolution: A Theory in Crisis* (Chevy Chase, MD: Adler & Adler, 1986), 358.

3. Charles Darwin, *The Origin of Species and The Voyage of the Beagle* (repr., New York: Random House, 2012), 17.

4. Charles Darwin, "Darwin, C. R. to Gray, Asa (22 May [1860])," Darwin Correspondence Project, http://www.darwinproject.ac.uk/letter/entry-2814, accessed January 14, 2014.

5. Herbert Spencer, *The Principles of Biology*, vol. 2 (New York: D. Appleton, 1891), 444.

6. Charles Darwin and Sir Francis Darwin, "Letter to Hugh Falconer," *The Life and Letters of Charles Darwin*, vol. 2 (New York: D. Appleton and Co., 1897), 12.

7. Charles Darwin, *On the Origin of Species by Means of Natural Selection or the Preservation of Favoured Races in the Struggle for Life* (New York: P. F. Collier & Son, 1909), 520.

8. Charles Darwin, "On the Development of the Intellectual and Moral Faculties during Primeval and Civilised Times," *The Descent of Man, and Selection in Relation to Sex*, 2nd ed. (London: John Murray, 1874), 133–34.

9. Charles Darwin, "Secondary Sexual Characters of Man," *The Descent of Man*, 327–28.

10. John van Wyhe, ed., *The Complete Works of Charles Darwin Online*, accessed June 17, 2014, http://darwin-online.org.uk/content/frameset?viewtype=side&itemID=CUL-DAR112.B3b--B3f&pageseq=8.

Chapter 22 *The Scofield Reference Bible* Is Published

1. Warren Wiersbe, *50 People Every Christian Should Know* (Grand Rapids: Baker, 2009), 204.

2. C. I. Scofield, *The Scofield Reference Bible* (New York: Oxford University Press, 1967), 4.

Chapter 23 The Fundamentals

1. "Historic Documents of American Presbyterianism: The Doctrinal Deliverance of 1910," PCA Historical Center, accessed January 15, 2014, www.pcahistory.org/documents/deliverance.html.

2. Curtis Lee Laws, "Fundamentalism in the Northern Convention," *The Watchman-Examiner* (July 1, 1920), 834.

3. Paul Enns, *The Moody Handbook of Theology* (Chicago: Moody Publishers, 2008), 651.

Chapter 24 The Scopes "Monkey Trial"

1. Jeffery P. Moran, *The Scopes Trial: A Brief History with Documents* (New York: Bedford/St. Martin's, 2002), 2.

2. Paul Amos Moody, *Introduction to Evolution* (New York: Harper & Row, 1970), 492–93.

3. Lowell Hayes Harrison, *A New History of Kentucky* (Lexington: University Press of Kentucky, 1997), 346.

4. Austin Peay, "Message from the Governor," *Tennessee House of Representatives House Journal*, no. 745, March 23, 1925.

5. The National Center for Education Statistics, "Table 9. Percentage of persons 25 to 29 years old with selected levels of educational attainment, by race/ethnicity and sex: Selected years, 1920 through 2012," *Digest of Education Statistics*, accessed January 15, 2014, http://nces.ed.gov/programs/digest/d12/tables/dt12_009.asp.

6. Edward J. Larson, "Before the Crusade: Evolution in American Secondary Education Before 1920," as quoted in Moran, *The Scopes Trial*, 20.

7. "Plan Assault on State Law on Evolution," *Chattanooga Daily Times* (May 4, 1925), 5.

8. "Arrest Under Evolution Law," *Nashville Banner* (May 6, 1925), 1.

9. "Darrow Ready to Aid Prof. Scopes," *Nashville Banner* (May 16, 1925), 1.

10. *Baltimore Sun* (July 14, 1925), 1.

11. William Safire, *Lend Me Your Ears: Great Speeches in History* (New York: W. W. Norton, 1997), 849–53.

12. "Scopes Trial: Excerpts from the Court Transcripts, Day 6," accessed May 16, 2014, http://faculty.smu.edu/jclam/science_religion/trial_transcripts.html.

Chapter 25 The Rise of the Neo-Evangelicals

1. National Association of Evangelicals, "Statement of Faith," accessed May 15, 2014, www.nae.net/about-us/statement-of-faith.

2. National Association of Evangelicals, "History," accessed May 15, 2014, http://www.nae.net/about-us/history/62.

3. NRB, "History," accessed May 20, 2014, http://nrb.org/about/history/.

4. Eric Tiansay, "Strong Sales Mark Updated NIV's Anniversary," *Christian Retailing*, March 28, 2013.

5. The Evangelical Theological Society, "ETS Constitution," accessed May 20, 2014, http://www.etsjets.org/about/constitution.

Chapter 26 The Dead Sea Scrolls Discovered

1. Harold Scanlin, *The Dead Sea Scrolls & Modern Translations of the Old Testament* (Wheaton: Tyndale, 1993), 3.

2. The Leon Levy Dead Sea Scrolls Digital Library, "Discovery and Publication," accessed May 20, 2014, http://www.deadseascrolls.org.il/learn-about-the-scrolls/discovery-and-publication.

Chapter 27 The Jesus Movement

1. Erwin Fahlbusch and Geoffrey William Bromiley, eds., *The Encyclopedia of Christianity*, vol. 3 (Grand Rapids: Eerdmans, 2003), 28.
2. Larry Eskridge, *God's Forever Family: The Jesus People Movement in America* (New York: Oxford University Press, 2013), 2.

Chapter 28 Vatican II

1. "Global Christianity: A Report on the Size and Distribution of the World's Christian Population," Pew Research Religion & Public Life Project, December 19, 2011, http://www.pewforum.org/2011/12/19/global-christianity-exec/.
2. Deacon Eric Stoltz, "John XXIII Convokes Second Vatican Council," *Conciliaria*, December 25, 2011, http://conciliaria.com/2011/12/john-xxiii-convokes-council/. English translation courtesy of eminent conciliar historian Rev. Joseph Komonchak.
3. "Pope John's Opening Speech to the Council," accessed May 20, 2014, http://web.archive.org/web/20070808180613/http:/www.rc.net/rcchurch/vatican2/j23open.txt.

Chapter 29 The Rise of the Christian Right

1. Jerry Falwell, untitled sermon, Lynchburg, Virginia, July 7, 1976.
2. Hans Johnson and William Eskridge, "The Legacy of Falwell's Bully Pulpit," *The Washington Post* (May 19, 2007).
3. Jimmy Carter, *Keeping Faith: Memoirs of a President* (New York: Bantam Books, 1982), 561–62.
4. Faith Popcorn, *The Popcorn Report* (New York: Doubleday Currency, 1991), 27.

Chapter 30 The Rise of New Atheism

1. *Freedom From Religion Foundation, Inc. v. Chip Weber, United States Forest Service*, United States District Court for the District of Montana Missoula Division (Case 9:12-cv-00019-DLC, Document 104, filed June 24, 2013), 27.
2. Olivia B. Waxman, "Unveiling America's First Public Monument to Atheism," *Time*, June 28, 2013, http://newsfeed.time.com/2013/06/28/unveiling-americas-first-public-monument-to-atheism/.
3. Michael Lipka, "5 Facts about Atheists," Pew Research Center, October 23, 2013, http://www.pewresearch.org/fact-tank/2013/10/23/5-facts-about-atheists/.
4. Ibid.
5. Ibid.
6. Carl Sagan, *Broca's Brain: Reflections on the Romance of Science* (New York: Random House, 1974), 283.
7. Ronald L. Numbers, ed., *Galileo Goes to Jail and Other Myths about Science and Religion* (Cambridge: Harvard University Press, 2009), 6.
8. Sagan, *Broca's Brain*, 286.
9. Henry M. Morris, *Scientific Creationism* (Green Forest, AR: Master Books, 1974).
10. Robert F. Worth, "From Bible-Belt Pastor to Atheist Leader," *New York Times* (August 26, 2012), MM40.

Alton Gansky is the author of twenty-four novels and nine nonfiction books. He is a Carol Award and an Angel Award winner, and has been a Christy Award finalist. He holds a BA and an MA in biblical studies and has been granted a Doctor of Literature degree. He is the Director of the Blue Ridge Mountains Christian Writers Conference. Gansky has also served as editor and collaborator for top-tier authors. He lives with his wife in Central California.

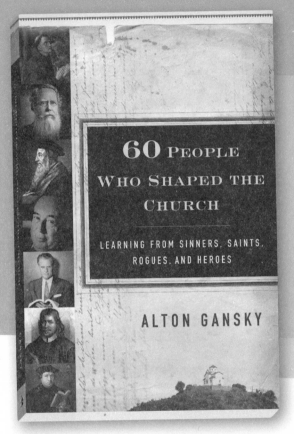